American Anatomies

New Americanists

A Series Edited by Donald E. Pease

American Anatomies

Theorizing Race and Gender

Robyn Wiegman

DUKE UNIVERSITY PRESS   *Durham and London 1995*

Chapters 3 and 4 are revised and expanded versions of
previously published articles. "The Anatomies of Lynching"
previously appeared in *Journal of the History of Sexuality* 3.3
(January 1993): 445-467 (reprinted by permission). "Bonds
of (In)Difference" first appeared in *Cultural Critique* as
"Negotiating AMERICA: Gender, Race and the Ideology of
the Interracial Male Bond," 13.4 (Fall 1989): 89-117 (reprinted
by permission). Portions of chapters 5 and 6 appeared in
very different forms in "Melville's Geography of Gender,"
American Literary History 1.4 (Winter 1989): 735-753, and
"Toward a Political Economy of Race and Gender," *Bucknell
Review* Special Issue "Turning the Century: Feminist Theory
in the 1990s," ed.Glynis Carr (Lewisburg, Pennsylvania:
Bucknell University Press, 1992): 47-67.
Printed in the United States of America on acid-free paper
Typeset in Minion by Tseng Information Systems, Inc.
Library of Congress Cataloging-in-Publication Data
appear on the last printed page of this book.
Third printing, 2002

Contents

Acknowledgments

To acknowledge is always in some sense to pay a debt, and while I would like, in the context of this study, to resist an uninterrogated language of economy, it seems to me that intellectual work is often about accumulation, though not of property but of generosity. Like all debts, mine have accumulated over time, but they take shape in my mind as locations, and it is remarkable to me how they seem now to both begin and end in the same place.

As my first mentors and now my colleagues, Cynthia Kinnard Dominick and Ray Hedin of Indiana University were crucial to my developing interest in American studies, and I am honored to be teaching with those — as with Jean Robinson — who first and most compellingly inspired me. I also count myself fortunate to have as colleagues in the English department a group of prolific young scholars, especially the Americanists Eva Cherniavsky, Jonathan Elmer, and Cary Wolfe, whose intellectual passions and pedagogical commitments have challenged me. To those who read in careful and tactful ways drafts of this manuscript — Kari Bloedel, Diane Elam, Mary Favret, Elena Glasberg, and Andrew Miller — I can only hope that my revisions reflect your contributions well. To Mary Jo Weaver and Susan Gubar, who have helped make possible whatever ease of inquiry feminists now enjoy, I am most grateful for both intellectual comraderie and friendship. And to Lynn Hudson, Theresa Kemp, Merrill Morris, and Jane Rhodes: appreciation is due for your collective creativities.

This book began as a dissertation under the direction of Susan Jeffords at the University of Washington and received generous commentary not only from her, but from a collection of committed and thoughtful teachers: Carolyn Allen, Mark Patterson, Sara VandenBerg, and Evan Watkins. At Syracuse University, the debates within the English department about politics and the profession compelled me into a broad range of theoretical reconsiderations, and I am pleased to now understand the significance of such difficult, but necessary, contentions. I am especially indebted to Steve Mailloux, Stephen Melville, Bill Readings, Margaret Himley, Steven Cohan, and the members of the Feminist Theory Colloquium, Linda Alcoff, Dympna Callaghan, and Ingeborg Majer O'Sickey. Tom Yingling was most crucial to the intellectual vitality of my years at Syracuse and although he died before any of our ideas for collaboration made it to the page, the theoretical contours of this book are nonetheless shaped by him.

At Duke University Press, I have been fortunate to work with Ken Wissoker, whose care for the manuscript and its political gestures, not to mention his sense of things more generally, have at crucial points invigorated me. And Cathy Davidson demonstrated to me what we mean when we talk about intellectual generosity.

And finally to those who cannot be tied to place—to Anne Fay, Phyllis Radke, Judith Roof, and Sharon Wiegman: in whatever ways you will, I thank you for knowing what this book means.

American Anatomies

Taking Refuge: An Introduction

There is really nothing more to say—except why. But since *why* is difficult to handle, one must take refuge in *how*. —Toni Morrison, *The Bluest Eye*

In her approach to the story of Pecola Breedlove in *The Bluest Eye,* Toni Morrison's narrator expresses the kind of apprehension about our ability to explain the social violences of race and gender that haunts this book. For while *American Anatomies* hopes to provide a compelling argument about the lengthy and often contradictory collusion of race and gender hierarchies in U.S. culture, it likewise invests in *how* as a response to the difficulties of handling *why*. Where such difficulties are for the narrator primarily emotional, my hesitations take place on methodological grounds as well. As critical debates about disciplinary study in the past twenty years have stressed, the practices we engage to define and explain social complexities condition whatever conclusions we might reach.[1] *Why* therefore emerges as the consequence of our narratives of *how,* and these narratives are neither innocent nor politically disinterested. To take refuge, as this book does, in the contingencies of *how* is to register these broader anxieties about knowledge, truth, and politics that are currently transforming our disciplinary understandings of and approaches to cultural critique.[2] *American Anatomies* is thus a book marked by limits: not only the history, politics, and disciplinary limits of race and gender as conceptual categories, but more specifically, the limits of its own theoretical claims to know.

Let me begin, then, with what this study will *not* do. It will not offer an analysis of the critical currency now accorded to race and gender without reading that analysis as both resistance to and complicity with late-twentieth-century formations of white supremacy and patriarchy. Instead, *American Anatomies* approaches its critical obsessions as both cultural and disciplinary ones, and while it hopes to contribute to an antiracist and anti-sexist critique, I maintain a deep skepticism toward the political and theoretical assumptions that seem most to motivate me. The political necessity of such skepticism is one of the primary arguments of this book, and it takes place alongside two interrelated sets of concerns: contemporary critical debates about multiculturalism and "difference" on one hand, and the broader reconfiguration of white racial supremacy since segregation's institutional demise on the other. To be part of an intellectual conversation that maps these historical changes is for me, as for others, to become a symptom of the very reconfigurations of which I speak, for in the integrationist terrain of contemporary culture, the post-racist possibility of America is too often figured by the centrality of Anglo-Americans as the heroic agents of racism's decline. This is not to forward an essentialist argument about who can or should speak, but it is to define the cultural contours and controversies that condition as well as limit my own speech.

The shuttling that I have just performed between contemporary critical and U.S. cultural contexts is characteristic of this study's strategy of investigation. It demonstrates most of all my concern with the epistemological frameworks that simultaneously enable and limit how and what we can know—not simply in the present, but in our construction of the past as well. In response to this concern, *American Anatomies* looks to various aspects of Western knowledge regimes since the late Renaissance as they have contributed to the articulation of race and gender differences. In the transformation from natural history to comparative anatomy, in particular, I trace the way social hierarchies have been rationalized, in both senses of the word, by locating in the body an epistemological framework for justifying inequality. At the same time, I challenge contemporary cultural criticism's continued investment in the epistemology of the body, especially as it comes to be figured in the faulty and politically disabling analogy between "blacks and women." By pursuing the history of this analogy and its consequences for both nineteenth- and twentieth-century social struggle, I stage what I call a feminist politics of "disloyalty": a disloyalty, that is, to the modern methodologies that often allow us to claim perspectives of political noncomplicity. In the difficulty of extracting our critical gaze from the very relations we hope to expose, *why* is impossible to handle. But in the *how* of race and gender, there is still a great deal to be told.

In using the notion of the critical gaze trapped in the frameworks of its own seeing, I have invoked a central concept that underlies this study: visibility. Such an invocation points to the difficulties of methodological perspective and political praxis that I mention above, foregrounding the relations of "sight" and "observation" that adhere to "theory" (the Greek *theoria* meaning literally "a looking at") and to the investigative terrain of modern disciplinarity itself. In the equation between theoretical investigation and sight, that sense through which observation as a definitive mode of analysis is both concretized and idealized, we encounter an important cornerstone of modernity, indeed one of its most anxious and contentious epistemological productions.[3] But while vision is the privileged sense of modernity, its ability to establish and guarantee both meaning and truth is repeatedly undermined not only by modernity's own philosophical and representational preoccupations but also by its relationship to technological production and reproduction. Twentieth-century critics have been especially, one could even say obsessively, concerned with vision and visuality precisely because of these insecurities and contradictions, *and* because contemporary culture is itself definitively premised on visual knowledge regimes. Even a brief catalogue of current titles demonstrates this overarching concern: *Modernity and the Hegemony of Vision, Vision and Textuality, Vision and Visuality, Ways of Seeing, Visible Fictions, Hard Core: Power, Pleasure, and the "Frenzy of the Visible," Stolen Glances, Signatures of the Visible, Vision and Difference,* and *Downcast Eyes: The Denigration of Vision.*[4]

But the relationship between the critic's interest in and skepticism of the primacy of vision and visuality on the one hand and the ascendancy of the visual as contemporary culture's most overwhelming characteristic on the other needs rather careful explication, especially because the popular realm of the visual functions in the twentieth century as a newly configured public sphere. What does it mean, for instance, that the visual apparatuses of photography, film, television, and video (as well as the many offshoots of computer technologies) serve as our primary public domain, our main shared context for the contestations of contemporary cultural politics? And perhaps more important, what does it mean that within these technologies, the body is figured as the primary locus of representation, mediation, and/or interpretation? These questions form the backdrop to the investigations undertaken in this study, where the emphasis on the visual shifts among considerations of epistemologies of vision, the representational ideologies of visual technologies, and the appropriations and significations of the body as the determinative site of visible differences.

Such shifts—from vision to the visual to the visible—point to the various cultural modalities and historical contexts through which issues of race and gender (and their convergences and divergences) will be read. These modalities, understood as *economies* of visibility, are clearly part of the development and deployment of the economic arrangements of capitalism, but this study hopes to approach the concept of visual economies in more expansive terms. In Western racial discourse, for instance, the production of the African subject as non- or subhuman, as an object and property, arises not simply through the economic necessities of the slave trade, but according to the epistemologies attending vision and their logics of corporeal inscription: making the African "black" reduces the racial meanings attached to flesh to a binary structure of vision, and it is this structure that precedes the disciplinary emergence of the humanities and its methodological pursuits of knowledge and truth. This does not mean that imperialism was not well served by the negative equation between "blackness" and an ontological difference, but that the framework for such an equation must be approached in terms broader and more historically and culturally comprehensive than the slave trade and its necessity for ideological and economic justification. By defining the visual as both an economic system and a representational economy, and by refusing to explain their relationship as a simple correspondence, this study mediates between the complexities of Western racial formations and the specificities of their U.S. figurations.

In addition, I hope to set forth the variety of cultural contexts in which specific racial categories are rendered "real" (and therefore justifiable) through the naturalizing discourses of the body, those discourses that locate difference in a pre-cultural realm where corporeal significations supposedly speak a truth which the body inherently means. But the significations attached to the body — the culturally specific, fetishistic attention to skin, hair, breast, brain size, and skull shape, for instance — are not the predetermined loci of difference, but a deeply problematical and asymmetrical production. To imagine ourselves outside such regimes of corporeal visibility is not only at some level unthinkable but also intolerable to our own conceptions of who and what we "are." In this sense, the economies of visibility that produce the network of meanings attached to bodies (their specific race, gender, ethnic, sexual, and national demarcations) are more than political and hierarchical practices: they are indelibly subjective ones as well. It is precisely this that has given both power and substance to identity politics in the last two hundred years.

More recently, identity politics have come under attack from within some of their most politically effective social formations and resistant organizations. While linked to the postmodern critique of the humanist subject but in no way reducible to it, the conversation about the limits and possibilities of identity politics moves in a variety of directions.[5] In one, critics consider the ability of contemporary market relations to harness identity categories as a means of expanding capitalism, thereby undermining the utopian dream of identity politics by producing cultural representation where civil rights and black nationalist liberation struggle had pursued and envisioned political representation. In the Bush-Reagan era in particular, we witnessed a deft appropriation of the liberationist demand to make "visible" the subjectivities and histories of the cultural margins, as consumer culture harnessed ethnic, racial, and national specificities for its expanding global purposes. While the visibility garnered here replaces, at the popular level, historical invisibility and the visual apartheid of segregation, this subsequent integrationist representational regime does not demonstrate an advance toward democracy's "inherent" equalities. Rather, this new visibility in popular culture reveals the profound transformations that underlie both the form and structure of contemporary white supremacy.[6] The demise of segregation *as a national policy,* in short, has entailed a heightened propulsion to diversified consumption. As Stuart Hall laments, "there is always a price of incorporation to be paid when the cutting edge of difference and transgression is blunted into spectacularization" ("What Is This 'Black' . . . ?" 24).

For various cultural critics, the appropriation of identity politics by contemporary capitalism does not mean that identity politics were somehow wrong all along, but that the structure of "the cultural dominant," to quote Hall again, has not remained, even in the past two decades, the same. Its changes are clearly due to the effect and success of identity politics and the social movements that coalesced in the second half of the twentieth century within such an organizing framework. At the same time, the contemporary deployment of the cultural dominant demands a rethinking of the force and function of identity as the primary framework for articulating disempowerment and inequality today, since we now live in a cultural moment of increasingly adept resistance to the insurgencies of identity-based political organization. For this reason, cultural workers of all kinds have been enmeshed in the critical move to deessentialize identity.[7] Such a project involves critiquing the way counter-identity formations may contribute to the naturalization of difference that accompanies modernity by making inherent those properties that signify culturally as markers of difference and subordination. With this work, critics have hoped to intervene in the decontextualized and specular incorporation and absorption of identities that now characterize the popular visual realm. If identities are not metaphysical, timeless categories of being; if they point not to ontologies but to historical specificities and contingencies; if their mappings of bodies and

subjectivities are forms of and not simply resistances to practices of domination—then a politics based on identity must carefully negotiate the risk
of reinscribing the logic of the system it hopes to defeat.

This task is, of course, not simple, and it is perhaps a mark of our own
tie to oppositional thinking that the turn toward anti-essentialism has been
sought by some as a newly found political guarantee. But the work of contemporary political engagement does not end with the critique of identity's
relationship to modernity and its reliance on essentialist, humanist epistemologies—even though it is important, as this study hopes to demonstrate,
to begin precisely there. By doing this, we can explore the asymmetry of
corporeal identity that underlies the category of citizenship within modernity. Modern citizenship functions as a disproportionate system in which
the universalism ascribed to certain bodies (white, male, propertied) is protected and subtended by the infinite particularity assigned to others (black,
female, unpropertied). That this system is itself contingent on certain visual
relations, where only those particularities associated with the Other are,
quite literally, *seen,* demonstrates the political importance of unveiling,
in a variety of registers, Western economies of visibility. Therefore, while
cultural workers have critiqued the oversaturated, visual signification attending those bodies particularized by modernity, the critical gaze has also
been increasingly attentive to the unmarked and invisible, but no less specific, corporeality that hides beneath the abstraction of universality.[8] These
two gestures—challenging the visual scripting of identities while imposing
a visibility on the explicit hierarchies of entitlement cloaked by the universal—complicate the critical terrain in which identity as a politics might
move. For very different reasons, then, identity proves to be dangerous to
minority and majority alike.

But these are not the only dangers. The starkly oppositional framework
of minority and majority in which I have just situated identity proves
problematical, indeed deeply inaccurate, as a way of articulating the complexities of social and subjective positioning. The terms are nothing if
not ironic: the very "majority" contained within the category (presumably
white, heterosexual, wealthy men) is clearly, overwhelmingly, a global minority, and the minority against which they wield their power is itself the
global majority. This irony is also an incongruity, however, since the oppositional framework for articulating power depends on a homogenization of
identities into singular figurations, the "straight-white-monied man" becoming the composite, fixed figure for defining social hierarchies. While
one does not want to abandon the ability to talk about the cultural hege-

mony of this category, the logic of "majority" reaches an impasse when the social subject cannot be aligned, without contradiction, on one side or the other of the minority-majority divide. Where, for instance, is the straight, black, working-class man or the gay, white, monied woman? As Hall writes, "We are always in negotiation, not with a single set of oppositions that place us always in the same relation to others, but with a series of different positionalities. Each has for us its point of profound subjective identification. And that is the most difficult thing . . . [that these identities] are often dislocating in relation to one another" ("What Is This 'Black' . . . ?" 31).

The problem of registering and attending to multiplicity, what we might understand as *the* central issue in contemporary cultural politics, requires new approaches and different kinds of critical thinking about the relationship among power, identity, and social subjectivity. This is especially true as the visual terrain of popular culture increasingly commodifies identities according to the logic of corporeal inscription. But how to do this? How do we encounter a cultural rhetoric about identity that has remained stranded (in political organization as well as the popular imagination) within singular trajectories of social being, trajectories that, while grounding twentieth-century social movement, have also inscribed a variety of new and damaging exclusions? Feminism, as is now well remarked, has repeatedly elided "woman" with whiteness, and the civil rights and Black Power movements (as well as contemporary nationalist discourses) operate(d) on often quite explicit masculinizations of the category of race. Contemporary cultural rhetoric attending such exclusions simply weds these identity categories together, writing "blacks and women" as the inclusivist gesture of post-1960s politics. Lost in the systematic reduction is the black woman, whose historical and theoretical presence has quite rightly been pursued in recent years as a way of rethinking the inherently compounded nature of social identity.[9]

But paying attention to the categorical elision of "blacks and women" does not necessarily pose an adequate explanation of the historical and social productions underlying the phrase. It is simply not enough to locate the exclusions of "blacks and women" in the rhetoric and practices of twentieth-century social movements, as if there were literally no feminist or black liberationist discussions of the specificities of black women's disempowerment and oppression in either this century or the last one. To do so reproduces a monolithic notion of both feminist and African-Americanist political struggle, undercutting the participation and leadership by black women for the past two hundred years.[10] In the process, the notion is tacitly upheld that feminism has always been white—that black female organizations were/are not themselves feminist political enterprises. The inability of the phrase "blacks and women" to signify culturally as "black women" must therefore be figured in ways that both historicize and exceed the rhetoric and representation of political struggle in the late twentieth century.

In recognizing that the exclusiveness of "blacks and women" is related but not reducible to twentieth-century social movements organized on their behalf, this study approaches the rhetorical figure of post-1960s inclusion as the symptomatic site for a number of cultural excavations of the specificities of race and gender. Most simply, I ask: What constitutes the historical convergence of "blacks and women," not just as an affirmative action couple in the contemporary era, but within the broader philosophical and cultural discourses of modernity? Precisely how have "blacks and women" become wedded in the cultural symbolic as our primary figure for the complicated relationships of race and gender? What underwrites the sense that each posits something which the other cannot possibly be? What relations of analogy and differentiation subtend this metaphoric "wedding"? And what critical frameworks might begin to undo the standoff of these categories, undermining the ease with which "blacks and women" can be posed as exclusive, almost oppositional singularities? In short, how do we articulate the historical and contextual productions of "blacks and women"? These questions and their circulation within issues of public culture, modernity, visuality, identity, and political movement serve as the motivating foci for this inquiry, and it is toward their unraveling that the conversations about race and gender in this text, collectively and often elliptically, move.

How

Part 1 of this book, "Economies of Visibility," concerns the epistemology of the visual that underlies both race and gender: that process of corporeal inscription that defines each as a binary, wholly visible affair. In particular, I interrogate the status of the body as the primary readable "text" and question the formations of identities and individualization inaugurated there. Central to this analysis is a deterritorialization of the binary figuration of black/white that shapes not only the very concept of race in the United States but my discourse here as well.[11] Such a deterritorialization entails examining the history, function, and structure of visibility that underwrites the binary formation, producing the epistemology of perception that simultaneously equates the racial body with a perceptible blackness, while defining, in its absence, whiteness as whatever an African blackness is not. By exposing the visible relation that collapses social subjectivity with skin and marks an epidermal hierarchy as the domain of natural difference, I want to explore how the black/white axis works to secure the tenuousness of race to a framework of stable boundaries, which in turn provides the necessary grounding for the ideology of white supremacy.[12]

Of course, bodies are neither black nor white, and the range of possibilities accruing to either designation contradicts the assurance of these categories to represent, mimetically, the observable body. Our cultural trust in the objectivity of observation and the seemingly positive ascription we grant representation are part of the history of race's discursive production, and both embroil us in questions that have now become central to contemporary cultural studies. These questions, already implicit in my commentary, begin by foregrounding the difficulty of discussing a mode of difference and hierarchy that relies on the body without reinscribing that mode's logic of bodily essence. In the context of race, it extends to broader issues concerning the relationship between the rise of the human sciences, the economic program of imperialism and New World slavery, and the ideals of the Enlightenment as a political commitment to the innate rights of "man." Such issues are certainly not new, especially for those interested in the history of race and the subsequent forms of racism it has shaped. But if, as I would like to suggest, the construction of race is predicated on its obsessive performance, our refusal to grant that performance its centrality as "real" and observable truth is perhaps more than a mere academic pursuit.

In formulating an analysis of the powerful array of prescriptions and practices that have accompanied this society's investment in race, it becomes apparent that the binary construction of race reiterates the logic of our culture's other, often competing visual paradigm: sexual difference. By focusing on the confluence of these bodily scripts, I hope to demonstrate, from the outset, that the study of race and gender must be more than a correction, via categories, to America's quite violent and damaging historical exclusions. In this focus, I hope to resist what is often disturbing about contemporary theory's approach to race and gender: its assumption that the circulation of categories can adequately explain—by way of a reference to compounded social identity—either the cultural dynamics of race and gender or their various and contradictory historical productions. Instead, I want to explore more historically partial and contingent articulations of race and gender, not to discount the contemporary need to marshal these categories as aspects of a politically engaged cultural critique, but to diversify the contexts in which we claim and explore their meanings. I want, in short, to post their epistemological, corporeal, and visual modernity.

Rather than beginning this study in the midst of the contemporary condensation of race and gender into "blacks and women," however, chapter 1, "Visual Modernity," focuses on the emergence of race as a corporeal inscription by reading it in the context of the economy of the visual that attends modernity. Here, the skepticism in various trajectories of postmodern critical theory toward the primacy of vision in Western culture will be useful to trace the historical contours of race's discursive production and its increasing imbrication with sexual difference.[13] In particular, Michel Foucault's *The Order of Things,* which focuses on the transformations underwriting Western organizations of knowledge since the Renaissance, offers a preliminary framework for reading the economies of visibility that have crafted, in a variety of contradictory ways, the historical production of race. Through the Foucauldian framework, "race" emerges as the effect of specific organizations of Western knowledge in which scientific and aesthetic approaches to vision, as well as philosophical delineations of (dis)embodiment, assume prominent roles. By disentangling race from the security of a natural reading of skin and placing it squarely within the broad contours of Western knowledge regimes, this chapter demonstrates how the powerful materiality of race is structured by our historically shifting understandings of perception and cultural representation, from the first appearance of the English on African shores to the logic of observation that rationalizes the human sciences and spawns the anatomical and political analogies between race and gender to which Americans are the most immediate heirs.

To begin in this way is to foreground a specific narrative mapping of race and gender, one that purposely does not locate the *why* of social inequality in the primacy of sexual difference as the originary form on which other modes of hierarchy, including race, have been founded.[14] As a counter to various feminist assumptions and methodological practices in which race becomes the additive to gender, this study reads figurations of sexual difference as they emerge within scientific debates about race in the eighteenth and nineteenth centuries. In chapter 2, "Sexing the Difference," gender is linked to modernity and the disciplinary shifts it encodes at the same time that the contemporary collaboration "blacks and women" is read as taking shape within the legacy and epistemology established by scientific discourses of racial measurement. Contrary to feminist assumptions about the transhistorical primacy of gender, race within *this* discursive nexus founds the paradigmatic production of gender, thus generating a series of analogies and differentiations between Africans and women that characterize feminist abolitionist discourse in that century and the race/gender axis of difference in the twentieth century as well.

To argue that the relationship between race and gender is not transhistorically the same—is not a "natural" reading of bodies in their obvious and unchanging visual differentiations—demonstrates that differences are contextual and contingent productions. This means that the nexus of race and gender that emerges from the rise of race science and its obsession with delineations of "being" cannot become paradigmatic for other productions of difference or even for other configurations of race and gender.[15] Feminism's political need for an explanatory mechanism that can read the complexities and contradictions of social hierarchy cannot be satisfied in such a singular or overarching way. Indeed, even the differences we think we know are bound to a variety of often conflicting discursive and institutional contexts for their construction. A compelling example of this, and one that I explore in the context of sexing racial differences, can be found in early African-American writing where sexual difference actually functions as a rhetorical means for rescuing the slave from the prisonhouse of epidermal inferiority. In the conflict between scientific and popular constructions of the African(-American)[16] as a species beneath "man" and the political struggle for enfranchisement and human status, the claim to sexual difference—to be a "man" or "woman"—works to define and invoke a social subjectivity (and hence psychic interiority) previously denied the slave. Abolitionist discourse, feminist and nonfeminist, routinely stressed the gendered aspects of enslavement, marking a similarity or sameness among all social subjects that strategically placed the slave on the side of humanity. The slave's rhetorical claim to enfranchisement can thus be read as hinging, in part, on sexual difference.

The implications for contemporary feminist theory of this kind of formation of race and gender are numerous, and it is one of the tasks of this study to forge a broad reconsideration of such terrain. What does it mean that for African-American female and male slaves the possibilities of escaping the category of the inhuman took shape under a bizarrely liberating figuration of gendered subjectivity—that to be *female* or to be *male* provided a rhetorical possibility for entering the determinations of modern social subjectivity? For a feminism schooled in the assumption that sexual differences are the foundation of women's disempowerment and oppression, the challenge of this possibility is far reaching. After all, the Anglophilic feminist tradition often traces its contemporary identity to Mary Wollstonecraft's *A Vindication of the Rights of Woman*, where the argument for liberation is articulated in the context of the impossible strictures of femininity that attend modern political theory and social organization. While one does not want to undermine the necessity of that critique, it is no small irony how significant the category of gender Wollstonecraft already occupied could be. This is not to say that gender was solely a liberating category for the African-American woman, as the asymmetry of patriarchal gender relations clearly worked to encode specific kinds of abuse and violence toward the female slave whose body became the commodified technology of the slave economy's reproduction. But to move from a perceived and legalized inhumanity—a chattel—to those categories of human identity defined by gender is not in this context a simple or singular defeat.

And what of the black male? This is the question that guides the transition into part 2 of this book, "The Ends of 'Man,'" where my disloyalty to one of second-wave feminism's central tenents takes central stage. Here I provide an extended reading of the contradictions that attend the black male's social positioning and, with it, the limitations of feminist theory's conception of the masculine (and of patriarchy) as well. Such an approach shifts the methodological framework of feminist research by demonstrating that gender works to adjudicate the relations of domination and subordination not just between men and women, but among men themselves. Chapter 3, "The Anatomy of Lynching," explores the contradiction that resides within all patriarchal relations: that empowerment based on maleness is not automatically conferred but can be, and frequently is, quite violently deferred. In the case of the black male, who occupies an empowered "masculine" and disempowered "racial" positioning, this deferral has often taken the form of explicit feminizations in the disciplinary activity of castration that has accompanied lynching. By looking more closely at this terrain of violence and desire, where white men repeatedly touch and discuss the penis they so determinedly destroy, I approach a variety of theoretical impasses now attending feminist thought. For in reading multiplicity and heterogeneity at the reportedly deessentialized (but always female) body and finding unicity and homogeneity at the un(der)theorized (but always male) body, feminist theory has both guaranteed the primacy of gender and discussed its complexities in very narrow terms.

By approaching gendered subjectivity as a complicated, even paradoxical project for the African-American who is negotiating the various racist representational and institutional regimes of white supremacy, and by entertaining what Eve Kosofsky Sedgwick in *Between Men* has compellingly shown — that feminism can speak to and learn from examinations of relationships among men — the middle part of this book moves to the question of the masculine in order to reconfigure feminism's political interventions into and theorizations of race and gender difference. For some readers, any focus away from the feminine will be read as a negation of current investigations of women. Nevertheless, I want to pay attention to the way the discourse of sexual difference defines, constructs, enforces, and negotiates hierarchies within the masculine, that locus most often left unattended by feminist interrogation. How else, for instance, might we read the two most prominent and contradictory images attending the African-American male unless we situate these within the paradoxes of race and gender: the feminized, bumbling black "coon" on the one hand (Sambo, Tambo, Uncle Remus, and Jim Crow) and the hypermasculinized black male rapist on the other (Willie Horton, Bigger Thomas, and Gus from *Birth of a Nation*)?

That these images emerge in concert with a burgeoning consumer culture in the late eighteenth and nineteenth centuries demonstrates the link between the cultural rhetoric of the black male and the oversaturation of the visual that increasingly comes to dominate the popular realm; but the shift to the black male as rapist as the narrative around which the practice of lynching becomes racialized at the end of the nineteenth century points as well toward a reinvigoration of the disciplinary structures of white supremacy. Here lynching must be viewed in its performative, specular dimension, as a disciplinary activity that communalizes white power while territorializing the black body and its movement through social space. Where Foucault makes a distinction between the spectacle of public torture and execution of the seventeenth and eighteenth centuries and the strategies of surveillance that increasingly accompany the production of subjects in the nineteenth, lynching proves to be an interesting link between the two. Because the terror of the white lynch mob arises from both its function as a panoptic mode of surveillance and its materialization of violence in public displays of torture and castration, the black subject is disciplined in two powerful ways: by the threat of always being seen *and* by the specular scene.

We might understand the panoptic and corporeal violence of lynching and castration as a disciplinary practice linked historically to the political and economic reorganizations that accompanied Reconstruction, when the antebellum figure of the male slave as docile, passive Uncle Tom failed to subdue the anxieties posed by the new conditions attending Emancipation. The legal enfranchisement of the black male slave made more urgent the prevailing threat to white masculine supremacy always underlying images of African-American males: their ability to enter the cultural symbolic as *men,* with all the rights and privileges that their new status as bearers of a "black" patronymic might grant. No longer tied to a slave economy that alternatively wrote him as the feminine or the savage inhuman, the black male emerged in popular discourses during Reconstruction as the mythic embodiment of phallic (and hence masculine) potentiality as the black rapist. This representational narrative, which cast the white man as the defender of white female sexuality, translated the economic crisis wrought by the transformation from slavery to freedom into sexual and gendered terms. By offering the dominant culture a very powerful means through which not only black men but the entire black population could be disciplined as innately—if no longer legally—inferior, the myth of the black man as rapist became, as Richard Wright would later depict, that "death before death came" (*Native Son* 228).

It is significant that this death was often wrought through violences tied to the discursive delineations of sexual difference, where the phallic lack characteristic of the feminine was quite literally imposed onto the black male through the frequent accompaniment of castration with lynching. Such attempts to deny the black male the primary sign of power in patriarchal culture demonstrate the fact that the black male is precisely *not* a woman. If his lack must be corporeally *achieved,* his threat to white masculine power arises from the frightening possibility of a masculine sameness and not simply from a fear of racial difference. This potential masculine sameness governs the black male's contradictory position in the cultural symbolic and underlies the various representational attempts to align him with the feminine. As Richard Dyer writes, "the treatment of black men . . . constantly puts them into 'feminine' positions, that is, places them structurally . . . in the same positions as women typically occupy" (*Heavenly Bodies* 116–117). To enforce passivity where the possibility of masculine activity resides "permits the fantasy of power over them to be exercised . . . justif[ying] their subordination ideologically" and averting as well the possibilities of change (116). In aligning representations of black men with the constructed position of women, dominant discourses routinely neutralized black male images, exchanging potential claims for patriarchal inclusion for a structurally passive or literally castrated realm of sexual objectification and denigration.

Of course, there are important distinctions between castration and symbolic emasculation, regardless of the extent to which the threat underlying

each is a product of the tension between patriarchy and white racial supremacy. And yet, it was precisely the elision between material and symbolic feminization that underwrote a great deal of Black Power rhetoric in
the 1960s and 1970s, begetting the turn in popular culture toward images
of a powerfully masculine black male. While the Superfly and Shaft figures
of the 1970s are hardly without their own linkage to stereotypes and reinvigorated racisms, their successors in the popular imagination — the black
male as the integral double in male bonding narratives — proves a crucial
ideological shift in the broader transformation from segregation to integration. Where the post–Civil War period hypermasculinizes the black male
through the image of the overly endowed black male rapist, the post–World
War II Reconstruction period of the twentieth century offers a struggling,
but soon-to-be (if not already) integrated masculine figure. This shift occupies my attention in chapter 4, "Bonds of (In)Difference," since the 1980s
witnessed an unprecedented proliferation of interracial "buddy" movies.
These films simultaneously assent to and resist Black Power analogies between masculinity and equality by defying the legacy of emasculation that
attends black male representation, while recasting white masculinity as a
disempowered and embattled marginality itself. In an ironic twist, incorporation of the black male into the reign of the visual that characterizes
commodity culture becomes a mechanism through which the history of
racism among men is revised and denied. The very demands for representational inclusion and for a repertoire of images that resist the stereotypes
of enslavement become, in the post–civil rights era, what Kobena Mercer
and Isaac Julien wryly call "'positive images' with a neo-conservative ven-
geance" ("Introduction" 2).[17]

By foregrounding popular culture's appropriation of the political demands and rhetorics of identity politics, chapter 4 establishes the historical context for rethinking the strategies of critical reading adopted in the
postsegregation era by Americanists and feminists alike. In part 3, "White
Mythologies," I explore the broad scope of the problem of paradigms that
attends contemporary critical discussion of race and gender. These chapters
examine two specific reiterations of the nostalgia for an interracial sameness
that anchors itself in gender and thereby threatens to reiterate the popular contemporary formula of "blacks and women." Chapter 5, "Canonical
Architecture," reads Leslie Fiedler's 1960 interpretation of interracial configurations in the context of contemporary bonding narratives before turning to recent rereadings of Fiedler and the male bond from an emergent gay
studies perspective. Where Fiedler's earliest formulation of an interracial

male bonding tradition in American literature linked the "negro and the homosexual" — figuring homosexuality in the process as arrested psychosexual development — contemporary critics such as Robert K. Martin and Joseph A. Boone work to retrieve the antihomophobic and antipatriarchal possibilities that attend the mythic scene of bonded men. But like feminism's own illusory sisterhood, this retrieval, no matter how bound up with utopian investments, has dire consequences for the minoritized male, whose position in the integrationist narrative of contemporary criticism inadvertently stages a reinvigoration of the racial supremacy of the white male. At the same time, the domain of literary production is overwritten by an equation between "America" as a symbolic founding and paternal rights and practices themselves.

That these effects can be read in part as an inversion of one of feminism's most repeated rhetorics, sisterhood, demonstrates how feminism has itself been tied to an integrationist ethos which likewise carries, as in the popular realm, its own narrative of historical transcendence. The contemporary turn toward the specificities of monolithic Woman — her race, class, sexual, and national demarcations — has been assumed, after all, to post feminism's historical complicities, but it is precisely in this gesture toward the methodological fix that feminism misrecognizes the complex anxieties that might in political terms more generatively motivate it. By challenging this continued faith in methodology as a political guarantee, chapter 6, "The Alchemy of Disloyalty," undoes the logic of this study's own analytical trajectory, refusing all gestures of categorical retrieval by staging a host of theoretical disloyalties. In this context, the "black woman," so elided by the categorical logics of "blacks and women," does not emerge as my study's ultimate destination, as such an arrival would threaten to reinvest in the corporeal identities that adhere to modern disciplinarity. Instead, the final chapter both meditates on the way feminists currently shape the history of feminism within (or against) the contestatory relations of race and gender and sketches in broader detail the implications of the conversation about methodology and politics that this study has engaged.

Taken together, the final two chapters move the book toward a reflection on contemporary critical theory as both a political vision and a utopic hope in which the desire to transcend the contingencies of historical perspective are alternatively confronted and disavowed. For those loyal to feminism's historical dream of transcendence — of the possibility of a political discourse wholly unanchored from complicity with dominant epistemologies, visualities, or social relations — such a reading of culture will no doubt

lack the ingredients so often necessary to the continuation of political belief. But by drawing on a broad array of cultural discourses through which
to pursue a discussion of the categorical constructs of race and gender, this
study simultaneously ponders the limits of our current thinking about difference on one hand, while questioning the assumptions that captivate our
intellectual inquiry and wed us to methodology as our political guarantee
on the other. This means that while I demonstrate how categorical unities
and monoliths are themselves part of a particular history in which vision,
visuality, and modernity play crucial roles, I cannot assume that my engagement in an antiracist feminist critique does not also betray my greatest
sincerities. Such a betrayal, it seems to me, is both the risk and the inevitability of existing within the anxieties of discipline that simultaneously
shape and deform our cultural critique.

Economies of Visibility

1   Visual Modernity

Did that woman, could that woman, somehow know that here before her very eyes on the roof of the Drayton sat a Negro?

Absurd! Impossible! White people were so stupid about such things for all that they usually asserted that they were able to tell; and by the most ridiculous means, finger-nails, palms of hands, shapes of ears, teeth, and other equally silly rot. . . . Never, when she was alone, had they even remotely seemed to suspect that she was a Negro. — Nella Larsen, *Passing* 40–41

Under critique in this passage from Nella Larsen's *Passing* is the visible economy of race, an economy of parts that enables the viewer to ascertain the subject's rightful place in a racial chain of being. While not the only means for the articulation of racial essence, the visible has a long, contested, and highly contradictory role as the primary vehicle for making race "real" in the United States. Its function, to cite the body as the inevitable locus of "being," depends on a series of bodily fictions assumed to unproblematically reflect the natural meaning of flesh.[1] But as Irene Redfield's meditation here reveals, the seeming veracity of flesh can fail to register itself, and it is significant that Larsen represents this failure by foregrounding corporeal signs that *do not* appear.[2] Without these signs — without the significations attached to skin, hair, and palms — Irene is able to claim an implicit and highly privileged whiteness, moving with deliberate ease through the unofficial segregation of Chicago. The visible negation of "blackness," in other words, prefigures her racial indeterminacy, demonstrating how the "logic" of race in U.S. culture anchors whiteness in the visible epistemology of black skin. Such an epistemological relationship circumscribes our cultural conception of race, contributing above all to the recurrent and discursively, if not always materially, violent equation between the idea of "race" and the "black" body.[3]

To interrupt this equation is crucial to the political articulation of an antiracist cultural critique, and scholars from a variety of disciplines have become increasingly attentive to the social construction of whiteness and the forms and privileges that construction entails.[4] To unveil whiteness as its own racial specificity, however, does not necessarily explain the way race has been constituted as a visual phenomenon, with all the political and ideological force that the seemingly naturalness of the body as the locus of difference can claim. After all, does "the fact of blackness" (*Black Skin, White Masks* 109), as Frantz Fanon terms Western racial obsessions, lie in the body and its epidermis or in the cultural training that quite literally teaches the eye not only how but what to see?[5] This question, framed by the contemporary archive of postmodern thought, sets up the investigative path of this chapter, which traces the visible economies that accompany both the "logic" of race and the broader legacy of modernity that has most powerfully disciplined the body across a range of specificities. While such specificities neither begin nor end with racial difference, it is evident that contemporary critics have only begun to elaborate the relationship between the emergence of modernity and the forms of race and racism that its emergence shaped.[6]

Such an elaboration, of course, is in no way simple, entering as it does the highly contentious conversation about the meaning of modernity and its historical, philosophical, aesthetic, and political contours.[7] While this chapter does not seek to settle such debates, it must nonetheless engage them in order to consider how the tensions within Western knowledge regimes give to race a shifting and often contradictory corporeal epistemology. In particular, I use Michel Foucault's discussion of the rise of the human sciences to analyze the way the visible has achieved a complicated methodological primacy since the late Renaissance, though it is toward the radically different notions of vision and visibility *and* of the body and "being" within this period that my conversation will turn. By placing race at the center of Foucault's examination of the discontinuities between "classical" organizations of knowledge (what most historians recognize as the Enlightenment), and their subsequent demise with the birth of "man" as an object of study in the early nineteenth century (what Foucault calls the modern), this chapter explores the reorganization of knowledge that underwrites the transformation from natural history to the human sciences. Through this reorganization, the human being acquires for the first time in history an organic body and an interior psychic depth, becoming the primary object of investigation and making possible a host of new technologies, institutions, and disciplines. Most crucially, the theoretical assumptions on which race is apprehended undergo a profound rearticulation, a simultaneous strengthening of the corporeal as the bearer of race's meaning *and* a deepening of that meaning as ultimately lodged beyond the assessing gaze of the unaided eye. The epistemology of the visual that enables natural history is thus displaced (though not abandoned) by an emphasis on the organic nature of the body, on its invisibly organized and seemingly definitive biological functioning.

It is this emphasis on race as a constituted "fact" of the body—as a truth that not only can but must be pursued beyond the realm of visible similarities and differences—that characterizes the methodological proclivities of the modern episteme, and it is under its disciplinary gaze that an elaborate discourse purporting the African's inherent inhumanity is most productively, though not originally, waged.[8] In such a methodological context, which begins by generating comparative anatomy and its argument over the biological basis of social hierarchy, we can weigh the political stakes of Foucault's conversation about modernity. At the same time, we can explore, as I do in the final stages of this chapter, the various technologies of race that accompany the subject's newly formed epistemological centrality—technologies that produce, in Foucauldian terms, various cultural practices of subjection. I thus read the contestation over racial order and being as a central feature of the epistemic turn toward what we now call modernity, that process by which, in Foucault's words, "the mode of being of things, and of the order that divided them up before presenting them to the understanding, was profoundly altered" (*The Order of Things* xxii). In the disciplinary displacement of natural history by the human sciences, in short, race in Western culture is constituted as far more than skin.

The Eye of the Beholder

Although England had various sources attesting to the existence of dark-skinned people, from biblical narrative to ancient mythologies, it is not until the sixteenth century that the English and African are known to have come face to face.[9] This meeting, now so embedded in the history of imperialism and so completely overdetermined by the legacy the "facial" figuration implies, pivots in nearly all accounts on the African's arresting "black" visage; as Winthrop D. Jordan notes, explorers "rarely failed to comment upon it" (*White over Black* 4). But simple commentary does not necessarily lead to the enslavement of a group of people based on the color of their skin, and it would be erroneous to assume that the program of exportation to be accelerated in the seventeenth century can be accounted for by the "fact" of a perceptible difference, as though the latter has substance enough to fully determine the former. As Jordan indicates, "English contact with Africans did not take place primarily in a context which prejudged the Negro as slave. . . . Rather, Englishmen met Negroes merely as another sort of men" (ibid.). Before the fifteenth century, in fact, "the question of the Negro's color can hardly be said to have drawn the attention of Englishmen or indeed Europeans generally" (12). By the late seventeenth century, however, color had become the primary organizing principle around which the natural historian classified human differences, and a century later, it functioned as the visible precondition for anatomical investigations into the newly emergent object of knowledge, "man."

How do we understand this broad scope of Western thought that began in earnest to define race as a visible economy in the sixteenth century and continued to confer upon it a central position in subsequent articulations of race, up to and including the present day? To answer this question, we must take seriously the notion of race as a fiction — as a profound ordering of difference instantiated at the sight of the body — in order to jettison the security of the visible as an obvious and unacculturated phenomenon. For what the eye sees, and how we understand that seeing in relation to physical embodiment and philosophical and linguistic assumptions, necessitates a broader inquiry into the articulation of race, one that takes the visual moment as itself a complicated and historically contingent production. In the process, we must rethink the seeming progression often attributed to the production of race in Western culture, where the initial sighting of the African's "blackness" functions as the economic and epistemological origin for institutions of enslavement, as well as subsequent delineations of difference based on cranial capacity and anatomical form.[10] The history of the visible that undergirds these fashionings of race is not, as our assurance in the visible may often lead us to believe, always the same.[11]

To accept race as a complex aspect of social formation and not as a visible truth is particularly difficult from within Western ideologies that render the body "natural" in its "different" meanings.[12] Much evidence can be marshaled, however, to demonstrate that this naturalization, implicit in the equation between skin color and enslavement, is part of a late-flowering racist discourse in the Anglophilic West. As David Brion Davis notes in his far-ranging study, *The Problem of Slavery in Western Culture,* "slaves in most ancient societies were not distinguishable by skin color or other racial characteristics" (48). Instead their "lowly status" was indicated in other ways: by shorn heads, identification tablets, branding, and tattooing. Davis reads these visual symbols as part of a historical continuity of the corporeal logic of race: "in later centuries," he writes, "men would come to regard darkness of skin as a brand which God or nature impressed upon an inferior people" (49). But, while an imposed sign crafted by the master and a "natural" sign based on skin share the similarity of signifying inferiority, Winthrop Jordan's assertion that, prior to the fifteenth century, color failed to function as a perplexing and controversial aspect of human being weighs heavily here. To mark the body is not the same as *being* a bodily mark. Each involves a vastly different understanding of the substance of the body, regardless of the extent to which a visible decoding has been brought to bear.[13] This distinction is important in arguing against the assumption that Davis makes of a vast continuity underwriting Western discourses on blackness, where the logic of the visible ascribed to the corporeal in ancient societies is simply updated in the equation between black skin and enslavement.[14]

This does not mean that the visible is not crucial, at all points, to the construction and perpetuation of Western racial productions, but that the distinction between an imposed mark (such as a tattoo) and the idea of difference as lodged in the skin must be understood in broader terms. Here, Foucault becomes especially useful, since his focus on the rise of natural history demonstrates a transformation in Western epistemological modes wrought by the economic, scientific, and religious upheavals of the late Renaissance — transformations that are in turn reconfigured by the displacement of natural history by biology in the nineteenth century. In particular, Foucault looks at the way natural history compensated for the loosening of religious authority by setting as its task the articulation of a comprehensive classification system of nature. The epistemological assumptions underwriting such a project demonstrate the demise of the "preclassical" regime in which resemblances among phenomena were emphasized to evince the preordained unity between nature and the institution of God. But in the seventeenth century, Foucault argues, the "classical" mind disengaged from this activity of "*drawing things together*" and instead subjected every resemblance "to proof by comparison" (*The Order of Things* 55). Such comparison pivoted on "the apparent simplicity of a *description of the visible*," and in this, natural history's methodological reliance on rationalized vision was born (137). Visibility, in short, was no longer linked to the other senses as the eye was resituated "to see and only to see" (43).

In defining the characteristics of the rationalization of vision, Foucault discusses how the emphasis on comparison forged a structure of thinking that pivoted on two primary and exclusionary figures: identity and difference. Within this framework, relationships between entities in the natural world were investigated by relying on a disengaged process of observation, one that significantly carried with it a definitional range "restricted . . . to black and white" (*The Order of Things* 133). Foucault's language here, his marking of the binary of black and white that structured the classical knowledge regime of the seventeenth and eighteenth centuries, is not simply a fortuitous metaphor for my own examination of the production of racial discourse, but it is an important description of the consequences of natural history's methodological reliance on rationalized vision. Such a reliance disavowed the binocular physiology of vision in favor of the authority of a singular eye that purportedly took its place in visual space suspended from the body, observing but not interpreting.[15] The epistemological basis of natural history rests in this mathematical vision, as it provided the methodological certainty on which the natural historian established a clear and unambiguous description of "the system of identities and the order of differences existing between natural entities" (Foucault, *The Order of Things* 136). It is in this context, with the observer's neutrality seemingly guaranteed by the methodological emphasis on observation, that natural history's increasing interest in human classification must be approached, since it is here that the rendering of race as an epiphenomenon of skin is most damagingly drawn.

Of course, natural history was not alone in securing the process of vision to a highly ordered and regularized material realm. Indeed, its systematical understanding of vision and form was remarkably similar to what Martin Jay in "Scopic Regimes of Modernity") calls Cartesian perspectivalism (6). Jay demonstrates a relationship between the English Renaissance's aesthetic understanding of vision and the scientific perspective founded on the researcher's dispassionate eye, a relationship that outlines for me the broad context in which the African's definitive "blackness" came quite literally to be seen. Linked to the "objective optical order" heralded by the artistic theory and practice of the Italian Quattrocento, Cartesian perspectivalism is characterized as "a lone eye looking through a peephole at the scene in front of it . . . static, unblinking, and fixated" (6, 7). The lone quality of this observing eye and its relation to an ordered exterior reiterates the scenario of observation within the classical episteme where vision constituted itself, in a feat of emotional withdrawal and bodily repression, at the radiating edge of the monocular eye. As Jay says, Cartesian perspectivalism was "in league with a scientific world view that no longer hermeneutically read the world as a divine text, but rather saw it as situated in a mathematically regular spatio-temporal order filled with natural objects that could only be observed from without by the dispassionate eye of the neutral researcher" (9).

The image of the peephole that Jay uses to describe the neutral moment of observation is a variation on what, by the Renaissance, had been known for hundreds of years: light passing through a small hole into an enclosed, unlighted space would cast an inverted image on the wall opposite the hole. As Jonathan Crary discusses, the representational relations underlying this phenomenon served not only as a central figuration of visual relations from the late Renaissance to the early nineteenth century, but were technologized in various instruments of observation sharing the same name: camera obscura. As an instrument "within an arrangement of technical and cultural practices," the camera obscura guaranteed for "scientists or artists, empiricists or rationalists . . . access to an objective truth about the world" ("Modernizing Vision" 31). In tracing the dynamics of the camera obscura structure of vision, Crary significantly delineates the kind of epistemic break posited by Foucault in the early nineteenth century, where the disembodied vision of the classical episteme gave way to organicity and the study of the body was wrenched (however incompletely) from the rationalized visibilities of Cartesianism. But prior to this moment, as Crary notes, the Cartesian paradigm, for at least two centuries, "stood as model . . . of how observation leads to truthful inferences about the world" (*Techniques of the Observer* 29).

This is the visual system that conditioned the natural historian's quest to define a classification system that established and explained the order of nature, and it was in the process of such ordering that a most damaging racial question would be formed: How many species comprised the field generally known as "man"? There was, however, no single route to the emergence of this question, and while it seems to demand (and has elicited) deeply racist answers, we would be wrong to assume that the motivating force of natural history was to establish scientific proof for white supremacy in a theory of multiple creations. Still, natural history's eventual turn to the identification of skin as the primary characteristic for classifying human beings in the late seventeenth century was no insignificant methodological move, demonstrating as it did a shift away from geography to the body as the locus of identity and difference. It was François Bernier, a physician and traveler, who first eschewed the prevailing geographical classificatory system of human beings by locating skin as the single characteristic on which human organization would depend. Although he discussed a variety of classificatory means—hair, nose, stature—his primary focus on skin color initiated the kind of reduction of human organization to a singular, determining, and ultimately visual terrain that now has a well-known history in the Anglophilic West.[16] But like other naturalists working in his tradition, Bernier was adamant that skin differences did not constitute hierarchical orders of being, even as his methodological choice could be turned to sanction the growing popular sense that race had a corporeal foundation: that the body was the origin of racial truth.

The contradiction between Bernier's appeal to the body and his subsequent refusal to grant that appeal a hierarchical meaning was itself characteristic of natural history's approach to human organization in the seventeenth and eighteenth centuries. The primary figures—Bernier, Carolus Linnaeus, George Louis Leclerc Buffon, and Johann Friedrich Blumenbach—all argued against understanding racial differences as inherent hierarchies.[17] And yet, the assumptions underlying their methodologies—their reliance on observation and notions of orders based on comparisons of identity and difference—evinced more complicated and contradictory positions about the origin and meaning of race. For instance, in crafting descriptions of the primary divisions he observed within the human species, Bernier failed to provide an account of the division that he occupied, proceeding instead from the assumption of an already known European norm (Gossett, Race 32). This Buffon did as well, though he emphasized environmental factors discerning the African's blackness; in his schema, whiteness served as the classificatory norm, "the real and natural color of man" (quoted in Gossett, Race 36).[18] In these and other cases (such as Blumenbach's naming of the caucasian as the original type of man from which all others diverged[19]), we witness the asymmetry of the classical episteme where the rationalization of observation underwrote the European's claim to a universal, normative position and the specificity of race was increasingly elided with "black."

In the United States, where the debate about skin color and hierarchical arrangements would become more heated under the pressure of abolitionist reform, various explanations of race followed in the Buffon and Blumenbach tradition, revolving around climate, custom, and other changing conditions. In 1787, for instance, the Reverend Mr. Samuel Stanhope Smith posited that because race was caused by climate, the European and African must be innately the same. To Smith, the culturally disparaged intellectual and moral condition of Africans(-Americans) evinced "the humiliating circumstances in which they find themselves" (An Essay on the Causes of the Variety of Complexion and Figure in the Human Species 105), and hence he believed that in freedom even bodily signs, such as skin, would change.[20] Implicit in Smith's discussion was an assumption of whiteness as the civilized status of skin, an assumption that twentieth-century readers no doubt find more congruent with theories of black inferiority than many eighteenth-century advocates of abolition did. But it is crucial to recognize that commentators on race who worked within the methodological tradition of natural history remained for the most part tied to an understanding of race as mutable and of the human species as part of a larger continuity of order and meaning.

This emphasis on mutability was especially important in the context of eighteenth-century obsessions with the Great Chain of Being, that ancient notion of harmonious and continuous order that moved by ascending complexity from the simplest to the most intricate. In its reemergence as a racially based delineation, the Great Chain propelled countless discussions about the relationship between man and ape, crafting specific arguments for the African's cosmic subordinacy by positioning him as intervening between the two. When Peter Camper invented the "facial angle" in the 1770s, he brought a methodological focus to the Great Chain theory by "demonstrating" a scale of being that passed from the European to the African to the chimpanzee.[21] For Blumenbach and other naturalists, however, the concept and procedure of the facial angle eclipsed crucial distinctions between animals and humans, undermining to great detriment natural history's overarching emphasis on the homogeneity of "man." It was perhaps this emphasis that functioned throughout the remainder of the eighteenth century to stave off the force of the Great Chain theory from moving fully in the direction inaugurated by Camper, though comparative anatomy in the early nineteenth century took up in many ways where Camper left off.

In this regard, one might read comparative anatomy as an extension of the logic of the visible that adhered to natural history, since both seemed to rely on similar elaborations of the body and its "being." But as Nancy Stepan suggests, there was no simple line of development from natural history to nineteenth-century race science. Instead, we must read this relationship as a broad and definitively radical reorganization of knowledge:

[T]he changes that occurred in racial science [in the late eighteenth and nineteenth centuries] were at the same time rather more than a move towards racial typology and polygenism. [They] involved a change from an emphasis on the fundamental physical and moral homogeneity of man, despite superficial differences, to an emphasis on the essential heterogeneity of mankind, despite superficial similarities.

> It was a shift . . . to a sense of man as primarily a biological being, em-
> bedded in nature and governed by biological laws. (*The Idea of Race
> in Science* 4)

In the ascendancy of biology, as we shall see, the concept of "race" will undergo significant transformation, losing the kind of fluidity it achieved in natural history as a product of climate and civilization, as a variation within the human species, to become a rather stable and primary characteristic for defining the nature of the body, both its organic and ontological consistency. This is not to say that in its emphasis on skin, natural history did not contribute to the strengthening of Western racist discourse, but to suggest that something more than rationalized vision and the reduction of the scale of nature to binary relations was necessary for the full flourishing of race science in the nineteenth century—a flourishing on which, this chapter argues, some of the broadest and what have become for us most damaging productions of "race" in American culture depend.

The Seen and the Unseen

It is, in fact, toward the emergence of the human sciences that we must turn in order to explore how race becomes increasingly defined as an inherent corporeal difference in the nineteenth century. Foucault's only address to the legacy of debate concerning the meaning, form, and order of races since the Renaissance significantly occurs in demonstrating the epistemic distinctions that separated the new human sciences from their predecessor, natural history. While he agrees that "the natural sciences dealt with man as with a species or a genus: the controversy about the problem of races in the eighteenth century testifies to that," he maintains that the formation of a table of relations based on what the eye sees did not "isolate, in any way, a specific domain proper to man" (*The Order of Things* 308–309). But comparative anatomy begins to break with the assurance of the visible to craft interior space, to open the body to the possibilities of subterranean and invisible truths and meanings, and to define the particular physical domain through which the human being will gain increasing specificity and biological coherence. For Foucault, this means that comparative anatomy was not "merely a deepening of the descriptive techniques employed in the Classical age," for its investigative pursuit extended beyond the "surface of the body at which the naturalist's gaze had once halted" (269, 294). Natural history, in other words, was replaced by biology and in this, face was situated as potentially more than skin deep.

While the first anatomical investigations of the human body predate by hundreds of years the period that Foucault defines as marking the birth of the modern episteme, comparative anatomy's formulation in the work of Georges Cuvier in the late eighteenth century demonstrates various methodological differences between natural history and the new disciplines devoted to the study of "man." Most crucially, Cuvier introduced the idea of organic coherence within the processes of an organism, its governance, that is, by biological laws. While Foucault does not chart the implications of Cuvier's work for a discourse of race, and fails to indicate that much like his contemporaries, Cuvier was interested in accounting for the origins of racial differences, the reorganization of the living being around "nuclei of coherence" (*The Order of Things* 273) underwrote claims throughout the nineteenth century for the permanency of racial characteristics, biological in origin, and connected to the organic coherence of the organism as a whole. Shorn of the climate and cultivation theories of the natural historian, race became, as George W. Stocking Jr. notes, "the permanent inherited physical differences which distinguish human groups" (*Race, Culture, and Evolution* 30). In the emergence of race as a biological category, Cuvier's work had weighty implications: his primary interest was the brain and skull and he posited that the function and role of one organ could differ greatly from its function and role in another organism. "[O]ne organ [can be] at its highest degree of perfection in one species, while another reaches that same degree of perfection in a different species" (quoted in Foucault, *The Order of Things* 271). For the investigative pursuits of nineteenth-century physiognomy, phrenology, and craniology, Cuvier offered both the locus— the brain and skull—and the rationale for constituting racial differences as evolutionary and hierarchical.[22] As biology assigned to "man" a new sphere of specificity, the racial determinations wrought through this sphere produced not simply the constancy of race as an unchanging, biological feature, but an inherent and incontrovertible difference of which skin was only the most visible indication. The move from the visible epidermal terrain to the articulation of the interior structure of human bodies thus extrapolated in both broader and more distinct terms the parameters of white supremacy, giving it a logic lodged fully in the body.

While the visible must be understood as giving way to the authority of the invisible recesses of the body, to organs and functions, the full force of this production of racial discourse was nonetheless contingent on the status of an observer, whose relation to the object under investigation was mediated and deepened by newly developed technologies for rendering the invisible visible. To a great degree, the inauguration of biology rested on the inadequacy of the eye to penetrate surfaces, requiring instead the enhancement of apparatuses that perfected its limitations and enabled it to exceed the boundaries of its own physicality. For this reason, we witness in the nineteenth century the invention of numerous kinds of mechanisms—in race science alone, callipers, cephalometers, craniometers, craniophores, craniostats, and parietal goniometers—that overcame the limited specificity of the "naked" eye (Stepan, "Race and Gender" 43). In this, the geometrical optics of the seventeenth and eighteenth centuries gave way to physiological optics in the nineteenth as "knowledge was accumulated," as Jonathan Crary writes, "about the constitutive role of the body in the apprehension of a visible world" (*Techniques of the Observer* 16). Vision, in short, was linked to the centrality of the nervous system, and the assurance of an unmediated and realistic relationship between the thing perceived and the processes of its perception was wholly undermined.

At the same time, with vision now understood as a "referential illusion" (Crary, *Techniques of the Observer* 91), cultural practices of representation and signification were themselves altered, and it is in this process that analogy surfaced as a definitive mechanism for positing relations between things that were, from the level of appearances, seemingly unconnected. In the context of the nineteenth century's production of racial discourse, the privilege accorded to analogy enabled a host of other cultural determinants to be linked to and organically defined within the sphere of the body. Through the crafting of analogic relations, the deployment of race was multiplied, radiating outward to constitute new identities of bodies as sexual, gendered, and criminal excesses. In "Race and Gender: The Role of Analogy in Science," Nancy Stepan reads the theoretical supposition that linked the brain and the skull along the lines of function as the primary means for the emergence of broad analyses of the similarities and differences that existed among individuals and groups. By the 1820s, in fact, the phrenological literature demonstrated direct comparison between "women and lower races . . . on the basis of their skull formations" and, a decade later, "a specialized system of implications based on the similarities between brains and skulls appeared for the first time" (46). These implications were fundamentally different from previous suggestions of the relationship between race and gender, where reproductive function and sexuality connected "black females (the 'sign' of sexuality) and lower-class or 'degenerate' white women" (ibid.).

In using the skull and brain as the measure for intelligence, comparisons between race and gender were made available for cross-gender formulations for the first time. Here, as Stepan writes,

women's low brain weights and deficient brain structures were analogous to those of lower races, and . . . [women] shared with Negroes a
narrow, childlike, and delicate skull, so different from the more robust
and rounded heads characteristic of males of "superior" races. Similarly, women of higher races tended to have slightly protruding jaws,
analogous to, if not as exaggerated as, the apelike jutting jaws of lower
races. . . . In short, lower races represented the "female" type of the
human species, and females the "lower race" of gender. ("Race and
Gender" 39–40)

Though these analogies, the African male could be aligned with the feminine, positioned within a hierarchy of bodily functions on a level approxi-
mating that of the Anglo-American woman — a figuration that precedes, as
I will discuss in detail in the next chapter, twentieth-century couplings of
"blacks and women."

While neurophysiology would eventually challenge the conclusions of
phrenology and discredit it well before the end of the century, the legacy
of measurement would proceed undaunted, more rigorously in fact, in the
empirical desire to found the basis and scope of human difference in un-
assailable biological terms. As the century wore on, craniometrists continued to develop new means for extending the analogic relations phrenology had worked so hard to establish. In time, the smaller brains of
women and the so-called lower races became de rigueur for craniologists,
and the larger brain sizes of the European male accounted for his intellectual and cultural superiority. It was really not until the twentieth century,
and then quite well into it, before the scientific community began to question and ultimately undermine the assumption, according to Stepan, "that
some measure, whether of cranial capacity, the facial angle, the brain vol-
ume, or brain weight, would be found that would provide a true indicator
of innate capacity" (Stepan, "Race and Gender" 46).

In the turn from the visible taxonomy of skin to the comparative anatomists' obsession with organology and corporeal measurement, we witness
the changing disciplinary structures of knowledge that have governed race
since the late Renaissance and mark for Foucault the epistemic transformations that inaugurated the human sciences. But a caution is warranted
here: to remain too definitively wed to the notion of the epistemic leap
is to potentially underrepresent the contestations around the category of
humanity that framed both the modern and the classical epistemes. In the
United States, for instance, the classical emphasis on environmentalism as
explanation for the racial determinant of skin retained a prominent place

in various writings throughout the nineteenth century. As late as the 1840s and 1850s, in fact, the preeminent authority on race in the states was still Samuel Stanhope Smith, whose 1787 theoretical treatise on the origin of race, which he posited as climate and custom, had been reprinted in 1810 and did not incur a threatening challenge until the 1830s. This challenge came from Dr. Charles Caldwell, whose *Thoughts on the Original Unity of the Human Race* established the polygenesis argument as credible science in the United States. Instead of founding his discussion on the kind of argument of function taking place in scientific circles in Europe, however, Caldwell returned to biblical documentation to make a case that the African's existence postdated the flood—not enough time, as George M. Fredrickson remarks, "for a new race to come into existence through the effects of climate" (*The Black Image in the White Mind* 73). Caldwell's work would be succeeded at mid-century by the founding of American ethnology, and the craniologic analyses of George Morton, George R. Gliddon, Dr. Josiah Nott, and Louis Agassiz would fashion, on the basis of anatomical function, the necessary proof for the theory of separate creation.[23]

The intensification of scientific efforts to ascertain the origin and bodily foundation for race in the nineteenth century, alongside the persistence of environmentalism as a key explanation for racial difference in the United States in the antebellum period, indicates a less emphatic break, a more troubled confusion, between classical and modern apprehensions of race. To a large extent, such an intensification points to the importance of thinking about epistemic organizations as heterogeneous, containing subcultural formations of knowledge that exist in contradiction or tension with each regime's primary features. If we return to Martin Jay's discussion of vision and modernity, for instance, we might note that he places the rationalized vision of the classical regime in an earlier period than does Foucault, demonstrating how the objective vision of the late seventeenth and eighteenth centuries had theoretical underpinnings in articulations of linear perspective in the fourteenth century. While Foucault might argue that Renaissance perspective never managed to fully disentangle itself from the significatory system of the preclassical episteme where the relation between observer and observed was set within a framework "coeval with the institution of God" (*The Order of Things* 34), Descartes's own meditations on rationality and substance in the seventeenth century, to which the classical episteme is indebted, were part of an excursus on divine existence as well. Renaissance work on linear perspective, thought within the context of Foucault's epistemes, might be characterized as a subcultural formation of knowledge in the preclassical era, initiating the rationalization of space and vision that would emerge, in the wake of Descartes's philosophical anchoring, as foundational for Enlightenment science.

Such an emergence was not an inevitability, however, no matter how seemingly progressive or developmental one may want to construct these historical relationships. Similarly, the strengthening of racist discourse through biology in the nineteenth century was no simple or inevitable "outgrowth" of early craniology, no matter what mutual effect they may have shared. Such a perspective on the historical is perhaps the cornerstone of the Foucauldian method and ultimately an influential one for approaching questions about the production of racial discourse and its attendant hierarchies. After all, part of the naturalness of any discourse of difference is its ability to marshal a history whose features seem both inevitable and incontrovertible, freezing the future into a sequential unfolding of the dominant modes of knowledge governing what comes to us as—and what we invent to be—the narrative of an evolutionary past. In locating the preeminent assumptions of a particular knowledge regime and the tensions within that regime that threaten, at various points, to undermine and circumvent its reigning logic, we may be able to ascertain other kinds of historical possibilities. And yet, the task of understanding the past differently is overwhelming, as is the necessity of confronting the present and its new deployments of racial discourse. If rethinking the historical contours of Western racial discourse matters as a political project, it is not as a manifestation of an other truth that has previously been denied, but as a vehicle for shifting the frame of reference in such a way that the present can emerge as somehow less familiar, less natural in its categories, its political delineations, and its epistemological foundations.

Technologies of Race

The "if" at the outset of the preceding sentence is a pressing consideration, one not easy to negotiate because of the often quite clear disparity between critical analysis and political transformation that, to many, constitutes the impasse of "theory" in academia today. That it seems as if we have no choice but to believe in critical thought as a mode of transformative action underscores for me what Foucault means when he uses the word *subjection* to describe the broad consequences of "man's" emergence as human subject in the modern episteme. For here, without the classical assurance of an observational neutrality, the modern human subject must necessarily exist within the complications of "representations by means of which he lives, and on the basis of which he possesses that strange capacity of being able to represent to himself precisely that life" (*The Order of Things* 352). Of course, that life cannot simply be conferred the status of a new overarching truth that invests the human being with meaning and renders our epistemological framework secure. In the Foucauldian universe, when the human subject enters into existence from the simplicity of classical taxonomy, bound to a representational grid of our own making, we have not reached the culminating point of a narrative of progress, some remythologized liberatory moment heralded as the "birth of man." Instead, we have merely begun to comprehend our "ambiguous position as an object of knowledge and as a subject that knows: enslaved sovereign, observed spectator" (312).

Such a rendering of modernity breaks with more humanist explanations to establish a vastly different understanding of the relationship between the scientific, industrial, and technological "revolutions," one that does not announce "man's" epistemological centrality as an incontrovertible step toward democratic emancipations. In the context of Western discourses of race and the hierarchical social arrangements they inscribe, the failure of modernity to exact a transcendent subjectivity is crucial to rethinking the forms of political resistance undertaken in the contemporary period, and it is one of the aims of this study to fully engage just such a discussion. First and most immediately, however, I need to sketch in broad terms the implications of Foucault's take on modernity for reading the disciplinary practices attending race in nineteenth- and twentieth-century American culture. For while the emergence of the human being as both subject and object of knowledge characterizes the epistemic specificity of modernity, other attending transformations in the social order are central to the cultural practices of discipline through which white supremacy has negotiated itself, not only under the aegis of slavery but also in the various historical configurations that follow it in the twentieth century. To trace the racial technologies of power that create, address, and proscribe modernity's emergent subject entails returning to the question of vision and visibility, and to a more precise explanation of the impact of the dissolution of the classical regime on cultural epistemologies.[24]

In his discussion of the science of physiology in the early nineteenth century, Jonathan Crary relates how explorations of the nerve structure of the eye contributed to new ways of thinking about knowledge and its limitations, as well as to the increasing insertion of the human being into mass systems of both production and consumption. As part of the broader scientific quest of the body's organic complexity, physiology concentrated on those aspects of vision that were sublimated in perspectival and classical accounts: the existence of afterimages and peripheral vision, the effects of the curvature of the retina, the dilation and contraction of the pupil, the consequences of direct and indirect viewing, and the operational processes of binocular vision. Such a pursuit reflected the disciplinary demands of industrialization, in which more sophisticated understandings of eye and hand coordination, as well as visual fatigue, were necessary to increase productivity. Most important perhaps, in defining the eye's organic functioning, physiologists would conclude that vision was itself a referential illusion, by demonstrating that a variety of stimuli could create the same visual sensation or, conversely, that the same stimulus could create a variety of sensations. Vision was conceived, in short, "without any necessary connection to the act of looking at all" ("Modernizing Vision" 38).

This is indeed a far cry from the classical regime and its faith in optical verity, and it begins to demonstrate an essential component of modern vision: what the eye sees is not a neutral moment of reception but an arbitrary and disciplinary operation, one in which experience is actually produced in the subject. As Foucault suggests in *Discipline and Punish,* the referential illusion of modern vision underlies a host of cultural arrangements and apparatuses, and we might, to extrapolate from his argument, include as examples the distribution of bodies in urban space, the architectural structure of the factory, or even the invention of increasingly more realist technologies, such as photography, cinema, television, and of course virtual reality.[25] Readers familiar with Foucault know that his primary concern is with penal practices as an exploration of various techniques of power that organize and discipline the social body. As the prevailing method of penal legislation of the sixteenth and seventeenth centuries, he assigns "spectacle": the appearance of the "tortured, dismembered, amputated body, symbolically branded on face or shoulder, exposed alive or dead to public view" (8). To the eighteenth century and its rationalism he ascribes panopticism and surveillance. As his terms suggest, the organization of vision and the relationship between visibility and invisibility are central, and it is in drawing out the significance of these relationships that Foucault's analysis becomes most useful to any conversation concerning American racial hierarchies as practices of subjection.

Spectacle, as Foucault explains, involved public torture, the scene of the scaffold, the excess of violence; it was a ritual that marked the victim; its visible economy was its claim to truth: "the condemned man published his crime and the justice that had been meted out to him by bearing them physically on his body" (*Discipline and Punish* 43). But in the eighteenth century, through the philosophies of the Enlightenment, penal reform began to dispose of the specular exposure of pain in which the condemned function as the communal abject for a public thereby witnessing the material force of the sovereign's power. Instead, what was "maximized [was] the representation of the penalty, not its corporal reality," or as Foucault says a bit later, "the idea of the offence [was] enough to arouse the sign of the punishment" (95, 105). By making the criminal wear placards and clothing to signify the crime, the public incorporated the sign of the punishment into its image of the crime, and hence the disciplining effect was exacted not from the horror of torture but from the more benign but still visible mark conferring criminality (and the exercising of justice) on the individual. The "gentle way of punishment," as Foucault ironically calls it, was thus achieved through "a mechanism that coerce[d] by means of observation," where the subject's internalization of discipline constituted the coercive mechanism through which the social body was traversed by power (104, 170).[26]

The model on which Foucault bases his reading of the compulsory visibility attending surveillance is the Panoptican, an architectural form that demonstrates both materially and metaphorically the new relations of visibility that enmeshed the disciplinary subject:

> [A]t the periphery, an annular building; at the centre, a tower. . . . [T]he peripheric building is divided into cells. . . . [T]hey have two windows, one on the inside, corresponding to the windows of the tower; the other, on the outside, allows the light to cross the cell. . . . They are like so many cages, so many small theatres, in which each actor is alone, perfectly individualized and constantly visible. (*Discipline and Punish* 200)

Significantly, the disembodied position of the panoptic observer is compared by Foucault to the work of the naturalist, whose metaphorical if not literal enclosure in a tower of observation decorporealizes the gaze, rendering an exterior or outer world fully open to view. And like the naturalist, the panoptic observer was committed to classification, hierarchy, and relations of identity and difference. As Foucault writes, the Panoptican made "it possible to observe performances[,] . . . to map aptitudes, to assess characters, [and] to draw up rigorous classifications" (203); the panoptic was not a reiteration of the regime of visibility attending the classical age, however, since the power of the gaze significantly functioned in lieu of the act of looking by inscribing visibility everywhere.

In time, this panoptic system was generalized throughout the Western world, no longer bound to a specific architecture but wrought within a broader configuration of social space, visual technologies, and disciplinary exercise. Assuming the form of an omnipresent surveillance, power was itself invisible, but "capable of making all visible . . . a faceless gaze that transformed the whole social body into a field of perception: thousands of eyes posted everywhere" (*Discipline and Punish* 214). This insertion of the social body into a field of permanent and self-incorporated visibility took place alongside various economic upheavals that accompanied the production of the discourse of race, demonstrating the colluding specular and panoptic frameworks through which race was deployed as a technique of disciplinary power in both the nineteenth and twentieth centuries. Indeed, the shift from the socially inscribed mark of visibility attending spectacle to the self-incorporated vision of the panoptic relation coalesced in the United States, not in successive stages but as intertwined technologies that worked simultaneously to stage the hierarchical relations of race. While we might attribute to the slave system many of the features of the society of spectacle, for instance, from the dynamic of the auction block to brandings, whippings, and other rituals of public torture, the panoptic can be located in such phenomenon as the organizing layout of the plantation, the ideological elision between slavery and dark skin, and the legalization of miscegenation as an abstracted property relation. The disciplinary power of race, in short, must be read as implicated in both specular and panoptic regimes.

Two particular periods in U.S. history are especially telling in this regard, and they form, as students of the history of race well know, a bizarre kind of symmetry, coming in two successive stages: the first, chasmic disruption of the Civil War and the revisionist aftermath of Reconstruction in the 1880s and 1890s; and the civil rights movement in the mid-twentieth century and the conservative retrenchment of the 1980s and 1990s. When we turn to the late nineteenth and early twentieth centuries, we encounter the landscape overseen by the Ku Klux Klan: lynched, castrated, raped, and charred bodies ceremoniously strung up for public view—images that would increasingly circulate as detailed descriptions of torture found their way into local newspapers and as photographs of the event were mass produced for commercial entertainment value.[27] But unlike public executions in the seventeenth century, this program of torture functioned within a panoptic logic, as the perpetuators of dismemberment and murder were ritually veiled and acted not in the service of a lone sovereign but for a now-homogenized, known-but-never-individuated, power. Here, the spectacle becomes the culminating moment for the panoptic's reinforcement, a lasting demonstration of the power of the eyes that watched, that rarely had to offer up their own name. The white hoods and the capes of the Klan: these were the means for translating the practices of torture into instruments for the panoptic's effect, multiplying the significatory value of white skin as the invisible, but everywhere seen, locus of panoptic power. Simultaneously known and unknowable, the rituals of the Klan maximized the relationship between specular and panoptic modes of punishment, translating the possibilities of public execution into psychological structures of servitude and assumed inferiority and drawing the contours of social space in such a way that the African-American subject took up a cellular existence, "like so many cages," within the omnipresent gaze of the white eye.

Certainly the cellular existence posited here did not rely solely on the ritualistic terror of the Klan, no matter how thoroughly the practices of the Klan may have marked the excesses, insecurities, and liminal zones of the logic and discipline of white racial supremacy. The Klan was only the extreme moment in a broad systemization of social space, one whose propensity for segregation (in housing, education, public transportation, hospitals, prisons, and even cemeteries) began in the northern, "free" states as custom before the Civil War brought on the end of chattel slavery. In the south, according to C. Vann Woodward, 1877 marked the official beginning of the Jim Crow era, whose dissolution in law, if not in certain primary configurations of social life, waited until the 1954 Supreme Court decision outlawing segregation in public schools.[28] The legally instituted segregation of space and services established a panoptic regime (in whose service the Klan's specular practices functioned): from the complicated definitions of blood relations as indices of racial categorization to the multiple public warnings "No Colored Allowed" and their affirmative inversion "For Whites Only." The binary cleavage of race to which this panoptic system applies radiated its significatory value through the ever-present production of community gazes, inscriptions that read and rendered the truth of the body and, in doing so, produced the experiential truth of the subject as well. This experience has and continues to situate every subject in U.S. culture within the panoptic vision of racial meanings, regardless of the extent to which whiteness prefigures its own seeming invisibility.[29]

In the long struggle against segregation in the mid-twentieth century, the specular scene of torture and dismemberment would emerge once again as a central feature of white resistance to the panoptic's segregatory decline. From bombings and beatings, lynchings and tauntings, the entire response to civil rights brought forth the full arsenal of the spectacle's appeal. In its aftermath, a number of significant reorganizations of the social body began to take place, as institutional integration destabilized the formal structure of the panoptic and threatened to subvert segregation's tenuous geometry of public gazes. While nineteenth-century Reconstruction would feature, as a mythic "Old South" was being born, the proliferation of racial icons (Sambo and Mammy figures adorning everything from greeting cards to soap dishes and match covers), the deployment of race at work in the second reconstruction also evinced its own mass production.[30] But gone were the bug-eyed, large-lipped faces gracing kitchen wares. Instead, the new mode of cultural surveillance — a disciplinarity so deeply woven in systems of representation that it would come to signify, by the late 1980s, political representation as well — was defined according to the developing possibilities of visual technology dominating late-twentieth-century life. Here, one turns to cinema, television, and video where the circulation of representational images partake in a panoptic terrain by serving up bodies as narrative commodities, detached from the old economy of corporeal enslavement and situated instead in the panoply of signs, texts, and images through which the discourse of race functions now to affirm the referential illusion of an organic real.

This illusion is predicated on the ascendancy of a visual regime in which the very framework of "black" and "white" designates authentic, natural races. But the conformation of the body to a racial script that precedes and instantiates the subject in a relation of subjection does not depend, in any uncomplicated way, on what the eye sees: as I have discussed, the primary characteristic of the modern panoptic regime is its reliance on a visual production that exceeds the limited boundaries of the eye thereby dispersing the realist relation underlying classical vision. In the increasing production of simulated visual fields, in the deeply wrenching knowledge of an eye that constitutionally misperceives, in the loss of epistemological assurance in the referent — in all of these, the logic of race attached to a corporeal essence is challenged at its most fundamental level of bodily belief. It is for this reason that the signs of race, the inscriptions of bodies, and the signifiers of various cultural determinations are today seemingly unleashed in a proliferation of circulating images: integration beckons now the rising primacy of difference as commodity, the manufacturing of multiple national and international markets, and the repetition of bodies constituted and defined in the visual field.

This is a primary figuration of the processes of subjection we now live within, visible economies that too often feature integration without equality, representation without power, presence without the confirming possibility of emancipation. Ours is a white supremacist system asymmetrical in its economic and political allotments, triumphant in its ability to mask deep disparity on the one hand, and yet thoroughly rigid in its maintenance of naive individualism and rhetorical democracy on the other. Its reliance on visual technologies cannot be underestimated, for in the shift toward mass cultural production and in the demise of official segregation, the apparatus of the visible as representational terrain engenders a disparagingly rejuvenated, though visibly different, deployment of racial power. The long historical transformation from a slave economy, so often heralded as the linear progression of the unstoppable, self-perpetuating, democratic ethos, emerges instead as part of the massive transformation in Western knowledge regimes that have produced modern subjects in all of their visual density. In this sense, the enfranchisement of the slave was only one kind of liberation, and slavery itself was only a particular economic form for the instantiation of racial hierarchies.[31]

In presenting such a broad sweep of the nineteenth- and twentieth-century cultural terrains and their various avenues for deploying the power of race, I am necessarily postponing until subsequent chapters discussions of the complexities of representation and the differences among visual technologies, issues that crucially qualify and specify the relationship between a cultural apparatus and its articulation of power. Here I hope I have been able to render a sense of the necessarily complicated production of the discourse of race that relies not simply on an economic or biological compulsion to exploitation, but on configurations of vision and visuality through which bodies are invested with social meaning in relationship with, but without final reduction to, any singular formation of economic determination. And while I'd like to close this discussion with a pretense toward resolution, if not the high hope of revolution, I can make no gesture of unqualified insight, as though the position I have occupied as observer to these historical fashionings of race can be disentangled from the privilege of my own cultural scripting. Nor can I posit some mythic relief by offering an alternative visual economy, one that can liberate, in a swift and assured transformation, the subject from the shackles of race's dual specular and panoptic regimes. These gestures we make to compensate for the potential liminality of scholastic endeavor — for the difficulties of *why* — seem rather self-indulgent in the context of the overdetermining historical deployment of race. Instead, I want to leave open the question of methodological and intellectual transcendence — not to suspend the political in an indeterminate realm, but to simultaneously foreground and defend against the easy turn in contemporary cultural criticism toward an emancipatory rhetoric that rings increasingly hollow to many ears.

Let me begin by returning to a brief moment in the last chapter where I simultaneously raised and suspended the question of sexual difference. I was exploring, if you recall, the transformations in the study of human differences wrought by biology's ascension, pointing to the analogic relations between race and gender that would come to underlie comparative anatomy in the nineteenth century. I was, in short, forecasting the trajectory of this chapter, in which sexual difference is traced from within the discursive structures of comparativist race science, bound to the corporealizing logic that sought to anchor the indeterminacies of race to organic organization. But why would the turn toward organs and organic function not establish, once and for all, the similarity, the precarious human embodiment, that ties together the family of "man"? After all, to discern differences is not only to defend against but also to inscribe the possibility of a universal human sameness, and it is this possibility that might just as easily have emerged to challenge social hierarchies.

Or could it have? Did comparative anatomy cloak within its methodology the possibility of a transformative humanism, a disassembling of the very logic of the body that achieved epistemological primacy within its disciplinary demands? Or does any comparative reading, whether positively or negatively inflected, invest too heavily in scripting the body as the definitive locus of human "being," contesting when it does *only* the interpretative force and not the essentialist logic that underlies discourses of social (in)equality? These questions point to the complexities of reading the body in our contemporary moment where the theoretical demand for jettisoning the essentialism of corporeal identities and differences arises alongside a postmodern skepticism toward the transformative possibilities of any critical methodology, even (perhaps especially) those we invest with the utopic hope to remake our world. In such a critical context, I approach comparative anatomy and the logics of race and gender it has simultaneously shaped and appropriated by a particular understanding of the historical: not as a text that simply precedes us, but as itself a crucially contested realm of cultural struggle. In this realm, in the pursuit of what Toni Morrison depicts as a *how* that can never fully explain *why,* this chapter offers a curious, perhaps awkward, and certainly contradictory set of theoretical claims.

At the outset, I briefly consider the context in which issues of enlightened citizenship, corporeal identity, and public visibility have been and continue to be defined, thereby establishing in a preliminary way the tie between modernity and its anatomization of both the individual and social body. Such a conversation is a necessary precursor to the investigations of comparative anatomy where debates about the origin and scale of human being produced a series of analogies between blackness and other kinds of seemingly visible bodily differences. Through the analogic relationship among differences, in fact, comparative anatomy drew nearly the full range of social hierarchies in the nineteenth century into race's well-entrenched logic of essential meaning, defining gender, sexuality, nationality, and class differences as consistent with race's corporeal distinctions. Most important for my purposes, the analogizing process generated that now-familiar couple, "blacks and women," whose reign in the twentieth century as the figure for social protest and affirmative action was preceded in less politically progressive ways by comparative anatomy's obsessive interest in the brain and sexual organs—those corporeal locations in which race and gender differences appeared to the nineteenth-century investigator as most definitive. Through analogies between the smaller brain capacities and the perversely developed sexuality of black and female bodies, comparative anatomy read the African's difference through the twin registers of sexual difference: as both a stereotypically feminized category and the preeminently sexual.

The assimilation of sexual differences to comparative anatomy's historical focus on race demonstrates what I take to be a broader and more profound transformation in the nineteenth century in which the discourse of sexual difference was increasingly used to articulate the social complexities of race and racial hierarchies. But comparative anatomy does not provide the only context for this contentious claim, as race science alone fails to reveal the contradictory discursive maneuvers accompanying the analogic wedding of blacks and women in either the nineteenth century or our own. What does it mean, for instance, that both feminist-abolitionist and early African-American writings were overwhelmingly concerned with the slave as a gendered being, finding in the possibilities of sexual difference a rhetorical strategy for marking the African(-American)'s equal humanity? From the perspective of race science, it is nearly incomprehensible that sexual difference could be claimed as a means for resisting constructions of the slave as a species beneath "man," and yet, marking slaves as both socially and politically gendered in the nineteenth century proves to inhabit a far more contradictory terrain. From the perspective of the human being defined as property, in fact, the gendered significations attending the elision between white and human convey deeply significant sociopolitical subjectivities, inscribing a variety of social privileges and priorities to *both* masculine and feminine as part of the rhetoric and organization of nineteenth-century "civil" society. These complexities are explored in the later stage of this chapter, which indirectly sets abolition-oriented writing against comparative anatomy in order to demonstrate the historical contestations and contradictions in which any analysis of "blacks and women" must be made.

For a feminism schooled in the language and conceptualization of gender's transhistoric — if differently configured — disempowerment, the postulation that sexual difference can decisively contribute to the transformation of the African(-American)'s status from chattel to human being forces a broad and potentially disturbing rearticulation of the history of marginality and especially of the paths of political revolt and resistance employed in the nineteenth and twentieth centuries. Most important perhaps, it underscores the potential political currency of our own challenge to feminism's accepted traditions, drawing into the orbit of feminist inquiry a host of questions about the structure of white supremacy on which hierarchies among women have dwelled. The cult of true womanhood demonstrates, for instance, how widely prized was the white woman for her civic roles and responsibilities, as her reproductive activities and domestic occupations were themselves crucial elements within narratives of social progress and national identity throughout the nineteenth century.[1] To be excluded from the public sphere of citizenship was not to be uniformly cast as inhuman, and it was this difference in human status between the white woman and the enslaved — both female and male — that became crucial to articulating the relationship between gender and modern social and political subjectivity. In the incompatible convergence between the white woman's excision from the public domain of enlightened citizenship and the slave's corporealization as the inhuman, we approach one of the most powerful and consequential asymmetries through which the coupling of "blacks and women" has been historically framed.

Although the rhetoric of sexual difference as a liberating subjectivity for the slave was incommensurable with the white woman's political quest for the rights of the public sphere, it is also the case that by the end of the nineteenth century the slave system's primary attachment to the axis of racial difference gave way to a new social arrangement, one that significantly privileged gender. Here, the black male was ushered, however violently, into the potentialities of citizenship while the female slave's emancipation carried no public entitlement and the white woman's struggle for public inclusion continued to fail. The asymmetry thus forged within the identity category of the African-American, reiterating the logic of patriarchal gender, represents the nineteenth century's most extreme shaping of the struggle for black liberation within the contours of sexual difference. By privileging the gendered structures of public citizenship, the tenuous abolitionist analogy between "blacks and women," forged as a political imperative against patriarchy and slavery, became instead a figure marking the mutual exclusions and contestations between race and gender that governed in a variety of ways the political rights of the public sphere until at least the 1920s—and that continue to hold a powerful influence in the liberalized discourse of "blacks and women" on which late-twentieth-century civil rights dwell. As this chapter demonstrates, to follow the transformations and dispersals in which the slave's emergence from the prisonhouse of epidermal authority was simultaneously protested and pursued through sexual difference is to enter one of the most contradictory and troubled arenas attending the theorization of race and gender today.

Modern Anatomies

When Irene Redfield contemplates the signifying practice of race as a catalogue of anatomical parts in the passage from Nella Larsen's *Passing* that opened chapter 1, it is to the history of comparative anatomy that her meditation specifically turns: "[w]hite people were so stupid about such things," she thinks, "for all that they usually asserted that they were able to tell; and by the most ridiculous means, finger-nails, palms of hands, shapes of ears, teeth, and other equally silly rot" (40). The parody here operates in the register of race's significatory extremes, where even the inconsequential minutiae of the body speak the truth that race supposedly, inherently means. While the "classical" methods of decoding (skin, hair, lips, and buttocks) are superseded (because absent), anatomy is nonetheless emphasized as the definitive locus of racial meaning—all this at the very moment that Irene's passing is most successfully achieved. But while Irene's parody undermines the production of race as a corporeal truth, thereby resisting the status of the body as the determination of race, it simultaneously demonstrates the popularization of the logic of comparative anatomy in American racial ideology. This popularization, still a dominant mode of racial meaning in the late twentieth century, took shape under the twin pressures of abolitionism and evolutionary science in the nineteenth century when the battle over the significance of race and human "being" achieved its most pitched and contested extreme.

That the intensity of the debate was reached here at a historical moment later than that witnessed in those European nations (England, France, and Germany) where race science began speaks to the specific force and tenor of the controversy over slavery and to the implications of slavery's demise for the form and function of white supremacy in the United States. The intra-colonial nature of the slave trade and the deeply familial and familiarizing structures of southern patriarchal organization coalesced to distinguish this system of racial hierarchy from the imperialist and colonialist systems established elsewhere in the seventeenth and eighteenth centuries.[2] With the slave trade outlawed in 1808, it was the increasing emphasis on reproduction as the foundation of the labor force and the visible, progressive "whitening" of the slave body throughout the century that marks in particular and urgent ways the crisis of race in nineteenth-century America. In fact, the cultural anxiety around the growing demographic proportion of African-Americans and the obvious though socially despised specter of interracial "breeding" must be understood as important elements in the ideological contexts that attend scientific investigations, which set as one of the century's primary tasks the final adjudication of the natural order of racial being. But if the truth of race could escape the visual, if the hallmarks of corporeal significations were increasingly and ultimately unstable, if the binary structure of racial thinking could dissolve at the sight of the body, how then could the necessary clarity of differentiation be found to ascertain once and for all the hierarchy of being?

The instability of race was, of course, not new to the scientific investigator. As I discussed in chapter 1, the natural historian had rather routinely relied on an understanding of race as a surfacial relation, not a permanent difference but an element of variation (climate and custom) that could change over time. For the comparative anatomist, however, race was to be pursued as a way of achieving greater corporeal security, of translating the logic of epidermal inferiority to interior, invisible differences. In looking to organs and their various forms and functions, the anatomist began a rigid classification of the body, but it was in its comparative dimension that the structure of the visible as a distinctly racial paradigm took on its most significant nineteenth-century meaning. As Nancy Stepan has observed, "[b]y analogy with the so-called lower races, women, the sexually deviate, the criminal, the urban poor, and the insane were in one way or another constructed as biological 'races apart' whose differences from the white male, and likenesses to each other, 'explained' their different and lower position in the social hierarchy" ("Race and Gender" 40–41). In discussing how such analogies emerged to ground the study of human differentiation in the nineteenth century, Stepan notes that the "origin of many of the 'root metaphors' of human difference are obscure" (42), and yet she points out that Aristotle compared women and slaves in ancient Greece and that the theological writings of the Middle Ages routinely associated blackness with sin and evil, associations that would seem to be refigured as part of the ideological structures of both modern slavery and contemporary white supremacy.[3]

In the context of Foucault's differentiation between the classical and modern epistemes, however, these associations cannot adequately explain the theoretical assumptions that underlie comparative science, even if they do point to the ideological contexts in which racial discourse was (and continues to be) produced. Instead, we need to be more specific in understanding the way modernity inaugurates a language concerning difference that increasingly specifies the body as the locus of subjective and social discipline—for it is in this kind of disciplinary structure that the taxonomic tasks undertaken by comparative anatomy become part of solidifying the human being as the primary object of knowledge in modernity, foregrounding the crisis of the subject-object relation that underlies the rise of the disciplines and their methodological quest for transcendence. To posit this quest within the context of racial hierarchies, both social and economic, is to demonstrate how the specification of difference functions to allay the deeply threatening potential of human sameness: of a cosmic order in which the ascendancy of the white masculine is no longer universalized, but reduced to its own corporeal particularities.

It is just such particularity that the philosophical and political discourses of Enlightenment worked so hard to negate, crafting the white masculine as the disembodied norm against which a definitive body of difference could be specifically engaged. Given the conversations about the relationship between blackness and (in)humanity since the late seventeenth century, we can approach this body as explicitly raced, regardless of the extent to which the public sphere imagined by Enlightenment political theory offered a rhetoric of democratic citizenship that pivoted on an abstracted, disembodied equality. As Michael Warner discusses, the arrival of the citizen into free, open, and rational public debate — the hallmark of democratic organization — was made possible by a decorporealizing public abstraction, an abstraction that, while theorized as universal, was not universally available. He writes, "[t]he subject who could master this rhetoric . . . was implicitly, even explicitly, white, male, literate, and propertied. These traits could go unmarked, even grammatically, while other features of bodies could only be acknowledged . . . as the humiliating positivity of the particular" ("The Mass Public and the Mass Subject" 382). For those trapped by the discipline of the particular (women, slaves, the poor), the unmarked and universalized particularity of the white masculine prohibited their entrance into the abstraction of personhood that democratic equality supposedly entailed. Their overmarked particularity served instead to signify their distinctly minoritized social positions, writing their bodies as an incontrovertible difference.

In the contemporary post-segregationist/post-feminist era, the cultural emphasis on a technologized public sphere (on a mass-mediated public) clearly shifts the representational and discursive grounds on which the complexities of citizenship and publicity in the nineteenth century appeared. Not that the corporeal abstraction that accrued to white masculinity has been displaced as the universal condition of political entitlement, but now this abstraction exists in overt contradiction with a visual culture predicated on the commodification of those very identities minoritized by the discourses and social organization of enlightened democracy. Under the pressure of contemporary commodity culture, the mythic Habermasian public sphere of open, rational debate, of a decorporealized, supposedly equal citizenship, is filled with bodies hailed in a variety of cultural registers according to, and not in abandonment of, their corporeal specificity. "To be public in the West," Warner says, "[is] to have an iconicity" ("The Mass Public and the Mass Subject" 385). But the cost of this iconicity is high, not simply because political agency in the realm of identity-as-commodity appears more difficult to grasp, but because the specificities of bodies, while seeming to signify everywhere, still do not signify the same. The minoritized African-American subject, for instance, can enter a public discourse previously closed to her, but the differential of "blackness" continues to mark and carry its modern double burden: signifying itself, it also anchors the differential meaning of whiteness by lodging it, as I have discussed, in the epistemology of black skin.

The asymmetry of these relations — of an iconicity that gestures toward

the body as universally particular on one hand, while privileging the public's historical reliance on disembodiment on the other — can be linked to
modernity's emphasis on disciplinary knowledge, and to the effect, as Foucault would say, of "man's" entrance into culture as its primary object of
investigation. With this new status, the human being is approached as an
organic body and an interior psychic depth, and a variety of new technologies, institutions, and academic disciplines are formed around the human's
epistemological centrality. As might be clear, the abstraction of personhood
that underlies the democratic public sphere is in many ways in contradiction with this increasingly specified structure of disciplinary knowledges, though the disciplines have tried to keep these contradictions at bay
through canonical formations and objectivist methodologies. Nevertheless,
contemporary pressures within institutionalized structures of knowledge,
what some call poststructuralist, others postmodernist, demonstrate that
the borders through which "man's" centrality has been formed are wrought
with tension and increasingly less secure. These tensions arise from modernity's own internal impossibilities: to hold to a political philosophy of corporeal abstraction at the same time that disciplinary knowledge necessitates
the particularization of human being in a variety of explanatory registers.

For a number of cultural observers, the ascendancy of technological corporealities sounds the death knell for democratic possibility, emphasizing as
it does iconicity instead of corporeal abstraction and thereby foregrounding commodified identities as the primary signifying form of the public
sphere. According to Warner, the tension between the visual's increasing
demand for difference and citizenship's philosophic dis-corporation "is the
legacy of the bourgeois public sphere's founding logic, the contradictions
of which become visible whenever the public sphere can no longer turn a
blind eye to its privileged bodies" ("The Mass Public and the Mass Subject"
397). But how to unveil the privileged body? This is no simple task, for
as the history of social protest in this country attests, nearly every political movement's confrontation with the privileged body has been built on
contradictory (re)investments in the minoritized body, figured newly as a
positive identity, to ground the struggle for liberation. The difficulties encountered here, in the realm of a public sphere reliant on the body and its
(in)visible majoritized and minoritized significations, can be linked to the
disciplinary fragmentation of human being that attends modernity, demonstrating how deeply overburdened the incremental anatomization of the
body is from within.

Brain Matters

It is precisely in the context of the political necessity of revealing the privileged body of modernity that we can return to issues of the corporeal in the nineteenth century. Here, the battle between the disciplined minoritized body and its privileged counterpart underlies not simply the proliferation of abolitionist and scientific discourses, but their relationship to one another as well. Even Georges Cuvier, whom Foucault cites as at the forefront of the transition from natural history to biology, was concerned with the raging debate about racial origins and the potential multiplicity of the species, if only to dismiss any suggestion that social hierarchies could either be explained or rationalized through investigations of human biology. In turning from the taxonomic tasks of the natural historian to the focus on organs and internal organization, however, Cuvier's central interest, the brain and skull, would become the cornerstone of race science on both sides of the Atlantic in the century following the American Revolution. In the United States, newly saturated by Enlightenment egalitarian rhetoric, the postulation that the size and shape of the brain and skull could determine the evolutionary status of human beings was more than ironic. Without the assurances of the African(-American)'s status as human, the democratic ethos of bourgeois citizenship was not simply unavailable, but incomprehensible as a theoretical or political concept. For this reason, the relationship between America's celebration of its democratic freedom and its continued tie to the slave system with its broad and damaging hierarchies remained for many white Americans a contradiction whose resolution was impossible to pursue.

Of course, the anxiety arising from the cultural repression of such incongruities had far-reaching effects, and it is no accident that the work of comparative anatomy throughout the century would so frantically seek to settle the question of the African(-American)'s difference as if scientific discourse could found the truth of human being even if religious and political discourses could not. With the proliferation of polygenesis theories in the United States implicitly challenging the stance of religious orthodoxy — that tidy monogenist rendition of humanity as the reflection of God's singular and perfect image — the nineteenth century witnessed a persistent conflict between Christian teachings and scientific investigations of human anatomy.[4] In short, the turn toward anatomically based gradations of human being in the nineteenth century, with its powerful racist discourse condemning the African(-American) to separate origins and primitivity

alike, frequently displaced both the democratic rhetoric of the Enlightenment and natural history's epistemic organization of knowledge. This displacement, occurring in the United States at the same time that the unity-
diversity debate lost its intensity in Europe, forged a widespread acceptance
of the theory of separate creation. As Thomas F. Gossett explains, "the idea
that the Negroes might be a separate species . . . came near dominating the
thinking of [nineteenth-century American] scientific men on the subject"
(*Race* 58).

While the concept of separate species most often challenged the documents of Christianity, various investigators of racial difference sought nonetheless to align their perspective with church teachings. George Robins
Gliddon, for instance, justified the concept of separate species by "proving"
that God had created human beings with distinct racial characteristics,
that any claim to environmental or evolutionary changes was heresy to the
originary, multiple creation.[5] So adamant was Gliddon on this point that he
spent a great deal of energy trying to demonstrate that the Egyptians were
white, that any "Negroid lineaments in the Sphinx . . . resulted from its
having been peppered with grapeshot and musket balls for five centuries"
(Stanton, *The Leopard's Spots* 50). By denying the African origins of Egyptian civilization, Gliddon hoped to demonstrate that the hierarchies of the
American slave system were not only natural, but quite divinely ordained.
In the process, he resorted to craniology, teaming up with Dr. Samuel
George Morton, whose 1839 *Crania Americana* established the field in the
United States by demonstrating the craniologic differences among Native
Americans, Anglo-Americans, and Africa's New World descendants. Mor-
ton had also recovered skulls from Egypt and differentiated along with
Gliddon between the negro and the Egyptian on the lines of immutable
anatomical racial distinctions. Such distinctions laid to rest for many in the
American scientific community the climate and custom theories of natural
history.[6]

The fascination with Egypt and the question of the racial category that
the Egyptian occupied points toward the ideological linkage between race
and civilization, a linkage that has played a central role in crafting a variety
of racist discourses throughout the Western world. Through the postulation that those of African descent were incapable of producing anything
but the most primitive of civilizations — those devoid of complex social
structures, philosophy, and high art — the paternalistic function of the slave
system was often affirmed. But the focus on the African(-American)'s incapacity for civilization has further implications than the justification of

slavery, as the articulation of black inferiority produced a social and subjec-tive position — whiteness — virtually unfigured, as Jordan suggests, before the Renaissance. The heightening of this production during the Enlighten-ment, the specific turn toward questions of innate capacity and civilizing potential, demonstrates how ideologically wrought was the emergence of "man" as the disciplinary object of study, how anxious the epistemologi-cal disruption. By seeking to affirm the priority of whiteness, even those Enlightenment philosophers most dedicated to the democratic relied on those assumptions about the negative intelligence, creativity, and civilizing potential of the African(-American) that nineteenth-century race science would definitively affirm.[7]

The comparative anatomist's focus on the brain and skull was very much a part of the elaboration of the question of the African(-American)'s ca-pacity for civilization, as the relationship between the brain and intelligence had been well established by phrenology in the eighteenth century.[8] When science moved beneath the skin, measuring the size of the skull, phrenology was abandoned as I have discussed for a deeper economy of visibility, a more definitive assertion of the body's truth. By 1840, Morton was confi-dent that the brains of the five races he had classified (Caucasian, Mon-golian, Malay, American, and Negro) were successively smaller, thereby proving the general superiority in intelligence (and hence civilization) of the caucasian race. In the extension of the logic of this superiority to en-compass, through analogy, the realm of sexual difference, the ideological framework governing phrenology was not simply displaced by comparative anatomy, but more fully and technologically elaborated. As Stepan notes, "the specific conclusions of the phrenologists concerning the anatomical structure and functions of the brain were rejected [by the 1840s, but] the principle that differences in individual and group function were products of differences in the shape and size of the head were not" ("Race and Gen-der" 46). In this context, the comparison between women and the "lower" races drawn by phrenology in the 1820s became the basis for comparative anatomy's analogic wedding of blacks and women. Such an analogy simul-taneously differentiated and linked two of the nineteenth century's pri-mary forms of social difference, instantiating and perpetuating the visible economies of race and gender by locating their signification on bodies that could not claim the disembodied abstraction accorded those both white and male. The conclusions thus drawn by the comparative anatomist by mid-century about the smaller brain capacity of the "lower" races and the infantile skulls of the European woman demonstrate the powerful ideological feat that the science of human diversity achieved in a cultural context rife with contestations over the subordinancies of white women and both African(-American) males and females.

At the same time, however, the analogy between white women and the "lower" races posed a number of theoretical difficulties for the craniologist. If men were in general superior to women in the capacity of intelligence, how did one account for the subordinancy the African(-American) male was accorded? Why, in short, did only European men have large brains? For Carl Vogt, whose 1864 *Lectures on Man, His Place in Creation, and in the History of the Earth* occupied a prominent position in analyses of human difference, the answer lay in evolution: the disparity in head size between men and women, he argued, was supposedly largest in the "civilized" races and smallest in those of less advanced cultures. "It has long been observed," he writes, "that among peoples progressing in civilization, the men are in advance of the women whilst among those which are retrograding, the contrary is the case" (82). In ascertaining a high degree of similarity in the cranial capacities of men and women of African descent, Vogt advanced an understanding of race that pivoted on the paradigm of sexual difference. Because "woman preserves, in the formation of the head, the earliest stage from which the race or tribe has been developed, or into which it has relapsed" (ibid.), masculine domination was evidence of advanced civilization. In this way, the binary structure of race—that rigorously defended emphasis on the incommensurabilities between black and white—took on, through anatomic analysis, a double ideological function: the European male's large brain evinced not simply a racial superiority, but a quintessentially masculine one as well. Blackness, in short, was here feminized and the African(-American) male was disaffiliated from the masculine itself. According to Stepan, it was this production of blackness as sexual difference that made possible subsequent and prolific scientific "comparisons between a black male and a white female" ("Race and Gender" 47), comparisons that became ideologically concretized in twentieth-century liberal discourse (and its politically reactionary counterparts) as "blacks and women."

Vogt as well as others engaged in the comparison between the African(-American) male and the European woman rather routinely, although their standard for measurement shifted, depending on the analogic relationship under examination. For instance, Vogt would assess the shape of the brain and its various parts, arguing that "[b]y its rounded apex and less developed posterior lobe the Negro brain resembles that of our children, and by the protuberance of the parietal lobe, that of our females" (*Lectures on*

Man 183). For G. Herve, a colleague of the well-known anthropometricist Paul Broca, brain weight served as the key determinant. "Men of the black races," he writes, "have a brain scarcely heavier than that of white women" (quoted in Gould, *The Mismeasure of Man* 103). And Broca's successor, Paul Topinard, further established the mutual subordinancy and intellectual symmetry between black males and white females by returning to the index of the facial angle and brain size, concluding that, as Stepan writes, "Caucasian women were indeed more prognathous or apelike in their jaws than white men, and even the largest women's brains, from the 'English or Scotch' race, made them like the African male" ("Race and Gender" 43). Topinard's data, ranging across the compiled documentation of nearly four decades of measurement, firmly established the black male as the representative for his race in the analysis of intelligence, through which his analogic relationship to the white feminine would be secured as well.

The importance of these figurations of race and gender cannot be glossed over quickly, for it is here that the full force of the debate on human differences as investigations into the history, development, and origin of "man" become more than merely archaic grammatical formulations. My use of the generic masculine in reference to such scientific and philosophical queries foregrounds the conceptual parameters of a great many of these debates in order to connect the centrality of man (combined with the attendant observation of differences among men) to the patriarchal formation of both the classical and modern epistemes. Under the primary guise of exploring the order of man, in fact, early contributors to the discourse of race were essentially plotting the patriarchal grid of universal human relations when they sought to answer "What is blackness?" and "From whence does it come?" By figuring blackness as a feminine racial formation, the possibility of the African(-American) male assuming an equal position with the crusader for advanced civilization, the white male, was thwarted and racial hierarchies became further entrenched according to the corporeal inequalities inscribed by sexual difference. While the theoretical implications of this negotiation of masculine differences for feminism will be taken up in detail in subsequent chapters, it is clear that in anatomical assessments of the brain and skull, the black woman was signified only indirectly, as "blacks and women" were so thoroughly marked as corporeal identities challenging the consolidated power and disembodied abstraction of those *both* white and male.

Privy Parts

While the black woman may be definitively secondary in the affiliations of "blacks and women" wrought by comparative anatomies of the brain and skull, her increasing centrality to investigations of sexuality in the nineteenth century demonstrates the powerful patriarchal inscription of the sexualized body as itself feminine. This sexualization, as Londa Schiebinger discusses in *Nature's Body: Gender in the Making of Modern Science,* revolved around two primary anatomical features, the buttocks and genitals, and provided the means to draw two broad and damaging conclusions: that African and European women were essentially, corporeally different from one another *and* that the black male was part of a degenerated racial sexuality as well. This double effect demonstrates the black female's function to further the ideological linkage between the African and the ape — a linkage first drawn in scientific terms in natural history, but developed by comparative science in ways that emphasized both the primitivity of blackness and its incomplete humanity. At the same time, the focus on the black female body as the site for investigating the sexuality of the "race" reinforced discourses of feminine beauty as paradigmatically white, so thoroughly negative was the black female's sexual characterization. In the context of anatomical study of the black female body, the subordinate status of the "race" thus emerged through a dual rendering of the "sexual": as both a matter of quintessential gender differences and as a taxonomy of "deviant" sexual parts and practices.

   While this cultural narrativization of blackness as both feminine and aberrantly sexual can be traced to discourses circulating in Anglophilic cultures long before comparative anatomy's epistemic ascendancy,[9] its construction as definitively corporeal focused, as many readers of the archive of race and sexuality well know, on the southwestern African, the Hottentot. Such a focus was not a surprise, however, as natural historians were fascinated with the breasts and reproductive features of the Hottentot female, and in this, they generated a variety of meditations on the differences between human groups based on the relationship among skin color, secondary sex characteristics, and purported sexual behavior.[10] Winthrop D. Jordan links European obsession with the Hottentot to the resurgence of the Great Chain theory in the late seventeenth century when candidates for that unheralded position between man and ape were rigorously sought. Being, in Jordan's words, "the most primitive of all the aborgines [*sic*] well known to Europeans prior to the second half of the eighteenth century"

(*White over Black* 227), the Hottentot became a standard offering for just such a role. Jordan points to John Ovington's comments in *Voyage to Suratt, in the Year 1689* as paradigmatic: "of all People they are the most Bestial and sordid," indeed "the very Reverse of Human kind . . . so that if there's any medium between a Rational Animal and a Beast, the *Hotantot* lays the fairest Claim to that Species" (ibid.).

A great deal of European fascination with the Hottentot revolved around the question of interspecies sexuality between African and ape, a question that centrally emerged during the earliest Anglophilic contact with the continent. When the *Columbian Magazine* reprinted in 1788 various key passages from Edward Long's highly influential *History of Jamaica* (1774), the impact of the Hottentot and ape connection was perhaps enumerated in detail for the first time to a mass American audience. Here Long affirmed the sexual primitivity of the Hottentot, linking such physical features as the eyes, lips, and nipples to low intelligence, immorality, and laziness. At the same time, he lifted the orangutan to a height of quasi-human civility. Eating at tables and endowed with the ability to speak, these apes, Long believed, did not "seem at all inferior in the intellectual faculties to many of the negroe race . . . [and] in form [they bear] a much nearer resemblance to the Negroe race, than the latter bear to White men" (quoted in Jordan, *White over Black* 492–493). But the grandest proof, and the point to which all his formulations seemed to energetically run, was the sexual community among the Hottentot female and apes: "[l]udicrous as the opinion may seem, I do not think that an oran-outang husband would be any dishonour to an Hottentot female," he asserted (ibid.). In supposing a sexual attraction between the Hottentot and the chimpanzee, European observers benefited in a number of ways, not the least of which was to displace the threat (and actuality) of their own interracial sexual practices with African women onto a highly crafted representation of the black woman's degenerate desires. Marking her "bestial" nature established, in however unscientific terms, the ideological means for defining the African as the intermediary creature between man and beast.

In the century to follow Long's damaging report, comparative anatomists would display a heightened interest in the question of African sexuality, turning to the sexual organs of the Hottentot female, particularly her genitalia and buttocks, to define the primitive sexual physiology of the "race" in general. As Sander Gilman reports, the Hottentot female became the primary signifier for black sexuality in the nineteenth century ("Black Bodies, White Bodies" 231), and it was through both popular and scientific dismemberments of her body that a normative sexuality—heterosexual and quite specifically racialized—was pursued.[11] The key figure in the Hottentot's position of centrality as sexual icon was Saartjie Baartmann (often called Sarah Bartmann), who was routinely exhibited throughout Europe from 1810 to the time of her death in 1815 at the age of twenty-five. Dubbed "the Hottentot Venus," Baartman served as Europe's symbol of African sexuality, characterizing for the scientific and public communities alike the voluptuousness and lasciviousness of the black female whose sexual organs, according to the 1819 *Dictionnaire des sciences medicales*, "are much more developed than those of whites" (quoted in Gilman "Black Bodies, White Bodies" 232). In describing the Hottentot's genitalia and buttocks as hyper-developed, the dictionary account reflects the sexual inversion of those ideologies of anatomical size that governed investigations of brains and skulls where largeness was equated with superiority and civilizing potential. In the anatomical study of sexuality, however, developmental proportions were akin to inferiority, and it was here that the African body took on one of its most monstrous representations, being scripted as simultaneously corporeally and libidinally excessive.

The author of the dictionary account, J. J. Virey, drew his information on the Hottentot's supposedly "hideous" sexual form from the autopsy report issued on Baartmann by none other than Georges Cuvier. In his pictorial rendering of her body, Cuvier paid particular attention to what had become an object of intense speculation, the labia minora, or as they were then called "the Hottentot apron." Described as the elongation of the labia, the "apron" was first reported in the seventeenth century and was frequently hailed by early naturalists as a definitive measure of the primitivity and animality of the Hottentot. As Schiebinger reports, its physical existence was never definitively affirmed, though investigators of racial differences would spend the eighteenth century debating its anatomical specifications, producing in the absence of actual evidence a variety of phantasmatic representations. By the time of Cuvier's dissection of Baartmann, nothing, he wrote, was "more celebrated in natural history" than this part of Hottentot anatomy (quoted in Schiebinger, *Nature's Body* 168). Under such conditions, it is not surprising that nine of the sixteen pages of Cuvier's autopsy report were devoted to Baartmann's sexual anatomy—from her labia to the "elastic and shivering mass" of her buttocks to her ape-like pelvis—while only one paragraph, as Schiebinger tellingly notes, described her brain (171–172). Following the autopsy, Cuvier prepared Baartmann's dissected genital organs for display in the Musée de l'Homme in Paris, thereby offering for public consumption a record of the form and "nature" of her sexual difference.[12]

Thus reduced to her sexual organs by the methodological practices of comparative anatomy, Baartmann's representative body became the entombed counterpart to other European practices devoted to the circulation of the African for specular display. In traveling zoos and permanent colonies, Africans found themselves, individually and in groups, the objects of obsessive voyeuristic scrutiny in both Europe and America—commodities produced for a public overwhelmingly convinced that these bodies, above all, marked an affinity with animals that the caucasian's developed rationality disavowed. In focusing a great deal of this attention on the African female as the determining site for sexual definitions of the body's animal excess, racial differences were increasingly cast in the context of—and as—multivalenced sexual differences. But this does not mean that the African male's body had escaped scrutiny along the lines of its sexual proclivities and "private" parts. As Winthrop Jordan discusses, prior even to England's contact with Africa, European literature figured the African male in terms of both genital and libidinal extravagance, thereby drawing upon the kinds of European associations between savagery and wanton sexuality that comparative anatomists throughout the Anglophilic west would later scientifically seek to verify.[13]

One of the most damaging associations for the sexual representation of the black male was the emphasis in early natural history on the penis size of the tailless ape—an animal whose existence became known to Europeans at approximately the same time and place that Africans were themselves first encountered. This "tragic happenstance," as Jordan calls it, produced an affiliation in the minds of Europeans between the African "and the animal which in appearance most resemble[d] man" (*White over Black* 29). Edward Topsell's commentary on the baboon in his 1607 *Historie of Foure-Footed Beastes* epitomized the conversation that would come to dominate discussions of African male sexuality in subsequent centuries. The baboon, "above all loved the companie of women, and young maidens; his genitall member was greater than might match the quantity of his other parts" (quoted in ibid. 30). Topsell's "observations" even speculated on the sexual meaning of facial features. "Men who have low and flat nostrils are Libidinous as Apes that attempt women," he wrote, "and having thicke lippes the upper hanging over the neather, they are deemed fooles" (ibid.). One hardly needs to point out the confluence expressed here between physiology, sexuality, and intelligence—or to note that two centuries later, Anglophilic cultures would accept as commonsense these associations, newly lodged in the corporeal logic provided by phrenology and craniology.

Still, even as the discourse on the sexuality of racial difference demonstrates a common concern for the hyperdevelopment of both male and female anatomies and their libidinal proclivities and capacities, Schiebinger argues convincingly that natural history's investigation into the human-ape connection was not symmetrically gendered. Three of the four most well known illustrations of apes drawn by naturalists in the seventeenth century, for instance, featured the female of the species (*Nature's Body* 88), thereby inscribing broader cultural ideologies that linked animality to the body and the body to femininity. In such a context, it is not surprising that the focus on the female to ascertain the precise boundaries that divided the human and the ape would depend overwhelmingly on investigations of sexual difference. As Schiebinger reports, "[w]hen naturalists' attention turned to females, only sexual traits were considered" (ibid.). Studies delving into differences between human and simian males, on the other hand, focused on reason, speech, and other matters of culture building—those provinces of the masculine that would later become central to comparative anatomy's racialized reading of brains and skulls. Indeed, by the time comparative anatomy extended its taxonomic conquest of the body to sexual parts, "the fact of blackness" was inextricably saturated by natural history's lengthy discourse on the black female's sexual—and sexualized—associations with the ape.[14] This saturation predisposed comparative anatomists to find in the African woman's sexuality the definitive grounds for the further marking of both black and female differences.

But it is one of the signs of the political contestations underwriting comparative anatomy that the study of sex and sexuality never reached the pitched extreme—the paradigmatic example—that brains and skulls did as elements of nineteenth-century race science. "In most instances," writes Schiebinger, "sexual differences were considered secondary to racial differences" (*Nature's Body* 159). In comparative science's reiteration of the mind/body split endemic to patriarchal culture—where man assumes the head while woman is confined to the sensuous physical realm—the universalizing determinations of the body that governed the broader, "enlightened" political sphere were thus reinscribed: women of all races retained a secondary, highly particularized corporeal signification while the universalism of the masculine fractured to reveal an anatomized African(-American) male. It was precisely by situating "blackness" under the sign of the feminine in both domains of comparative science—the mind and the body—that the competing and complementary relations of patriarchy and white supremacy were finally adjudicated to the overarching privileges of white men. Together, the sexual monstrosity accorded the black female as the emblem of the "race" on one hand and the intellectual femininity accorded the black male as the racial standard of measurement on the other organized the corporeal and social inferiorities ascribed to the African in the discourses of comparative anatomy. Such organization linked, via an implicit gendering, the composite relation of blacks and women.

This is not to argue that sexual difference must be understood as the definitive, originary, or more salient political axis for approaching the nineteenth century's hierarchical inscriptions of racial difference, but it does suggest that the trajectory of analysis undertaken by comparative anatomy increasingly relied on the discourse of sexual difference to forge the corporeal particularities on which "blacks and women" would subsequently depend. As Nancy Stepan observes,

> from the late Enlightenment on students of human variation singled out racial differences as crucial aspects of reality, and an extensive discourse on racial inequality began to be elaborated. In the nineteenth century, as attention turned increasingly to sexual and gender differences as well, gender was found to be remarkably analogous to race. . . . It was race scientists who provided the new technologies of measurement. . . . ("Race and Gender" 39, 43) [15]

The first drawing of a female skeleton, for instance, was produced by Samuel Thomas von Soemmerring, himself a well-known anatomist of racial differences who sought in the study of bones a more permanent index of the body's fundamental (and global) racial organization than natural history's focus on skin.[16] In extending the *anatomical* investigation of race to sex and sexuality—in shifting the logic of the visible from the body's surface to its interior, organic domain—Soemmerring and other comparative scientists overthrew the segregatory structure underlying gender in natural history by making possible analogies between differently sexed bodies. While brains and skulls would take precedence as the most common analogic link between black men and white females, comparative analyses of the pelvis also contributed to the growing conversation that scripted race and gender as mutually determining to the African(-American)'s purported inferiorities.[17]

But we would be wrong, I think, to read the trajectory of analogic linkages forged by comparative anatomy as paradigmatic of either the historical or political relationship between race and gender in all U.S. cultural registers, either in the nineteenth century or our own. Feminist-abolitionist discourse, after all, relied on the same proposition propelling comparative science—that the African(-American) (of whatever gender) shared a commonality in social and often subjective position with white women, but it did so with vastly different political goals, if not with definitively different effects.[18] By recognizing that the analogic wedding of "blacks and women" emerged in politically resistant as well as complicit contexts in the nineteenth century, we might begin to comprehend how varied sexual differences have been in the context of race in the United States. What does it mean, for instance, that in discourses of civic inclusion and political rights, the social marks of gender have often provided the rhetorical means for *constructing* as well as depriving the slave's common humanity? How do we understand that gender might "liberate" the slave when it also contributed to the slave's degradation, both in the comparative literature offered by anatomical science and within the organization of plantation life itself? How might we comprehend, in short, the uneven, asymmetrical productions of race and gender through which "blacks and women" have historically emerged, drawing together as well as fragmenting the corporeal logics on which their hierarchies depend? To explore these questions, whose ideological force and investigatory path underlie the conversations throughout this study, I want to return to the father of craniology whose proclivity for heads was perhaps only matched by his obsession with arts and letters.

The Word and the Flesh

During his years as enthusiastic skull collector and classifier of humankind, Johann Friedrich Blumenbach privately assembled an extensive library of works written by Africans and their New World descendants in order to demonstrate the inaccuracy of scientific and cultural assumptions of their natural inferiority.[19] The association in place in this brief but telling eighteenth-century scenario links textual production with intelligence as an emblem of the African's potential for civilization, capturing the legacy of race and writing that shaped the emergence of nineteenth-century African-American discourse. As the primary lever for evincing the human sameness beneath the Western denigration of dark skin, this textual production became an important vehicle for extraditing those of African descent from the panoply of Western determinations that would cast them as a species beneath European "man." It is ironic that Blumenbach, who coined the term "caucasian" to specify that racial category which represented to him the original type of man, would also so adamantly hope to attest to the African's intellectual equality. The great skull collector who revolutionized the classificatory schema established by Linnaeus, in short, turned to the realm of the written to argue against the assertions of inferiority being advanced by the craniological analysis he worked to develop. Clearly, the relationship between methodological focus and assumptions about racial hierarchy was not guaranteed in advance, though from the perspective of the late twentieth century the emphasis on brain and skull can hardly seem disinterested in the articulation of racially coded determinations of being.

And yet, in being bound to the concept of single creation, Blumenbach's attempt at demonstrating the African's difference as part of human variety (and not an emblem of separate species) by focusing on the textual was itself consistent with developing abolitionist positions in both Europe and the United States. From these perspectives, the fact of the African's textual documentation — the creation of a countertext of blackness — could prove the fallacy of notions of inherent inferiority and cultural primitivity. Where proponents of slavery and African subserviency pointed to the paucity of written traditions in African cultures as signs of a racially definitive scale of being, abolitionists increasingly relied on the evidence of the textual to mark the African(-American)'s humanity. As Henry Louis Gates Jr. discusses in "Literary Theory and the Black Tradition," black formal writing in the West originates in the demand for and desire to document "the black's potential for 'culture' — that is, for manners and morals [in order to separate] . . . the slave from the ex-slave, titled property from fledgling human being" (4). The written, in other words, displaces the text of black inferiority crafted by scientific and popular discourses, offering instead a black textuality that attempts to remake the flesh by assenting to the privilege accorded the word throughout the Anglophilic West. "If blacks were to signify as full members of the Western human community," Gates explains, "they would have to do so in their writings" (6). But while the Enlightenment would raise the issue of the written as a primary index for weighing human identities and differences, it was not always toward equality that the measurement ran. As Gates documents, the "negro's" relationship to the written word was, as early as 1700, a feature of philosophical conversations about the nature, scale, and significance of difference, grounding arguments both in favor of and against assumptions of innate black inferiority.[20]

It is in the writings of Hegel that Gates finds the most damaging association between literacy as evidence of culture and racial hierarchy. As Gates writes, "[i]t is the absence of writing that [Hegel] takes to be the most salient indication that Africa is the land of ultimate difference" ("Literary Theory and the Black Tradition" 19). For Hegel, writing is a necessary ingredient in ascertaining the productivities of human culture, since it is through the written word that a human being demonstrates the objectivity necessary for self-consciousness. Without the ability to stand in an objective relation to self, culture, and a transcendent universal authority, "being" itself remains obscure. "What we properly understand by Africa, is the Unhistorical, Undeveloped Spirit," Hegel writes, "still involved in the conditions of mere nature . . . on the threshold of the World's History" (*The Philosophy of History* 99). As the Unhistorical, Africa is a land without memory, and hence, as Gates discusses, its inhabitants are assumed to be without the developments of mind and rationality that the Enlightenment so privileged. Unaware of the movement of time, capable only of transient memory, the African was cast in terms of emotional and intellectual infantilism, a body at the dawn of being, a continent awaiting history. Gates glosses this system of racial encodements: "[w]ithout writing, there could exist no repeatable sign of the workings of reason, of mind; without memory or mind, there could exist no history; without history, there could exist no 'humanity'" (21). And without humanity, one might add, there could exist no possibility of the requisite masculine supremacy for civilization.

In the context of Enlightenment thought, this last turn to humanity-as-masculinity is no phantasmatic association, even if, as already remarked, the rhetoric of enlightened democratic citizenship worked to deny the gendered specificity that lay within its concept of a universal humanity. As feminist philosophers have now well documented, the primacy accorded to rationality and intellect as conditions of a public sphere devoid of women betrayed an underlying masculinist assumption, an assumption that, as Gates suggests, was as definitively raced as it was gendered.[21] Therefore, the "burden of literacy" that Gates describes as the struggle to write one's way out of the inferiority conferred on blackness must be understood as a scene of multiple inscriptions: not only was the African(-American) the antithesis to Western human universalism, but the corporeal particularity of the feminine must be overwritten in the struggle for citizenship as well. And yet, it was not simply an equal, no matter how mutual, exclusion that crafted the philosophic negation of "blacks and women" from the rational and intellectual, from memory and time, from the self-consciousness of history. The asymmetries of gender, especially in the context of the nineteenth century's overwhelming attempt to demasculinize black men, were determinative features of the struggle for literacy. While Gates describes the cultural conditions that "both motivated the black slave to seek his or her text and defined the frame against which each black text would be read" ("Literary Theory and the Black Tradition" 17), the Enlightenment's correlation between political rights and literacy would seem to be weighted differently, depending on whether, in fact, one were talking about "his or her text."

Or would it? Can we say that in the context of bondage, where a human being is reduced to a property relation, gender signifies the commodified body in much the same way that it does the freed? Hortense J. Spillers's discussion in "Mama's Baby, Papa's Maybe: An American Grammar Book" suggests no, as the quantification of the African body under enslavement marks for her a process of "ungendering." As she describes it, the transformation of the African into an economic abstraction during the Middle Passage epoch of the slave trade displaced gendered subjectivity: "[t]he respective subject-positions of "female" and "male" adhere to no symbolic integrity," she writes, for in severing "the captive body from its motive will . . . we lose at least *gender* difference *in the outcome,* and the female body and the male body become a territory of cultural and political maneuver, not at all gender-related, gender-specific" (66, 67). Differences between male and female signified only in spatial terms, as discrete measurements for the storage of bodies in the slaver's hull. In one case, she reports, males were allowed six feet by one foot four inches and females five feet ten by one foot four inches (72). While these "scaled inequalities," as Spillers calls them, "reveal the application of the gender rule," she argues nonetheless that these distinctions were grounded in the logic of property, not finally in the social structure of sexual difference. This is because gender takes place "within the confines of the domestic . . . in the specificity of proper names, more exactly, a patronymic, which, in turn, situates those persons it 'covers' in a particular place" (ibid.). Stranded in the oceanic, commodified as property, devoid of the recognition of their names or cultures, slaves in transit were quite literally, she says, "*nowhere at all*" (ibid.).

To accept, even skeptically, Spillers's reading of the Middle Passage is, in some sense, to encounter the Gordian knot of difference that the importation of slaves in the New World occasioned, since it forces us to recognize how thoroughly saturated is the *socio-symbolic structure* of sexual difference with the determinants of white racial supremacy. This structure of sexual difference was (and is) not reducible to the "essential" components of male and female bodies, but refers instead to the processes and practices by which gendered subjectivity defines and inaugurates the modern subject, organizing "civil" society by scripting it according to highly gendered roles and functions. For Spillers, the concept of "ungendering" points to the absence of such a social system in which gender ascribed specific functions on the slave ship, thereby marking the slave woman's excision from the reproduction of mothering through which female gender routinely gains a symbolic location in patriarchy. Without the domestic organization of the reproduction of mothering, Spillers writes, the Middle Passage "carries few of the benefits of a *patriarchilized* female gender, which, from one point of view, is the *only* female gender there is" ("Mama's Baby, Papa's Maybe" 73). Later she explains that "even though the enslaved female reproduced other enslaved persons, we do not read 'birth' in this instance as a reproduction of mothering precisely because the female, like the male, has been robbed of the parental right, the parental function" (77–78). Without this right and function, the structure of patriarchy as a familial, domestic arrangement — as a program of civic roles and functions — is suspended, and the enslaved woman becomes, Spillers writes, "neuter-bound" (77).

By placing gender under this kind of intense theoretical pressure, Spillers's analysis works in tension with some of the trajectories of recent African-Americanist scholarship, which read the slave woman's maternal function — her reproduction of human beings as property, her role as nursemaid to the master's children, and her subversive participation in non-nuclear parenting structures within the slave community — as aspects of the complexities of sexual difference under which she lived.[22] For these scholars, the Middle Passage initiated the kind of gendered demarcations of enslaved flesh that would come to organize the productive roles and functions of slaves on the plantation. "Male and female slavery was different from the very beginning," writes Deborah Gray White. "[W]omen did not generally travel the middle passage in the holds of slave ships but took the dreaded journey on the quarter deck. . . . [W]omen and girls were [often] not shackled" (*Ar'n't I a Woman* 63). Such distinctions have been used to demonstrate the emphasis placed on the slave woman's sexual availability and hence on her overt sexualization since the earliest days of Anglophilic encounters with Africa. For Spillers, however, these gendered practices existed within a broader public discourse in which, as the juridical codes governing slave-holding attest, "[e]very feature of social and human differentiation disappears . . . regarding the African-American person" ("Mama's Baby, Papa's Maybe" 78). It is this reification of personhood that underwrites her concept of "ungendering," which marks the way gender's socio-symbolic structure ascribed certain meanings and privileges that failed to accrue to a body understood not as human, but as a propertied abstraction.

In differentiating between gender as a socio-symbolic structure and the descriptive terminology of male and female flesh that framed the discourse of the African(-American) as sexed property, Spillers's use of "ungendering" is not aimed at discounting the way the plantation economy maximized the (re)productivities of the enslaved based on the body's sexual differences. Nor is she dismissing the sexual violations imposed on the captive body, that body that became "the source of an irresistible, destructive sensuality" ("Mama's Baby, Papa's Maybe" 67). Instead, her concept of gender and its symbolic undoing seeks a different theoretical register, but one whose materiality must be viewed as no less violent than direct crimes (sexual and otherwise) against the flesh. If, as she suggests, the patriarchal symbolic relies on the patronymic and its organization of the domestic, then the denial of a black patronym—and the attendant displacement of the black female's maternity within the slave system—situated both black men and women as illegitimate subjects within the prescriptive field of patriarchal gender. The necessity of this production of illegitimacy to the economics of white racial supremacy was perhaps best epitomized by the slaver's imposition of a mother-bound kinship system onto the slave—a system in which the child followed the status of the mother, thereby guaranteeing paternal rights and privileges as definitively white racial ones.

While Spillers's essay seems to have as its political end a consideration of the implications of this "mother-right" system for the seeming private gender relationships between black women and black men, one can extend the discussion of the patronymic's domestic organization to the realm of the public as well, where the patronymic has served as the framework for defining the very possibility of citizenship throughout most of this country's history. After all, it was masculine lineage that constructed the legitimacy of the nineteenth-century citizen, whose claims to family, property, and the nation-state were wrought through the universal disembodiment attending white masculinity within enlightened democracy. In the context of the public sphere, the ungendering that Spillers ascribes to the translation of human beings into property was thus predicated on the impossibility of such beings claiming not simply gender in the abstract, but the specificities and privileges of *masculine* gender itself. As such, we might consider the ungendering of the enslaved male body in the public sphere as a process of feminizing blackness, even as such a figuration—of a simultaneous ungendering and feminization—appears decidedly contradictory. But such contradictions haunt in various ways all black bodies in modernity, especially as subjectivity, humanity, and the privileges of patriarchal gender were repeatedly cast as unintelligible aspects of the slave's being. That these unintelligibilities appeared to be equal in the context of black male and black female bodies under enslavement—while being definitively unequal in terms of the differing *potential* toward citizenship that gender difference entailed—marks the profound instabilities attending race and gender throughout the nineteenth century.

The difficulties of theorizing the specificities of race and gender in the context of the African-American's subjecthood are thus compounded by the incommensurabilities between male and female bodies in the public sphere where aspirations toward cultural legitimacy cannot be politically pursued, let alone described, in the same social or symbolic register. In the struggle for citizenship in the post–Civil War years, for instance, the black female could only be insinuated into enfranchisement, so thorough was her gendered disqualification from the public sphere. No longer chattel, she nonetheless was without recourse to the patronymic of citizenship—that right of self-possession—that governed the legal and political discourses of the public realm. The black male, on the other hand, entered enfranchisement through the symbolic possibilities that accrued to the masculine as the precondition of the patronymic, as the name that guaranteed legitimate lineage. That this entrance was marked by extreme and incontrovertible violence, often in the form of lynching and castration, demonstrates how unsettling was the possibility of the black male *as male*. Such a threat has clearly not lessened in the hundred years since black male enfranchisement, given not only the various levels of violence (economic, political, and representational) attending the prospect of black paternity in the late twentieth century but also the concomitant pathologizing of the mother-bound structure of the black family itself.[23]

From the perspective of these complexities, we can approach more clearly the central paradox attending the African(-American) within the terms of Western modernity: where the reduction of human being to chattel effects a reification of "personhood" that necessitates a rhetorical counterclaim to a distinctly gendered social and political subjectivity. For the African(-American) in the late eighteenth and nineteenth centuries, in other words, the ability to be gendered marked the entrance to the human, public community, providing both civic roles (such as the reproduction of mothering) while simultaneously fragmenting citizenship according to a deeply exclusive masculine universalism. While Spillers describes an equality between male and female bodies under slavery, such propertied equality dissolves at the discursive site of the African(-American)'s human signification, which installed a gendered being where the legal discourses of enslavement constituted, through commodification, the ungendered flesh. In this way, the slave's struggle to prove humanity necessarily involved a highly refined rhetoric of sexual difference, and it was this—this contorting and bizarrely liberatory framework of gender differences—that finally links abolitionist representations of the slave, as well as the slave's textual production, throughout the nineteenth century. The "burden of literacy" that Gates describes as the contradictory demand for black textuality in the master's tongue must thus be approached as the strategic locus for claiming an African-American subjectivity inseparable, as we shall see, from the distinctions of gender.

Engendering the Text

If disciplinarity always carries a methodological demand, then such a weighty claim—of the slave's need to forge a gendered subjectivity to counter slavery's commodified "ungendering"—would seem to require both a textual specificity (as in close reading) and evidence of critical scope (as in the broad survey). For the cultural critic, these are often contrary methodologies, elevating on one hand a textual instance as culturally paradigmatic, while shaping on the other hand continuities, repetitions, and disruptions as an overarching and most often coherent narrative of cultural meaning. In recent years, this methodological tug-of-war has been not so much lessened as dislocated by the greater attention paid to the political contestation that underlies all cultural critique. The authority of the text to contain the definitive truth of its own meaning, or the assemblage of texts to speak their narrative and symbolic affinities with each other, is cast as part of the crisis of the contemporary, with Truth exchanged for ideology, knowledge for the always-misperceived. It is only in this way that the contemporary becomes available to us as a site of productive agency, no matter how partial the possibilities may seem of shaping that which also makes us. From this perspective, the political force of this chapter's latest claim— that the delineation of a gendered subjectivity conditions the African(-American)'s rhetorical entrance into the human and that this delineation is deeply consequential for the twentieth-century figure "blacks and women" —is less a recovery of nineteenth-century social formations than an excavation of the historical present, of our own refracted mise-en-scène.

The theoretical stakes of this setting constitute what I think of as both an ecology of the past and an economy of being present—that is, both the reclamation and preservation of cultural materials rigorously cast as outside

Western regimes of knowledge *and* an attention to the violences, griefs, and privileges wrought by the social and (geo)political incommensurabilities that are culturally repressed in our fantasy of democratic becoming. To think of this ecology and economy in the context of race entails confronting the ideal of visibility—of representational presence and positive imagery—that has accompanied twentieth-century social struggle, where African-American political representation has been inextricably related to the complex interplay of gender, corporeality, and commodification. In the post-segregationist era, in particular, the crisis of commodification as both the status of identity and as the very condition of public discourse has dramatically recast the political possibilities that attended the visible's ideal. But this recasting is not a new complexity, as this chapter's conversation about modern anatomies has struggled to reveal. The domination of the visible that underwrote the slave's propertied status demonstrates that the problematic of visibility, corporeality, and commodification has routinely accompanied, in however different ways, the African's journey through the "new world." It is within this problematic that the slave's turn toward the textual to undo the commodification of bondage inextricably rests.

Explicating the difficulties of staging a human presence in the context of the African(-American)'s commodified negation requires paying attention to the social productivities and discriminations that gender inevitably inscribes. This is because the movement toward human signification pivots, as I have suggested, on the gendered assumptions that govern the relationship between the public and private spheres. In this relationship, it is the corporeal abstraction accorded white masculinity that underwrites a host of civic entitlements, serving as the veiled particular subject position on which the false universalism of democratic citizenship resides. For the African-American male slave, the rhetorical trajectory of emancipation entailed making claims to this masculine particularity, thereby disentangling his body both from the propertied ungendering of the legal ledger *and* from those popular and scientific discourses that equated blackness with the feminine and the deviantly sexual. In seeking masculine-gendered significations to undo the negations attending blackness in the public sphere, the black male thus encountered the asymmetries of gender in which both the promise and the denial of his equal citizenship was caught. Within this contradictory nexus, we can uncover the black woman's elision from signifying within the overtly racial component of "blacks and women."

To explore more fully the way the black male achieved his representative racial status, the closing meditation of this chapter turns to a paradigmatic textual instance, one whose production—as the first *known* short story published by an African-American male—marks simultaneously a literary-historical origin and the very impossibility of recoverable origins, an impossibility underscored by the necessity of the qualifier "known." The culture of loss that surrounds nineteenth-century black textual production and the difficulty of publication in a society overwhelmingly convinced of the African-American's incapacity for rational thought or imaginative creation—those indexes of civilization—highlight the material complexities under which the slave's textuality was born. More important perhaps, Frederick Douglass's 1853 "The Heroic Slave" demonstrates how deeply embedded was the quest for modern subjectivity in the textual economies of both race and gender, while also foregrounding the contradictions through which their corporeal logics and emancipatory rhetorics would routinely collide. In this collision, it is toward narratives of masculinity—of the heroic body, of democracy and the nation-state, of founding "fathers"—that Douglass's rhetoric turns. Such an attempt to grasp the civic entitlement of the public sphere characterizes the impossibly complicit effects that the asymmetries of gender in the nineteenth century inevitably conferred.

As those familiar with the story might remember, "The Heroic Slave" begins by establishing as its primary context the contradiction of enslavement that attends America's founding narrative of revolutionary emancipation:

> The State of Virginia is famous in American annals for the multitudinous array of her statesmen and heroes. . . . Yet . . . *one* of the truest, manliest, and bravest of her children . . . holds now no higher place in the records of that grand old Commonwealth than is held by a horse or an ox. Let those account for it who can, but there stands the fact, that a man who loved liberty as well as did Patrick Henry,—who deserved it as much as Thomas Jefferson,—and who fought for it with a valor as high, an arm as strong, and against odds as great, as he who led all the armies of the American colonies through the great war for freedom and independence, lives now only in the chattel records of his native State. (37–38)

By setting the mythology of national origin against the transaction of human being into property, Douglass casts an ironic addendum to the rhetoric of universal suffrage that accompanies America's nativity narrative, revealing the deeply profound ideological breach on which "liberty" under a slave economy rests. To repair this breach, "The Heroic Slave" seeks to reclaim the slave's unwritten human nativity, demonstrating, through geographical symbolics (Virginia) and heroic qualities (manliness, strength, and bravery), the slave's embodiment of the nation's revolutionary ideals. In doing so, Douglass appeals to the patriarchal symbolics of nineteenth-century gender relations in order to craft his slave's human and historical presence within the nation's paternal and filial narrative terms.

In this gendered redress of the slave's reduction to "the chattel records of his native State," "The Heroic Slave" encounters the problematic of visibility that accompanies both popular and scientific discourses of race throughout the nineteenth century. Such an encounter is inextricably para-doxical, as the scripting of the slave as gendered necessitates negotiating the very representational domain — the corporeal — on which the inherent inhumanity of "blackness," as I have shown, was routinely cast. The story's more awkward narrative moments evince the difficulty of forging just such a negotiation, as we witness "The Heroic Slave" struggling to reveal the slave as socially and subjectively familiar to a white audience without also reconvening the entrenched significations of the black body. As part of this struggle, Douglass adopts a strategy of deferral through which subjec-tive presence initially emerges in the context of both characterological and corporeal absence. These absences are highlighted by the narrator's com-mentary in the story's opening. "Glimpses of this great character are all that can now be presented," he writes of the protagonist, Madison Wash-ington. "He is brought to view only by a few transient incidents. . . . Like a guiding star on a stormy night, he is seen through the parted clouds . . . or like the gray peak of a menacing rock . . . he is seen by the quivering flash of lightening, and he again disappears covered with mystery" (38). In the metaphoric language of vision and (in)visibility, the narrator laments the impossibility of representation, turning instead to the remnants of the visible — of the "marks, traces, possibles, and probabilities" (ibid.) — as the means by which the protagonist, however partially, might be revealed.

Given the seeming contradiction between the subjective presence of the slave and his overdetermined corporeality, it is no wonder that "The Heroic Slave" initially introduces Madison Washington not as a physical narrative presence but as a disembodied voice. Engaged in soliloquy against the in-justices of enslavement, Washington is present as "a human voice" (38) in a pine forest, heard from the distance by Mr. Listwell, a white traveler from the north. So compelling is this human sound that Listwell edges into the forest in the hopes of discovering "what thoughts and feelings, or, it might be, high aspirations, guided those rich and mellow accents" (ibid.). As the paradigmatic reader, Listwell becomes convinced of the slave's humanity through the rhetorical eloquence of Washington's speech—a speech that significantly turns to the "generic" discourse of sexual difference to mark its speaker's human subjectivity:

> I am a *slave*, —born a slave, an abject slave. . . . That accursed and crawling snake . . . is freer and better off than I. He escaped my blow, and is safe. But here am I, a man, —yes, *a man!* —with thoughts and wishes, with powers and faculties . . . yet he is my superior. . . . I neither run nor fight. . . . I am galled with irons; but even these are more tolerable than the consciousness, the *galling* consciousness of cowardice and indecision. . . . When that young man struggled with the waves *for life* . . . did I not plunge in, forgetful of life, to save his? . . . Could a coward do that? *No, —no,* —I wrong myself, —I am no coward. (39)

In constructing the interaction between the slave and the always-free in the context of Washington's corporeal invisibility, Douglass fashions a version of the democratic public sphere, allowing the black body to achieve the disembodied abstraction that ascendancy to citizenship routinely confers. Such abstraction underwrites, if contradictorily, the rhetorical invocation of inalienable rights on which Washington's speech depends. "*Liberty* I will have, or die in the attempt to gain it," he ultimately exclaims. "I have nothing to lose. If I am caught, I shall only be a slave. If I am shot, I shall only lose a life which is a burden and a curse. If I get clear . . . liberty, the inalienable birth-right of every man . . . will be mine. My resolution is fixed. *I shall be free*" (39–40). In response to Washington's soliloquy, Listwell pledges his commitment to slavery's undoing: "[f]rom this hour," he exclaims, "I am an abolitionist" (42).

In emphasizing Washington's speech as the means for negotiating the corporeal text of black inferiority, "The Heroic Slave" draws an analogy between the slave's struggle for enfranchisement and the history of liberty's pursuit—a history characterized by great men (Patrick Henry and Thomas Jefferson) and heroic deeds (the birth of the nation). This analogy is literalized at the end of the story when Tom Grant, the sole white survivor of the narrative's slave revolt, testifies at length to Washington's character:

> The leader of the mutiny in question was just as shrewd a fellow as ever I met in my life, and was as well fitted to lead in a dangerous enterprise as any one white man in ten thousand. . . . I forgot his blackness in the dignity of his manner, and the eloquence of his speech. It seemed as if the souls of both the great dead men (whose names he bore) had

> entered him. . . . I felt myself in the presence of a superior man; one
> who, had he been a white man, I would have followed willingly and
> gladly in any honorable enterprise. (73, 75, 76–77)

In the context of his eloquent speech and dignified manner, Washington's
blackness is here thoroughly repressed—exchanged, that is, for those signifiers of similarity (his ability to lead for instance) that attend white supremacy's symbolics of civilized humanity. Through this strategy, Douglass
can envision the slave's participation in the dis-corporation that underwrites Enlightened democracy, even as such participation relies on the
white witness—he who has listened to the slave's humanity—to extend that
voice into the public sphere. By linking abolitionist identifications to the
centrality of the slave's speech and this speech to the demand for public
testimony in favor of the slave's humanity, Douglass offers a reconfigured
public sphere in which the slave's rhetorical mastery evinces the psychic
interiority and heroic masculinity necessary to civic entitlements. In doing
this, he demonstrates the slave's achievement of those hallmarks of white
superiority—speech, intelligence, and rationality—that significantly organized the taxonomic pursuits of race science, natural history, and comparative anatomy alike.

If we understand voice as serving, then, as the signification of human
equivalencies between black and white men, and thereby initiating Listwell's conversion to abolitionism and Tom Grant's de-racialized admira-
tion, it is significant that the narrative ultimately reveals Madison Washington as a physical presence—and it does so in ways that demonstrate the
white masculine precondition on which the dis-corporation of publicity
depends.

> Madison was of manly form. Tall, symmetrical, round, and strong. . . .
> His torn sleeves disclosed arms like polished iron. . . . His whole ap-
> pearance betokened Herculean strength; yet there was nothing savage
> or forbidding in his aspect. . . . A giant's strength, but not a giant's
> heart was in him. His broad mouth and nose spoke only of good
> nature and kindness. . . . He was . . . intelligent and brave. He had the
> head to conceive, and the hand to execute. ("The Heroic Slave" 40)

By aestheticizing the black body as a classical masculine form, "The Heroic
Slave" adjudicates the slave's social and specular particularity by evoking a
familiar aesthetic ideal. That this ideal reconvenes nineteenth-century obsessions with antiquity demonstrates not so much Douglass's capitulation

to Western fantasies of cultural supremacy, but the impossibility of uncovering an African(-American) presence where the universalized particularity of white masculinity routinely stands. From this perspective, it is significant that the narrative's description of the hero's blackness is figured in the poetic language of the Euro-American literary tradition. Quoting Shakespeare, Douglass writes, "[h]is face was 'black but comely'" while "[h]is eye, lit with emotion, kept guard under a brow as dark and as glossy as the raven's wing" (ibid.).

The shift from voice to corporeal visibility in the early pages of the narrative — and the movement back to dis-corporation provided by Tom Grant's testimonial to Washington's heroism and eloquent speech — demonstrates the paradoxes of representational presence that accompany the black male slave into literary identity. In displacing the visible economy of race by invoking the socio-symbolic structure of sexual difference, it is finally the masculinity of the slave that serves as the rhetorical ground for "The Heroic Slave"'s appeal to a common humanity, a masculinity that reveals the ideological framework of citizenry on which modernity's political vision of democracy is historically based. In the context of the story's articulation of white abolitionist identifications, the reader is solicited as masculine as well, with Listwell and Grant serving as paradigmatic witnesses to slavery's inherent immorality. Within the political structures of nineteenth-century power arrangements, such a circuit of homosocial bonds enables Douglass to forge a radical political vision of the slave's independently led, successful insurrection. Nevertheless, the utopic moment that symbolically heralds the ideological narrative of American revolution, of the heroic stand against undemocratic tyranny, takes place in a geographical elsewhere — the Bahamas — where violent slave revolt becomes the only guaranteed means for engendering the inalienable right to liberty.

And what of the slave woman? Does "The Heroic Slave" offer for her a paradigm of revolutionary participation, of speech and representational presence? Does it negotiate the text of "blackness" in which her claim to humanity is similarly exorcised? Does she emerge to claim her own significatory possibilities within the story's narration of revolutionary revolt? And if she does none of these, what then do we make of Douglass, himself a vigilant black male voice for women's rights in the nineteenth century? Or are the social incommensurabilities under which the slave as a gendered being could *and* could not wage political claims of import here? I am not suggesting that we dismiss the story's problematic sheltering of the female slave's narrative within the broad shape of the heroism of its heroic slave. Washington's wife, Susan, after all, is killed in the course of his attempt to rescue her from enslavement—and cast in the process in a most feminized and enfeebled way: "I ventured upon the desperate attempt to reach my poor wife's room by means of a ladder," Washington explains. "[B]ut the noise . . . frightened [her], and she screamed and fainted" (65, 66). As he carries the fainted woman from the master's house, she revives but "*too* late" to avert the whites in pursuit. Now, "assailed with '*Stop! stop! or be shot down*'" (66), they are fired upon and she is instantly killed. Following his apprehension, Washington finds himself aboard the *Creole,* bound for the dreaded New Orleans slave market, when he successfully engineers a slave revolt. What do we make of the narrative's inability to offer to Madison Washington's wife the revolutionary ideals of freedom and liberty that he obtains?

To answer such questions concerning the African(-American) woman's excision from the historical conjunction of modernity, humanity, and citizenry is to trace the conversations of this chapter. These conversations have demonstrated the contradictory and complicit mechanisms through which her body underwrites, as a sexual icon, the coupled emergence of "blacks and women" while retaining precious little political currency to signify as either of its representative members. Instead, she becomes the material ground for defining and ascertaining other social positions: in the development of her brain and skull, for instance, comparative science locates evidence for both the African(-American) male's masculine inferiorities and the white female's gendered priority; in the hyperextension of her sexual organs, "blackness" is saturated ontologically with animality and sexuality, thereby inscribing both black and female as deviant corporealities while forging sexual hierarchies among women. In the sphere of political rights, she further encounters a masculine universalism so weighty it severely limits her ability to grasp the possibility framing black male enfranchisement where the rhetorical invocation of a masculine humanity resists the negations of personhood that attend commodified flesh. Without the masculine characteristics underwriting the dis-corporation of the public sphere, without the racial supremacy idealized by nationalist narratives of civic duty and true womanhood, the African(-American) woman provides the framework for but fails to signify as a corporeal or symbolic presence in the contestations for political power figured by "blacks and women." In the nineteenth century as in our own, the conjunction—*and*—paradoxically establishes a relationship predicated on mutual exclusion.

How to undo this exclusionary figuration? How to signify the conjunctive body, simultaneously black *and* female? How to forge political affinities that traverse the hierarchical privileges and discursive logics of white or male? Feminists who have sought to answer these questions have recently turned to a methodological refashioning, countering the paradigmatic negation of "blacks and women" by situating the black woman at the center of investigative study.[24] Bell hooks's *Feminist Theory: From Margin to Center* characterizes such a methodological gesture, seeking in the repressions of American historical discourses the means for bringing to presence — to sight and to individual and collective voice — the black woman's critical centrality.[25] The current outpouring of academic research, perhaps unimaginable twenty years ago, is importantly reshaping the canons of knowledge available on the literary, historical, and theoretical contributions of black women. However, as much as one wants to herald these reconfigurations of knowledge formations as unqualifiably transformative, a variety of suspicions — about methodological transcendence, commodification, and the fetishization of marginality — remain. There is no assurance, after all, that methodological centrality retrieves the black woman from her historical erasure, no matter how politically crucial the project of reclamation may now be. In the context of the visible economies of race and gender in which she is entrapped, the movement from margin to center may in fact replicate the kind of commodification that has recently recuperated other identity-based political retrievals, undermining the contemporary political saliency of identity politics themselves.

In this context, we might ask whether the methodological shift can radically resist without remarketing, in modernist fashion, the logics of presence and visibility conditioning and contributing to the black woman's historical expulsion. For while the contours of contemporary feminist politics suggest that the only means for tracing and specifying the conjunctive body underlying "blacks and women" is a methodological recentering, it is not clear that only in this way can the cultural modes and disciplines that define and perpetuate her historic absence be explained. To achieve this may require investigative travel in an initially contradictory direction, into that domain of cultural relations most underwritten by the African-American woman's historical absence: those among black and white men. It is, after all, in the homosocial nexus of dread, violence, and a heightened erotic passion — or in the terms used in the following two chapters, in the ritualized practices of lynching and castration on one hand, and the repetitious narration of interracial masculine bonding on the other — that we witness the dilemma of sameness and difference that characterizes the political contestations between white supremacy and patriarchy so divisively encoded in the coupling of "blacks and women." The analyses of these struggles reveal the marks and traces of the black woman's historical absence in ways crucial to this project's broader elaboration of feminist disloyalties, even as it may risk reinscribing her methodological displacement. Risking this, risking disloyalty to the political priority now rightly given to black woman, this study moves haltingly toward her socio-symbolic return in a paradoxical but necessary investigative direction. First, then, the ends of Man.

The Ends of "Man"

3 The Anatomy of Lynching

When Matt lowered his eyes he noticed the ribs had been caved in.

The flesh was bruised and torn. [The birthmark] was just below [Willie's] navel, he thought. Then he gave a start: where it should have been was only a bloody mound of torn flesh and hair. Matt went weak. He felt as though he had been castrated himself. He thought he would fall when Clara stepped up beside him. Swiftly, he tried to push her back. . . . Then Clara was screaming. . . . Matt pushed [her] to go, feeling hot breath against the hand he held over her mouth.

"Just remember that a car hit 'im, and you'll be all right," the patrolman said. "We don't allow no lynching round here no more."

Matt felt Clara's fingers digging into his arm as his eyes flashed swiftly over the face of the towering patrolman, over the badge against the blue shirt, the fingers crooked in the belt above the gun butt. He swallowed hard . . . catching sight of Willie between the white men's legs.

"I'll remember," he said bitterly, "he was hit by a car." — Ralph Ellison, "The Birthmark" 16–17

Lynching is about the law — both the towering patrolman who renarrates the body and sadistically claims it as sign of his own power and the Symbolic as law, the site of normativity and sanctioned desire, of prohibition and taboo. In the circuit of relations that governs lynching in the United States, the law as legal discourse and disciplinary practice subtends the Symbolic arena, marking out a topos of bodies and identities that not only defines and circumscribes social and political behavior but also punishes transgression, from its wildest possibility to its most benign threat. Operating according to a logic of borders — racial, sexual, national, psychological, and biological as well as gendered — lynching figures its victims as the culturally abject — monstrosities of excess whose limp and hanging bodies function as the specular assurance that the racial threat has not simply been averted, but rendered incapable of return. The overdetermination of punishment in the lynching scenario demonstrates its profoundly psychological function, reinforcing the disciplinary range of white power that initiates the violent mechanism in all its complexity. How we understand this complexity—how we might approach the tableau of torture, dismemberment, and death that shapes lynching's specifically racialized deployment—provides the locus around which this chapter is organized and makes possible a discussion of the interesting relations of race and gender in U.S. culture.

In particular, this chapter extends the consideration of questions of the visible by focusing on the sexual economy that underlies lynching's emergence as a disciplinary practice for racial control at the end of the nineteenth century. Here, the de-commodification of the African-American body that accompanies the transformation from chattel to citizenry is mediated through a complicated process of sexualization and engendering. Not only does lynching enact a grotesquely symbolic, if not literal, sexual encounter between the white mob and its victim, but the increasing use of castration as a preferred form of mutilation for African-American men demonstrates lynching's connection to the socio-symbolic realm of sexual difference. That this realm pivots on scripting the body as a visible terrain is perhaps an incontestable assertion in the mid-1990s, given the proliferation of feminist attentions both to the structure of the gaze and to corporeal identities.[1] And yet, feminist theory's lengthy and crucial exploration of the visible economy that governs sexual difference has most often remained stranded within a reduction of the body to the figure of woman. To challenge this reduction and to become disloyal to feminism's moratorium on reading the category of men as anything other than patriarchal privilege—such motives underwrite this chapter's pursuit of the symbolic and specular anatomies of lynching, where differences among men are so violently foregrounded that one can no longer cling to the rhetorical homogeneity attached to the masculine in feminist and patriarchal discourses alike.

But why such disloyalty? After all, in the first heady decade of the contemporary women's movement, the assumption of masculinity as an undifferentiated position aided feminism's articulation of its own political subjectivity. Indeed, the representation of men as the common enemy worked to disrupt, at least provisionally, the arena of women's primary social bonding: the heterosexual. By bringing into question women's allegiances to men as products of heterosexuality's compulsory production, feminism made imperative political solidarity among women. Sisterhood became powerful, and the personal (with its multiple aspects of the everyday) took on a decidedly political signification. Like all utopic myths, however, this one of women's common sisterhood was quite fleeting, as the difficulties of political organization and differences among women emerged once again to challenge the foundational rhetoric of women's common oppression.[2] In the process, the concept of men as the common enemy was necessarily transformed to account for the way women's political solidarities often transgressed the sacrosanct boundaries of gender, especially in the cultural context of white racial supremacy. Because all men do not share equally in masculine rights and privileges—because some men are, in fact, oppressed by women of the prevailing race and class—assumptions about power as uniformly based on sexual difference (men as oppressor, women as oppressed) have been pressured to give way.

Lynching provides a crucial locus for exploring the implications of this necessary end of "man" by drawing out the contexts and crises of racial hierarchies on the form and function of late-nineteenth-century patriarchal relations. In the turn toward lynching as a white supremacist activity in the post-Emancipation years, we might recognize the symbolic force of the white mob's activity as a denial of the black male's newly articulated right to citizenship and, with it, the various privileges of patriarchal power that have historically accompanied such significations within the public sphere. The disciplinary fusion of castration with lynching makes this symbolic force a distinctly visible relation, not simply because of the public performance that attends the torture, but more important because of the corporeal interchange between genitals and skin. In the lynch scenario, the stereotypical fascination and abhorrence for blackness is literalized as a competition for masculinity and seminal power. In severing the black male's penis from his body, either as a narrative account or a material act, the mob aggressively denies the patriarchal sign and symbol of the masculine, interrupting the privilege of the phallus and thereby reclaiming, through the perversity of dismemberment, the black male's (masculine) potentiality for citizenship.[3]

Although this imposition of feminization works to align the black male, at the symbolic level of the body, with those still disenfranchised, it is significant that the narrative means for inciting and explaining the mob's violence takes the form of an intense masculinization in the figure of the black male as mythically endowed rapist. Through the discourse of the black male rapist, racial difference is cast not simply as sexual, but as a heightened sexual perversity. This figuration of blackness as primitive sexual appetite calls up a long associative history in Anglophilic culture where, as my previous discussions suggest, white supremacist discourses adjudicate the relations of domination and colonial imposition by shifting attention to the

sexual dynamics of the scene of conquest onto the bodies of those conquered. In the United States, the particular necessity of this shift in the late
nineteenth century may seem obvious, as the loss of miscegenation's economic rationalization under slavery turns the question of interracial sexuality toward the more tension-wrought domain of sexual desire. The myth
of the black male rapist serves to compensate for this economic loss, trans-
ferring the focus from the white man's quasi-sanctioned (because economi-
cally productive) sexual activities to the bodies, quite literally, of black men.
Located there, within the "logic" of an excessive hypermasculinization, the
black male's claims to citizenship—voting rights, employment, and more
abstract privileges of the patronymic—are violently denied.

This is not to suggest that lynching as a disciplinary practice has been
confined to the bodies of black men, even if it does recognize that the
very consciousness of lynching in U.S. culture figures decisively around
them. Black women were routinely lynched, burned, and summarily muti-
lated, and their public campaign against such terrorism was itself crucial
to the political articulations of African-American resistance in the early
twentieth century.[4] This chapter's emphasis on both the cultural narrative
and practice of lynching as a particularly contentious site for extrapolat-
ing the competing logics of patriarchy and white supremacy might best be
understood as an analysis of the mechanisms through which the corporeal violence attending black female bodies has been expulsed from public
view. Such expulsion is perhaps best epitomized by Clarence Thomas's invocation of the lynch metaphor during his confirmation hearings, which
simultaneously produced and reiterated the cultural memory of lynching
as terrorism solely against black men. The difficulty, some might say the
impossibility, for Anita Hill to signify as a body that had also been violated
by white supremacist practices, that had been similarly defined historically
in sexually discriminatory and inhumane terms, demonstrates the zero sum
of political currency against which black women have routinely fought. In
this context, a critical exploration of lynching that does not foreground the
violences leveled against black female bodies might seem to risk, at the very
least, political irresponsibility.

But as I have suggested in the previous chapter and as I hope to elaborate throughout the remainder of this study, the productive function of the
discourse of sexual difference as an increasingly deployed mechanism of
racial signification and control attaches in ways to black male bodies that
are crucial to a feminist politics of antiracist struggle—to a feminist politics
that is not simply invested in bringing the black woman into critical view,

[handwritten margin note: The double burden of race & gender oppression accounts for the historical elision of the black f from "blacks and women ..."]

but which traces the historical and theoretical contexts that shape her absence and that speak more broadly to the intertwining relationship between patriarchy and white supremacy. While we may know that the double burden of race and gender oppression accounts for the historical elision of the black woman from "blacks and women," and while we may routinely cite the political structures of race and gender in which the black woman has been forcefully and violently caught, the specificities and historical contingencies of these relations remain in many ways to be explored. Toward that end—but bound to a different, perhaps circuitous methodological focus—this chapter analyzes the interplay between the myth of the black rapist and the disciplinary mechanism of lynching and castration as a negotiation, through discourses of sexual difference, of the threat of African-American enfranchisement in the post–Civil War years. The gender asymmetry of this enfranchisement defines a difference between black women and black men that has important consequences to both the narrative and disciplinary (re)structuring of social power in the late nineteenth century.

It is in this context, too, that we can approach the variously gendered discourses of black liberation struggle in the twentieth century, where the cultural configuration of the black male's difference from white masculinity as a matter of sexuality and gender has most often focused liberationist critiques of white supremacy. Black Power discourses in the 1960s, for instance, turned repeatedly to the historical legacy of race and gender in order to define and articulate a strident black masculinity, one that worked specifically to negate lynching and castration's cultural and corporeal effect. In the attempt to "heal the wound of my Castration" (*Soul on Ice* 189), as Eldridge Cleaver framed the black male's struggle against the symbolic weight of white supremacy, Black Power asserted the priority of the black phallus and thereby reclaimed the imposition of feminization that has historically attended power relations between black and white men. At the same time, Black Power crafted the rhetorical figure of the white male as an emasculated one. As Imamu Baraka claimed in 1966, white men are "trained to be fags" (*Home* 216). By consigning the white male to the feminine, Black Power rhetoric inverts the representational economy of lynching and castration, articulating the space of the "real" masculine solely for the black male himself. The threat that this inversion poses to the cultural framework of white masculine power cannot be underestimated, as Black Power quite rightly read lynching and castration as disciplinary mechanisms saturated by the hierarchical logic of sexual difference.

In this regard, Black Power's overemphasis on masculinity and black

male entitlements might be viewed less as a simple re-creation of patriarchal logic than as an extrapolation and, to some degree, politically resistant
intensification of America's intersecting legacy of race, sexuality, and gender. At the same time, of course, Black Power's rhetorical inversion—to
assert the black phallus in the context of metaphorical and literal castration—elides black liberation struggle with a universal masculine position,
thereby displacing both the specificity and legitimacy of black female articulations of political disempowerment, as well as a variety of claims from
African-American sexual minorities. Most important perhaps, the equation
between a nationalist black liberation struggle and masculine rights reveals
the framing terms of citizenry and civil entitlements on which the constitutional documents of this country depend. To read the anatomy of lynching
from this perspective, both in its disciplinary practice and in its enduring
centrality to anti-segregationist and post-segregationist significations, is to
occupy, in however provisional and irretrievably partial ways, the complicated contestations in which race, sexuality, and gender are enmeshed.

Marking the Body

The corporeal inscriptions of race and gender that underlie the lynching
and castration scene can be located in a compelling shift in the production
of difference in U.S. history, based, as my preamble suggests, on changing material conditions in the post–Civil War years. While an elaboration
of these conditions is crucial to understanding the disciplinary practice of
lynching, I want to begin the discussion on more literary terrain. As readers
familiar with nineteenth-century U.S. literature no doubt have recognized,
my opening epigraph from a 1940 Ralph Ellison short story bears the same
title, "The Birthmark," as Nathaniel Hawthorne's now-canonical endeavor,
first published nearly a century earlier in 1843. In the relationship between
the two stories, we witness not only the symbolic weight given to the production of the body as the essential site of difference but also the translation
of castration from the metaphorics of the feminine to its literalization in
the dismemberment of black men.

   In each story, the figure of the birthmark establishes a system of corporeal inscription that links the body to cultural hierarchies of power: Hawthorne's birthmark being the "crimson stain upon the snow" (369) of the
beautiful Georgiana, while Ellison's is the mark below the navel of a young
black man, Willie. Significantly, both marks evoke castration. Georgiana's
"bloody hand" (370) functions as symbol of her feminine lack; Willie's

mark, through its disappearance into the "bloody mound of torn flesh and hair" (16) evinces his literal castration. While the antebellum story depicts the white female body as coterminous with sexual difference, Ellison's piece rearticulates the symbolics of gender and castration at the site of the black male body. Such a rearticulation is made possible by the shifting relations of race and sexual difference in the late nineteenth century, where Emancipation's theoretical effect — the black male's social sameness — is symbolically mediated by a disciplinary practice that seeks to literalize his affinity to the feminine. The intertextual connections between these two figurations of the birthmark offer an initial locus for tracing the highly sexual and gendered dimensions of difference that inhabit the anatomy of lynching.[5]

In Hawthorne's parable of sexual difference,[6] Aylmer, a man deeply committed to science, marries a beautiful woman, Georgiana, only to find that a small birthmark on her left cheek drives him mad. This "visible mark of earthly imperfection" (369), as he calls it, symbolizes in his mind her "liability to sin, sorrow, decay, and death" (370), those traditional attributes of the feminine that align her with materiality, the body, and the culturally abject. Through her articulation as quintessential difference, Aylmer's own psychological and scientific quest for transcendence begins. As the "frightful object" (371) that is cause of his "horror and disgust" (372), the birthmark carries the symbolic task of defining castration, not simply Georgiana's own, but the specter of Aylmer's as well. In what we might now call a paradigmatic scene of gender instruction, Aylmer's obsession with Georgiana's difference enables him the fantasy of his own universality and inherent completion and, in this, he escapes at least briefly the possibility of his own descent into material and mortal being. Georgiana's difference serves, in short, as Teresa de Lauretis might put it, as the very ground of Aylmer's representation, as "the looking-glass held up to man" (*Alice Doesn't* 15).

But while Georgiana's imperfect image grants Aylmer the fantasy of his own unbounded power and sets him in struggle with "our great creative Mother" (374), she remains the objectified spectacle of his desire, forever tied, in Laura Mulvey's terms, "to her place as bearer of meaning, not maker of meaning" ("Visual Pleasure" 58). In her function as the pivotal figure in Aylmer's subjective construction, Georgiana's ontological discreteness is wholly sacrificed, her alienation and negation so pervasive that we can hardly be surprised to know that "[n]ot even Aylmer . . . hated [the birthmark] so much as she" (379). In this, Georgiana's complicity with her own destruction is complete, for she has no means of constructing herself outside the place he has assigned for her. In the final stage of the story, when the enigma represented by woman and linked to the secrets of the natural world seems overcome, when "the last crimson tint of the birth-mark — that sole token of human imperfection — faded from her cheek" (386), Georgiana exhales her parting breath, leaving Aylmer with a dead but now perfect woman.

In the project of restoring woman to perfection, Hawthorne's story serves as a paradigm for the relations of sexual difference that underlie a variety of nineteenth-century discourses in which the recourse to the body and its ascribed inferiorities takes center stage. In the context of increasing cultural anxieties about "women's place" in the emergent public sphere and within the developing disciplinary mechanisms of modern medicine and science, the reduction of woman to her anatomy provides the difference against which masculine *disembodiment* can be achieved: the rationality of the mind surpasses, even as it appropriates, the physical limitations of the body. As my previous chapter has demonstrated, contestations over the disembodied privileges of the public sphere are not limited to gender, as feminist and abolitionist struggles throughout the nineteenth century simultaneously threaten a pervasive redistribution of bodies in social space, while industrialization increasingly pressures the dissolving agrarian-based slave system. From this perspective, the disembodied abstraction of masculine priority is as raced and classed as it is gendered, and the ensconcement of the feminine in the domestic serves as well to shape a bourgeois ideal from which the majority of women of all races are displaced. In Hawthorne's story, these race and class differences are inscribed in the contrast between Aylmer and his dark and dirty aide, Aminadab, on one hand, and in the figure of the birthmark as an imperfection embedded in the flesh of the beautifully fair Georgiana on the other. Sealed in the assumptions of domestic ideals and white feminine beauty, Georgiana's desire to undo the difference and disgust of her birthmark mark her as both affiliated with and differentiated from the white masculine and its achievement, through her, of disembodied abstraction. In the final turn of the story, in the moment of her perfection-in-death, even Aylmer must confront both the impossibility of retrieving the feminine from castration and the myth of his subjective construction: that the specter of his own castration can be averted through hers.

To the extent that the female body functions in Hawthorne's story to defer masculine castration by becoming its embodiment, it shares more than a coincidental affinity to the castrated body of the black male in Ellison's text written nearly a century later. For Ellison's literalization of castration pursues the logic of sexual difference from Hawthorne's foregrounded realm of masculine and feminine to that of racial difference and its inscription of corporeal and social division. In the process, the relationship between the body (as the designated site of certain specifically visible differences) and abstracted disembodiment (as social and subjective entitlement) can once again be seen. Most important perhaps, by depicting the black male within a symbolic system contingent on the discourse of sexual difference, Ellison's "The Birthmark" articulates the way lynching and castration stages the black male's relationship to masculine power itself.

Published the same year as Richard Wright's *Native Son*, Ellison's brief and little-known story opens at the scene of an accident, as Matt and Clara prepare to identify a body that has been purportedly hit by a car. But their brother, Willie, has been beaten and lynched, his face so thoroughly disfigured they must seek his birthmark, located beneath the navel, for positive recognition. In searching for the mark, Matt discovers castration instead: "where it should have been was only a bloody mound of torn flesh and hair" (17). This discovery establishes the interplay between birthmark and penis that activates the narrative's symbolic structure, allowing us to read castration as the remedy for the symbolic birthmark, the penis, that "flaws" black men. Such a remedy becomes necessary in the social transformation from enslavement to freedom, where the measure of the African-American's claim to citizenship is precisely his status as man — a status evinced by the penis, but ultimately rewarded in the symbolic exchange between penis and phallus. In castration, the correspondence between penis and phallus — between the masculine body and its potential for a dis-corporated power — is denied, and the symbolic realm of the phallus reveals its construction within the materialist determinations of white racial supremacy. This is not to say that the penis and the phallus are equivalent to one another, but to assert the opposite, that in the post–Civil War years, the contradictions between patriarchy and white supremacy are so deeply intensified that the irreducibility of phallus to penis must be repeatedly staged.

In Ellison's "The Birthmark," the relations of corporeal differentiation among male bodies functions through the familiar framework in which the feminine is cast as the visible difference against which masculine disembodiment is achieved. In the scene of racial hierarchies among men, however, the black male body takes on the "castrated" determinations of the feminine, becoming the site of both sex and sexual difference. For instance, when Matt searches for the birthmark and finds castration instead, it is significantly the symbolic structure of sexual difference that serves to identify Willie, his "being" reduced now to sex. Such a reduction enhances the subjective boundaries of white masculinity which, in its status within the story as the law, evinces the conflation of white male disembodiment and socio-symbolic power directly. The black male's signification as sexual and corporeal, however, averts the potential exchange of penis for phallus and, in this negation, he is placed within (consigned to and disciplined as) the feminine. As in Faulkner's *Light in August,* castration literalizes the association of "womanshenegro" that binds together the racial, sexual, and gendered (147).

While the affinity between the castrating marks in Hawthorne's and Ellison's stories demonstrates the dynamic of sexual difference at work in each, I am not positing these affinities as a full account of the political and ideological investments that underlie lynching and castration. Indeed, by ascribing the black male fully to the feminine, one runs the risk of reiterating the lynch scenario's cultural effect without further illuminating the historical and ideological mappings of race and sexual difference through which this effect has been achieved. For while U.S. culture has rather routinely posited the black male in relation to the feminine (as in the emasculated icons of nineteenth-century minstrelsy and their twentieth-century comic counterparts), race and sexual difference are not the same. If the phallic lack characteristic of the feminine must be physically and psychologically inscribed in order to deny the black male the primary sign of power in patriarchal culture, then his threat to white masculine power arises not simply from a perceived racial difference, but from the potential for masculine sameness. In the context of white supremacy, we must understand the threat of masculine sameness as so terrifying that only the reassertion of a gendered difference can provide the necessary disavowal. It is this that lynching and castration offer in their ritualized deployment, functioning as both a refusal and a negation of the possibility of extending the privileges of patriarchy to the black man.

In Ellison's "The Birthmark," this refusal is graphically depicted in the story's final image of the body of the castrated black man lying, bloody and brutalized, "between the white men's legs" (17). For here the black male body is figured in its relation to the power and privilege of white masculinity, becoming in its dismemberment the bearer of the white phallus's meaning. Through the gendered positionalities of castration and their relation to the patriarchal symbolic, then, the conflict presented by the African-American's masculine sameness is violently arbitrated in favor of the continued primacy of white masculine supremacy. To read the symbolic transposition of the birthmark from the stain of white femininity in Hawthorne's tale to the threat of the black phallus in Ellison's is to excavate not simply the powerful disciplinary function of race and sexual difference but their historically imbricated production.

Birth of a Nation

The political effect of the lynch scenario presented by Ralph Ellison in his brief but evocative story relies on the reader's awareness of the broader cultural context of "race relations" in the late nineteenth and early twentieth centuries, a context in which the system of economic, social, and political organization was profoundly altered by the African-American's emergence from slavery to (potential) citizenry. As a response to the ideological incommensurability between white supremacy and black enfranchisement, lynching marks the excess of discourses of race and rights, serving as a chief mechanism for defining and reinforcing white supremacist power in the post-war years. After all, the emancipation of five million slaves was neither a widespread cultural recognition of black humanity nor the proud achievement of the democratic ethos. As the late nineteenth century's turn toward the Ku Klux Klan and mob violence makes clear, the transformation from slavery to "freedom" was characterized by a rearticulation of cultural hierarchies in which terrorism provided the means for defining and securing the continuity of white supremacy.[7] The rise of black lynchings in the years following the war is indicative of a broader U.S. attitude toward African-American entrance into the political order: greeted by a few as the manifestation of a liberal ideal, "freedom," even for those literally enfranchised, was far from the reigning social reality.[8]

For the *New Masses* reader in 1940, the narrative of dismemberment and murder, overseen by the figure of the law, marked the repetitiousness of white supremacist discipline that greeted the "free" black subject in the 1860s, and it continued to reiterate his or her secondary social position throughout the twentieth century, including the present day.[9] Both mainstream and alternative newspapers regularly ran stories documenting the scenes of violence, often offering graphic detail of the practices of torture through which the entire African-American population could be defined and policed as innately, if no longer legally, inferior.[10] Such accounts extended the function of lynching as a mode of surveillance by reiterating its performative qualities, carving up the black body in the specular refiguration of slavery's initial, dismembering scene. For Trudier Harris, who has studied the legacy of lynching for African-American writers of the nineteenth and twentieth centuries, the imposition of a violent, bodily destruction worked "to keep Blacks contained politically and socially during the years of Reconstruction . . . convey[ing] to [them] that there was always someone watching over their shoulders ready to punish them for the slightest offense or the least deviation from acceptable lines of action" (*Exorcising Blackness* 19). What constituted "acceptable lines of action" for the newly emancipated slave depended, of course, on whose perspective was being articulated. In the conflict between a South deeply shocked by its lost hegemony and the slaves' euphoric desire to grasp for themselves the rights and privileges of citizenry, the full panorama of racist violence emerges as the defining conditions of "America" (as ideological trope and national body) itself.

For this reason, we might understand the end of slavery as marking in fuller and more complex ways the birth of the nation, where one of the questions that divided the delegates at the Continental Congress in 1776 was finally settled in favor of a rhetorical and legal, though not altogether economic or political equality.[11] As the rise of lynching in the post-war years indicates, this birth brings into crisis the definitional boundaries of "nation" that were implicit in the early constitutional documents: here, issues of generation, inheritance, and property rights are theoretically wrenched from their equation with the white masculine and made available, at least in the abstract, to a new body of citizens. The effect of this transformation is the dissolution of a particular kind of patriarchal order, for while the slave system ensured a propertied relation between laborer and master, and discursively and legally bound the African(-American) to the white father through the surname, emancipation represents the literal and symbolic loss of the security of the white patronym and an attendant displacement of the primacy of the white male. The many documented reports of slaves changing their names in the first moments of their freedom and the thematic value of naming itself in the African-American cultural tradition are indicative of the significance of the material and metaphorical eclipse of the white father's patronymic embrace.[12]

For the nonpropertied white male, the Civil War and Reconstruction represent important transformations in the historical articulation of a white underclass consciousness, offering on one hand the recognition of specific class-bound political interests, while often positing free African-Americans as competitors to the economic survival of the white working class. Andrew Johnson, Lincoln's successor to the White House, was a particularly prominent national spokesman for the racially inflected interests of nonproper-

tied whites. As Eric Foner discusses in his important reconsideration of the
Reconstruction era, Johnson, having grown up in poverty himself, identified with the Southern yeomanry. "He seems to have assumed," writes
Foner, "that the Confederacy's defeat had shattered the power of the "slave-
ocracy" and made possible the political ascendancy of loyal white yeomen.
The freedmen had no role to play in his vision of a reconstructed South"
(*Reconstruction* 181). Like other poor whites, Johnson saw slaves as complicit with their masters in maintaining economic and political power over
non-slaveholding whites. In this scenario, Foner writes, "[t]he most likely
result of black enfranchisement would therefore be an alliance of blacks
and planters, restoring the Slave Power's hegemony and effectively exclud-
ing the yeomanry from political power" (ibid.). Johnson's inability to read
the class interests of poor whites as aligned with the emergent black citizen — as in fact a multiracial underclass exploited by a feudalistic agrarian or
developing free market system — demonstrates how a class-conscious social
vision can work in complicity with white supremacy. Such a contradiction
contributed to the political fragmentation of the post-war years, producing
violent reprisals toward the emancipated slave from both the white yeoman
and the planter class.

In these reprisals for offenses more often imagined than real, lynching
was a primary disciplinary tool that took on over time an ideological narrative, as I have indicated, that both propelled the white crowd to action and
defined the methods of torture subsequently imposed: that of the mythically endowed rapist, the flower of civilization (the white woman) he intended to violently pluck, and the heroic interceptor (the white male) who
would restore order by thwarting the black phallic insurgence. But in the
early decades of the nineteenth century, lynching significantly did not function within this constellation of racial and sexual encodings. Instead, as
Trudier Harris discusses, it was a component of the system of frontier justice, operating in lieu of a legally sanctioned trial, and consisting of a variety
of punishments — most often whippings — without the final denouement of
death.[13] In fact, before 1840, writes James E. Cutler in his study of the history
of lynching in the United States, "the verb lynch was occasionally used to
include capital punishment, but. . . . '[t]o lynch' had not then undergone a
change in meaning and acquired the sense of 'to put to death.' . . . It was not
until a time subsequent to the Civil War that the verb lynch came to carry
the idea of putting to death" (*Lynch-Law* 116). And it was not until that time
as well that lynching became associated almost exclusively with acts of retri-
bution against the legally free population of African-American subjects.[14]

While the turn toward lynching as a racially coded practice owed its existence, as I have suggested, to the transformations attending Emancipation, its relationship to citizenry as a broader economy of the body in U.S. culture is significant as well. As I have discussed, the white male citizen of Enlightenment thought drew his particular suit of rights and privileges from the rhetorical disembodiment of the citizen as a social category. Within this category, in Lauren Berlant's words, "the generic 'person'" ("National Brands/National Body" 112) provided the abstraction necessary for replacing the historically located body with a national identity. As she explains:

> The American subject is privileged to suppress the fact of his historical situation in the abstract "person": but then, in return, the nation provides a kind of prophylaxis for the person, as it promises to protect his privileges and his local body in return for loyalty to the state. . . . [T]he implicit whiteness and maleness of the original American citizen is thus itself protected by national identity. . . . (113)

In other words, it was the repression of the specific racial and gender markers of privileged identity—of whiteness and maleness—that characterized the figure "American citizen" and inaugurated its rhetorical definition as an inclusive social body. In this constitution of the citizen as a disembodied entity, bound not to physical delineations but to national ones, the white male was (and continues to be) "freed" from the corporeality that might otherwise impede his insertion into the larger body of national identity.

For the African-American male subject, on the other hand, it was precisely the imposition of an extreme corporeality that defined his distance from the privileged ranks of citizenry. With the advent of Emancipation and its attendant loss of the slave system's marking of the African-American body as property, lynching emerged to reclaim and reassert the centrality of black male corporeality, deterring the now theoretically possible move toward citizenry and disembodied abstraction. Through the lynching scenario, "blackness" was cast as a subversive (and most often sexual) threat, an incontrovertible chaos whose challenge to the economic and social coherency of the nation could be psychologically, if not wholly politically, averted by corporeal abjection and death. That lynching became during Reconstruction and its aftermath an increasingly routine response to black male as well as black female attempts at education, self- and communal government, suffrage, and other indicators of cultural inclusion and equality attests to its powerful disciplinary function. As the most extreme deterritorialization of the body and its subjective boundaries, lynching guaranteed the white mob's privilege of physical and psychic penetration, granted it a definitional authority over social space, and encoded the vigilant and violent system of surveillance that underwrote late-nineteenth- and early-twentieth-century negotiations over race and cultural power.

The Offense of Sex

But why the charge of rape as the consolidating moment of lynching's justification? Why this sexualization of blackness as the precondition not just for mob action, but for lynching's broad cultural acceptance and appeal? The answer to this, like any historical accounting, is less apparent than the many contexts in which the evidence of lynching's sexualization appears. If we begin where I have suggested, with the narrative of rape (and its culmination in lynching) translating the crisis of Emancipation from economic to sexual and gendered terms, we encounter a very powerful means through which black men and the entire black community could be psychologically and physically contained. Most important, we witness the way the rape narrative simultaneously recognized and subverted the African-American male's theoretical equality in the sexual, political, and economic spheres. As those familiar with the late nineteenth century well know, the rape mythos, as an overwhelmingly southern response to enfranchisement, challenged the kind of social reform orchestrated by the Freedman's Bureau. The patriarchal logic of the dominant culture became the defining mechanism for organizing the newly freed slave: not only did the bureau appoint the husband as head of the household, assigning to him sole power to enter into contractual labor agreements for the entire family, but also it fought for the allotment of land for every freed "male," while granting only unmarried women access to this domain (Foner, *Reconstruction* 87).

In these pronouncements — as in the routine gender segregation attending voting, jury duty, the holding of political and Republican party office — the official program of Reconstruction understood the freedom of black men to entail a "natural" judicial and social superiority over African-American women. The nineteenth century's determination of public and private along strict gender lines thus provided a definitional structure through which social space and familial roles were shaped for a population no longer denied the right of maintaining family bonds.[15] Nevertheless, while the patriarchalization of the black family served to institutionalize it within the gender codes prevalent in white bourgeois ideology, thereby securing the black family to the formal dimensions of white social behavior, many whites were decidedly threatened by the definitional sameness accorded former slaves. The loss of one patriarchal organization of social life — that of slavery — and its replacement by the seeming egalitarianism of a masculine-dominated black family, then, had the effect of broadening the competitive dimensions of interracial masculine relations, especially as the black male's new property governance over black women threatened to extend its range of power to women of the dominant group as well.

It was in this climate that the mythology of the black man as rapist emerged, working the fault line of the slave's newly institutionalized masculinization by framing this masculinity as the bestial excess of an overly phallic primitivity. In the contours of Western racial discourse, of course, the primitive sexual appetite associated with blackness was not a new articulation at the end of the nineteenth century, but its crafting in the highly stylized and overdetermined narrative structure of the rape mythos — along with the sheer frequency of its deployment — marks a particular historical configuration of the sexual and gendered in their U.S. relation to issues of race and nation. Thus, while the slavery period often envisioned the Uncle Tom figure as the signification of the "positive good" of a system that protected and cared for its black "children," once emancipated, these children became virile men who wanted for themselves the ultimate symbol of white civilization: the white woman.[16] The transformation of the image of the black man from simple, docile Uncle Tom to violent sex offender characterizes the oppositional logic underwriting the representational structure of black male images in nineteenth- and twentieth-century U.S. culture, a logic in which the discourse of sexual difference — from feminized docility to hypermasculinized phallicity — comes to play a primary significatory role.

South Carolina Senator Ben Tillman demonstrates this oppositional logic in his 1907 speech before Congress, when he argues for the abandonment of due process for blacks accused of sex crimes against white women:

> [T]he white women of the South are in a state of seige. . . . Some lurking demon who has watched for the opportunity seizes her; she is choked or beaten into insensibility and ravished, her body prostituted, her purity destroyed, her chastity taken from her. . . . Shall men . . . demand for [the demon] the right to have a fair trial and be punished in the regular course of justice? So far as I am concerned he has put himself outside the pale of the law, human and divine. . . . Civilization peels off us . . . and we revert to the . . . impulses . . . to "kill! kill! kill!" ("The Black Peril" 181–182)

In proposing mob retaliation against the defilers of white womanhood, Tillman assures his listeners that he does not hate blacks by recalling "the negroes of the old slave days . . . the negroes who knew they were inferior and who never presumed to assert equality" (183). These blacks, with minds like "those of children," posed no sexual threat, as was witnessed, according to Tillman, during the Civil War when "there is not of record a solitary instance of one white woman having been wronged" by the 800,000 black men left on plantation land (181, 184). Only with Emancipation does rape follow; "the negro becomes a fiend in human form" (185).

In figuring the rape mythos in the context of economic and political transformation, Tillman reveals not only the force of the threat of black masculinization that accompanied emancipation but also the necessary negation of the threat that the turn to the rape charge fulfilled. In positing the bestial excess of black masculinity, however, Tillman establishes a racialized opposition between civilization and primitivity that significantly breaks down, in the face of the black brute, as the white man loses his civilized veneer. Like skin, civilization "peels off us" and only an aggressive impulse to kill remains. In the ethos of nineteenth-century racialism, the seeming reduction of the white man to such barbarity, to the violation of his own civilizing system of law, is rationalized by the figuration of the white woman, that pivotal player in the rape mythology. Through her emblem as the keeper of the purity of the race, white men cast themselves as protectors of civilization, reaffirming their role as social and familial "heads" and their paternal property rights as well. The white man thus maintained a position of superiority, as Trudier Harris observes, "not only in assigning a place to his women, but especially in keeping black people, particularly black men, in the place he had assigned for them" (*Exorcising Blackness* 20). In this way, the mythology of the black male rapist simultaneously engineered race and gender hierarchies, masking the white male's own historical participation in "miscegenating" sexual activities, while ensuring his disciplinary control over potential sexual—and one might add, political—liaisons between black men and white women. Within the context of nineteenth-century abolitionist and feminist movements, the necessity for disrupting such potential bonds was important indeed.

Still, the central figuration of the white woman's sexuality in the rape mythos must be understood as a displacement of the deeper and more culturally complex relation between black and white men. As Harris writes, "[t]he issue, then, really boils down to one between white men and black men and the mythic conception the former have of the latter" (*Exorcising Blackness* 20). Such a mythic conception works through the sexualization of blackness, in which as Frantz Fanon says, "the Negro is fixated at the genital" (*Black Skin, White Masks* 165). Caught there, within the framework of a subjectively reductive sexualization, the phallicized black male displays the anxieties and contradictions underlying the "logic" and disciplinary practices of white masculine supremacy: in reducing the black male to the body and further to the penis itself, white masculinity betrays a simultaneous desire for and disavowal of the black male's phallic inscription. To put this another way, the white male desires the image he must create in order to castrate, and it is precisely through the mythology of the black male as mythically endowed rapist that he has effectively done this.

In the process, the creation of a narrative of black male sexual excess simultaneously exposes and redirects the fear of castration from the white masculine to the black male body, and it is in the lynch scene that this transfer moves from the realm of the psychosexual to the material. Harris's descriptive account of the sexual undercurrent of lynching and castration is telling in this regard:

> For white males . . . there is a symbolic transfer of sexual power at the point of the executions. The black man is stripped of his prowess, but the very act of stripping brings symbolic power to the white man. His actions suggest that, subconsciously, he craves the very thing he is forced to destroy. Yet he destroys it as an indication of the political (sexual) power he has. . . . (*Exorcising Blackness* 22)

In this destruction of the phallic black beast, the white masculine reclaims the hypermasculinity that his own mythology of black sexual excess has denied him, finding in sexual violence the sexual pleasure necessary to uphold both his tenuous masculine and white racial identities.

Because lynching negates the black male's most visible claim to masculine power, Harris describes this ritual punishment as a "communal rape" (*Exorcising Blackness* 23), a description that inscribes within the lynching and castration scene the relations of power and disempowerment at work in the disciplinary practice most associated with sexual difference: male sexual violence toward women. Through the rape metaphor, the emasculation of the black male undertaken in lynching and castration emerges as the imposition of the binary figuration of gender, with the white masculine retaining hegemony over the entire field of masculine entitlements, while the black male is confined to the corporeal excess of a racial feminization. But, as I have suggested throughout my discussion and as my reading of *Native Son* will demonstrate in particular, it is important to maintain the distinction between the imposition of feminization onto male bodies and the historical framework of the feminine as part and parcel of being born female. Such a distinction enables us to understand the force of the discourse of sexual difference as it constructs and contains hierarchical relations among men without negating the specific materiality of gender oppression that accompanies women's variously raced positions in U.S. culture. In other words, the imposition of feminization onto male and female bodies is not, politically, theoretically, or historically, the same.

While castration may function as a means for enacting a gendered difference at the site of the black male body, it is also the case that such a practice of dismemberment enabled a perverse level of physical intimacy between the white male aggressor and his captive ex-slave, pointing to an underlying obsession not simply with gender sameness, but with a broader range of sexuality as well. Harris's report that "[i]n some historical accounts, the lynchers were reputed to have divided pieces of the black man's genitals among themselves" allows us to envision the castration scene as more than the perverse sexual encounter offered by the rape metaphor (*Exorcising Blackness* 22). In the image of white men embracing — with hate, fear, and a chilling form of empowered delight — the same penis they were so overdeterminedly driven to destroy, one encounters a sadistic enactment of the homoerotic at the very moment of its most extreme disavowal.

As Eve Kosofsky Sedgwick has discussed in *Between Men*, the male bonding relations that characterize patriarchal structures in nineteenth- and twentieth-century Anglo-American cultures depend on the panic image of the homosexual, whose same-sex desire provides the disciplinary terms for normalizing heterosexuality in its compulsory formation. From this perspective, we might understand the lynching scenario and its obsession with the sexual dismemberment of black men to mark the limit of the homosexual/heterosexual binary — that point at which the oppositional relation reveals its inherent and mutual dependence — and the heterosexuality of the black male "rapist" is transformed into a violently homoerotic exchange. "The homosociality of this world," Sedgwick writes in a discussion of the late Renaissance that is applicable to the history of Anglo and African men in U.S. culture, "is not that of brotherhood, but of extreme, compulsory, and intensely volatile mastery and subordination" (66).

In such a volatile and sexually charged realm, the mythology of the black male as rapist functioned to script the deeply disturbing transformations in U.S. racial relations in the late nineteenth century within the double registers of sexuality and gender, thereby granting to the white mob that captured and controlled the black body the psychological power of arbitrating life and death. In choosing death and accompanying it with the most extreme practices of corporeal abuse, whiteness enhanced its own significatory lack, filling the absence of meaning that defined it with the fully corporeal presence of a hated, feared, and now conquered blackness. The extremity of punishment in the lynching and castration scenario thus provided the necessary illusion of returning to the lost moment of slavery's totalized mastery—a moment never actually "full," though yearned for, indeed frantically sought after, through the disciplinarity of random mob violence.

White Beauty, Black Beast

The transformation of the economic into the sexual and its implications for reading gender and race emerge most fully in Richard Wright's *Native Son* (1940), our literature's most compelling story of the black man caught in the mythology of the rapist. Revolving around the fated life of Bigger, his employment by a liberal white family, his accidental murder of their daughter, Mary, and his subsequent flight and trial, the novel demonstrates what Wright considers the definitive pattern of U.S. race relations. As he writes in "How 'Bigger' Was Born," "[a]ny Negro . . . knows that times without number he has heard of some Negro boy being picked up . . . and carted off to jail and charged with 'rape.' This thing happens so often that to my mind it had become a representative symbol of the Negro's uncertain position in America" (xxviii). In *Native Son,* such uncertainty is explicitly linked to masculinity and to the competitive dimensions of black and white masculine relations. In the opening scene, for instance, Bigger's mother characterizes her son's failure as emasculinity: "[w]e wouldn't have to live in this garbage dump if you had any manhood in you" (12).

Through the metaphorics of emasculation, Wright simultaneously reiterates the disciplinary function of the rape mythos, while couching that function as symptomatic of African-American alienation in U.S. culture more broadly. As Bigger tells his friends: "[e]very time I think about it I feel like somebody's poking a red-hot iron down my throat. . . . We live here and they live there. . . . They got things we ain't. They do things and we can't" (23). In figuring segregation, racism, and poverty as the "red-hot iron down my throat," Wright casts Bigger's oppression in highly sexual and phallic terms, marking the force and effect of white supremacy as a negation of masculinity: "[y]ou ain't a man no more," Bigger finally says, "[White folks] after you so hot and hard. . . . They kill you before you die"

(326, 327). Being a "man" is thus equated with freedom and power, and the white world, so "hot and hard" against one, acts as the ultimate castrator of black claims to traditional manhood.

With the charge of rape, this pursuit — "the white folks after you so hot and hard" — becomes overtly sexualized, as the elaborate scene of Bigger's chase and capture demonstrates. Here, with Bigger trapped on a roof by white men wielding a fire hose, Wright depicts the white men's success as a horrific sexual encounter: "[t]he rushing stream jerked this way and that. . . . Then the water hit him. . . . He gasped, his mouth open. . . . The water left him; he lay gasping, spent. . . . The icy water clutched again at his body like a giant hand; the chill of it squeezed him like the circling coils of a monstrous boa constrictor" (251). In the contrast between the white men's exaggerated phallic power and Bigger's gasping submission, Wright reveals the sexualization of masculine relations underlying the rape mythos: in capturing Bigger, the white men — nearly eight thousand searching the city — have extended their own phallic reach beyond the confines of their bodies, laying claim to their property and paternity rights not merely by demonstrating ownership of white women but by forcing the black male to also submit to their masculine sexual supremacy. As the prosecutor, Buckley, says in his plea for the imposition of the death penalty: "[e]very decent white man in America ought to swoon with joy for the opportunity to crush with his heel the woolly head of this black lizard" (373).

Significantly, Wright offers Bigger's resistance to this disciplinary submission as an acceptance of Mary's death as a conscious act: "[t]hough he had killed by accident, not once did he feel the need to tell himself that it had been an accident. He was black and he had been alone in a room where a white girl had been killed; therefore he had killed her" (101). In accepting responsibility for Mary's death, Bigger sees himself not simply as refuting white masculine authority, but as gaining an advantage that had eluded him before: "[t]he knowledge that he had killed a white girl they loved and regarded as their symbol of beauty made him feel the equal of them, like a man who had been somehow cheated, but had now evened the score" (155). Through his destruction of the objectified symbol of white male rule, Bigger no longer needs the knife and gun, traditional symbols of masculinity, that had initially accompanied him to the Dalton home: "[w]hat his knife and gun had once meant to him, his knowledge of having secretly murdered Mary now meant" (141). For the first time he feels "a confidence, a fulness, a freedom; his whole life was caught up in a supreme and meaningful act" (111).

Bigger's acceptance of Mary's murder and his consequent sense of freedom are particularly meaningful when viewed in terms of an earlier and seemingly insignificant event in the novel. Before setting out for the Dalton home on the day of Mary's accidental death, Bigger gathers with friends at Doc's poolroom to discuss plans for robbing Blum's Delicatessen. While the men had pulled other "jobs," this was to be their first robbery of a white man and therefore "a violation of ultimate taboo . . . a symbolic challenge of the white world's rule over them, a challenge which they yearned to make, but were afraid to" (18). The language here of "violation," "taboo," and "symbolic challenge" scripts the robbing of Blum in the same terms as the mythic encounter between a black man and a white woman, pointing once again toward that more fundamental conflict that lies at the heart of the mythology of the black male rapist: the struggle over social, political, and sexual power between black and white men. In this sense, the role of the white woman as central to the rape mythos must be understood in the context of the negotiation of power among men, for her value lies in both her symbolic and reproductively literal role as bearer of the white phallus's meaning.

Thus it is in this context that we can understand the absence of the African-American woman from the cultural scripting of the rape mythos, for her reproductive value, historically appropriated as part of the master's property rights, reconfigured in the post-Emancipation era into no white phallic value at all. Instead, the African-American woman was condemned to a position of negativity as the symbolic excess of white womanhood. At the same time, of course, her negation and devaluation made possible the narrative casting of white women as both prize and pawn. Wright draws this quite clearly in *Native Son*, when the raped and murdered body of Bessie Mears, Bigger's girlfriend, is wheeled into the courtroom as graphic display of Bigger's violent criminality toward white womanhood. As he puts it, "[t]hough he had killed a black girl and a white girl, he knew that it would be for the death of the white girl that he would be punished. The black girl was merely 'evidence'" (306–307). As evidence, Bessie's value emerges to confirm Bigger's rape mentality, while the ironic, indeed tragic, displacement of violence against the black woman marks the dual—and dueling— hierarchies of race and gender through which the rape mythos plays.

While Bigger recognizes the asymmetrical value placed on black and white women, he casts Bessie's murder within the same contextual framework as that governing Mary's, finding both acts "the most meaningful things that had ever happened to him. He was living, truly and deeply . . . never had his will been so free" (225). In thus tying Bessie to the symbolic act of the white woman's murder—and in marking his violation of her as an equally cathartic trespass—Bigger redefines rape itself: "rape was not what one did to women. Rape was what one felt when one's back was against a wall and one had to strike out, whether one wanted to or not. . . . [I]t was rape when he cried out in hate deep in his heart as he felt the strain of living day by day" (214). By characterizing the psychological effects of racism as rape, Bigger inverts the cultural rhetoric of the mythology of the black male as rapist, drawing an equation between castration (both symbolic and literal) and the form of violence most overtly gendered in U.S. culture.[17] In the process, however, Wright casts the black male as rape's sole social and sexual victim, thereby establishing for Bigger an unqualified difference from the feminine that ultimately evacuates his affinity with black women altogether.[18] By expelling the feminine in this way, Wright features Bigger as the universalized emblem of black oppression, a universalization shaped by and predicated on the discourse of sexual difference as a negotiation of racial differences among men.

Although Wright's method of foregrounding the masculine stakes at work in the rapist mythos is depicted at the expense of both black women and the feminine more generally, his novel refuses the more traditional structure of male bonding that Sedgwick has defined, in which "the spectacle of the ruin of a woman . . . is just the right lubricant for an adjustment of differentials of power [among men]" (*Between Men* 76). This we witness in the final moments of the novel when Bigger makes an attempt, through his lawyer Boris Max, to connect with Jan, the white boyfriend of Mary Dalton. "Tell . . . Tell Mister . . . Tell Jan hello" (392), Bigger says, shifting from the servile "Mister" to the more familiar. But in his hesitation and in the novel's stark depiction of the chasms that separate white men and black, this attempt to form male bonds is a dim contrast to the image of 1930s progressive politics that was offered earlier in the novel where "a strong blinding sun sen[t] hot rays down . . . in the midst of a vast crowd of men, white men and black men and all men . . . melt[ing] away the many differences" (335). In the failure of male bonds to serve their utopic function, *Native Son* marks the extremity of hatred and violence that ushers the black male into the patriarchal province of the masculine. While it does not critique that initiation without reiterating the logics of sexual difference on which the masculine establishes itself, the novel nonetheless demonstrates the stakes of race and gender that capture Bigger in the definitional nexus of rape, lynching, and castration that Wright so defiantly wants to explore.

Black Beast, White Bitch

Throughout the twentieth century, black male writers have repeatedly turned to the figuration of the black rapist as both a protest and warning, purposely revising the mythic encounter between black men and white women as part of a challenge to the history of mutilation I have discussed above. Where Wright would cast Bigger Thomas's subjective and social crisis as the crime of blackness that precedes and ensures the crime of rape, Ralph Ellison's 1952 meditation on absence and invisibility moves the focus from the black man's sexual criminality to the white woman's. This shift in the production of a counterdiscourse on the rape mythos demonstrates a crucial reconfiguration of the impact and meaning of the black rapist in the second half of the twentieth century and points to the kind of rhetorical trajectory that Black Power discourses in the 1960s would themselves take.

In *Invisible Man*, two scenes in particular explore the sexual tensions that underlie the anatomy of lynching, demonstrating through their contrast the rhetorical revisions of the rape mythos from which black discourses in the latter part of the twentieth century would proceed. In the prelude to the "Battle Royal" in chapter 1, the town's prominent white civic leaders offer to the gaze of a group of young black men "a magnificent blonde — stark naked" (18). The sight of the white woman drives "a wave of irrational guilt and fear" (19) through the invisible man, the historical weight of the taboo against his looking at a white woman serving as the ultimate entertainment for the white men. In this positioning of bodies, we witness the representational strategy encoded in the rape mythos: through the specularization of both the white woman and the black man, the white man is empowered to "look," his look constructing the circuit of desire in which the body of the white woman serves as the mechanism for hierarchizing the space of looking among men. More important perhaps, such a configuration of bodies enables the white male spectator to displace his own desire for the black male body into a heterosexual frame, allowing the white men, for instance, to gaze at a young black man's erection (20) without defining a homosexual erotic position. Desire, power, and dread between black and white men are thus circulated in an asymmetrical paradigm of looking orchestrated across the body of the naked white woman.

Articulating his relationship to this scene, the invisible man is initially poised between two possibilities: identifying with the white woman as similarly exploited by the white men or invoking gender differences to distance himself from her. When he first sees the white woman, the protagonist admits that his guilt and fear are mixed with a strong desire—"[h]ad the price of looking been blindness," he says, "I would have looked" (19). In looking he feels, on the one hand, a desire forged through the recognition of similar roles in the circuit of white masculine desire—"I wanted . . . [to] go to her and cover her from my eyes and the eyes of the others with my body"—and, on the other hand, a desire formed by hate, by the need "to spit upon her," on her yellow hair, on her "face heavily powdered and rouged" (ibid.). Detached, empty, a crass portrait of the white man's civilization—a "small American flag tattooed upon her belly"—the white woman elicits ambivalence: "I wanted . . . to caress her and destroy her, to love her and murder her, to hide from her, and yet to stroke where . . . her thighs formed a capital V" (ibid.). Even in the context of this ambivalence, his commentary culminates in a moment of recognition: "I saw the terror and disgust in her eyes, almost like my own terror and that which I saw in some of the other boys" (20).

For the invisible man, this recognition cannot be sustained, and by the later stages of the novel, his encounter with the white woman will transform "the terror and disgust in her eyes almost like my own" into an extreme form of disavowal. This transformation occurs during the narrative's focus on the Brotherhood, that Marxist collectivity that seems destined to miscomprehend the complexity and significance of white supremacy as it competes with, contradicts, and confirms a capitalist mode of production. Here, the invisible man decides to sleep with a white woman to garner information about the Brotherhood, but unlike the earlier encounter, the white male gaze is now positioned beyond the frame of the scene. Instead, the circuit of desire pivots on her arousal at the thought of rape: "[t]hreaten to kill me if I don't give in. You know, talk rough to me, beautiful" (507), she coos, confessing that "ever since I first heard about it, even when I was a very little girl, I've wanted it to happen to me" (508). Through the white woman's reiteration of the black man as phallic beast, the protagonist overcomes his earlier and momentary recognition of her position as pawn and object of white men. Now it becomes the white woman who "had me on the ropes. . . . [S]he thinks [I'm] an entertainer" (509), a metaphor that harkens back to the Battle Royal where "we stood with our backs against the ropes" (21), where the spectacle of black bodies is "part of the entertainment" (17). Now the white woman has assumed the position of mastery: "[l]ie back and let me look at you against that white sheet. You're beautiful . . . [l]ike warm ebony against pure snow. . . . I feel so free with you" (509).

In describing the source of her feelings of freedom—"I can trust you . . .

you're not like other men. We're kind of alike" (509) — the white woman speaks the possibility suggested by the invisible man's recognition in the earlier scene. But the context of this speaking necessitates its disavowal, for *Invisible Man* founds the black man's liberation not on a social similarity with white women (or any women for that matter) but on the assertion of masculine sameness. By contending that the black man differs from other men, the white woman, in the throes of her sexual perversion for rape and physical abuse, ensures the opposite rhetorical effect: affirming not differences among men but their mutual and masculine sameness. This sameness is made possible by the extremity of the white woman's sexual and sexualized differences — by her narrativization of and desire for rape. It is this reconstruction around difference and sameness that is pivotal in *Invisible Man*, necessitating, when the white woman intones, "Come on, beat me, daddy — you — you big black bruiser," that the black man responds by slapping her and writing with lipstick across her stomach: "Sybil, you were raped by Santa Claus Surprise" (511). The joke of rape, which emerges as the secret fantasy of the white woman and the actual source of her sexual desire, constructs her as wholly alien to the black man. Through this alienation, the earlier sense of a mutual terror and disgust is averted: the invisible man now directs his disgust to the white woman, thereby reasserting not simply his gender difference from her, but the hierarchical power of his masculine position as well.

But why privilege that early moment of recognition? Is there nothing politically challenging about the black man's representational inscription as distinct from — perhaps even opposed to — the white feminine? In thinking about these issues, my assumption is that the moment of recognition early in *Invisible Man* is a powerful demonstration of how the sexual/textual dynamic of interracial masculine relationships functions first to stage black male desire for the white woman and then to punish the black male for that desire as part of reasserting and codifying white masculine sexual and social supremacy. Such supremacy and the circuit of desire it narrates rely on the mutual commodification and corporeal inscription of black and female difference. But in the novel's later relocation of the tensions of masculine sameness and racial difference at the sole site of white female bodies, Ellison's Santa Claus scene simply inverts the Battle Royal's nexus of race and gender, as well as its critique of the dynamics of the rape mythos, thereby establishing the mutual exclusion of — and indeed contestation between — "blacks and women." Such exclusion has serious consequences for black women, whose sexual specificity is negated whenever racial equality is cast, as it was in *Native Son,* in opposition to gender. The focus on the white woman in the later scene, in other words, evacuates Ellison's critique of the white male anxiety of masculine sameness that underlies, as I have been arguing, both the rape mythos and the lynching and castration scene.

This focus and its effect come to be repeated in radical black thought of the 1960s, where the ritualization of black mutilation characteristic of lynching and castration proved a crucial material and representational site around which anti-segregationist struggle proceeded. For Black Power, in particular, the mythology of the black man as rapist and the repeated sexual negation that accompanied the rape charge was central, offering a context in which black nationalist demands were simultaneously articulated and re-fined. Eldridge Cleaver's *Soul on Ice,* for instance, emphasized the reclama-tion of black masculinity as the usurpation of white supremacy by crafting the rape of the white woman as the prototypical insurrectionary act (26). By defining black masculinity in the context of symbolic and corporeal phallicization, Cleaver along with others asserted the primacy of a black phallic power, threatening not only the "sanctity" of white womanhood, but more important, the closed circuit of masculine relations on which U.S. patriarchal structures depend. In this way, Black Power marshaled the fear-induced imagery of black men as violent and potent to assert to white culture a bold and resistant political production, one that appropriated the fear that underwrote the mythology of the black rapist in order to recast the passive resistance school of civil rights reform. Thus articulating a political agenda of nationalist power, Black Power asserted black masculinity as co-terminous with racial emancipation.

In the process, the image of black men was rescued from the emasculat-ing history of enslavement and mutilation—what Cleaver calls "four hun-dred years minus my Balls" (*Soul on Ice* 189)—and the specter of a *white* masculine feminization was raised instead. As I stated at the outset, the work of Imamu Baraka is especially illustrative in this regard. Inverting the representational economy that depicts the black man as either literally or metaphorically less than a man, Baraka aligns feminization with whiteness, defining white men as "effeminate and perverted" at one point and more directly as "fags" at another (*Home* 220, 216).[19] By choosing homosexuality to characterize white men, Baraka highlights what is for him their cultural and procreative nonproductivity, and in this, he locates the struggle be-tween black and white men primarily in the body. Physical strength, in other words, emerges as the black male's claim to both power and a natural masculinity, while heterosexuality and reproduction become the essential components of virility. The white man, devoid on all counts, is metaphorically impotent: "[l]ife and creation (of life) are equally terrifying to [the white man]. ([Imagine] [t]he stuffing of the genitals into the mouth . . . making a man destroy his powers to create, destroying his seed, and his generations)" (*Home* 232).

But while Baraka captures the sexual jealousy that in part underlies the psychological motives for the mutilation of black men, his reinscription of the biologizing logic of gender posits creation as a singularly masculine production: future generations are contained in male "seed." As such, sperm functions as the definitive marker of the black man's superiority, for he "can send out no other kind of seed. And that seed, anywhere [even in white wombs], makes black" (*Home* 233). Appropriating reproduction as a masculine enterprise, Baraka relies on the discourse of sexual difference to redefine, through inversion, racial hierarchies among men. By doing this, the black masculine emerges once again as symbolic stand-in for black humanity itself:

> [T]he white man has tried to keep the black *man* hidden. . . . These were heathens that were brought over in the slave ships, or savages, or animals . . . definitely not men, not human. And when the possibility arose that these animals really might be men, then the ballcutting ceremony was trotted out immediately. . . . So the white man has tried to cover black *people's humanity.* (emphasis added, *Home* 226)

This movement from "black man" to "black people's humanity" conceives of the "human" only in terms of the struggle of the masculine itself.[20]

It was this masculinization of the discourse of black power that concerned Michele Wallace in her once-controversial study, *Black Macho and the Myth of the Superwoman,* a feminist rereading of the consequences of such a gendering of the black struggle on not only black men but, more specifically, black women. Published in 1979, *Black Macho* analyzes the sexism at the heart of the Black Power movement where, in the now infamous phrasing of Stokely Carmichael, black women were told to lie prone for the revolution. Arguing that this macho originated in white culture, Wallace views the black man as having "lost [his] grip on a black perspective, [and] as he lost track of his original intentions, and adopted a white perspective . . . he began to think . . . he was not a man" (77). By refuting those cultural historians who have viewed the black man's role in slavery as a completely "unmanly" one—unmanly precisely because black men did not have traditional patriarchal rights over black women[21]—Wallace challenges what she sees as Black Power's implicit lament: "that the black woman, [the black man's] woman, was not *his* slave, that his right to expect her complete service and devotion was usurped[,] [that] [s]he *was,* after all, the white man's slave" (23).

In particular, Wallace is concerned with the ideological and political fracturing that arises when black disenfranchisement is cast in terms of a denied masculinity, as the capitulation of Black Power to patriarchal notions of masculinity consequently cast the black woman as matriarch, willing helpmate to the black man's cultural castration. As Wallace writes, black women

> had a hell of a history to live down. We had been rolling around in bed with the slave master while the black man was having his penis cut off; we had never been able to close our legs to a white man nor deny our breasts to a white child; we had been too eagerly loyal to our white male employer . . . cleaning his house with love and attention while our man was being lynched. . . . We had not allowed the black man to be a man in his own house. We had . . . questioned his masculinity . . . driven him to alcohol, to drugs, to crime . . . because our eyes had not reflected his manhood. (*Black Macho* 92)

In constructing the black woman as complicit in the larger project of black male oppression, Black Power failed to capture the complexities of race and gender and ironically reaffirmed, through inversion, the very ideologies of difference that had entrapped black men. To cast this in other terms: black nationalism's negotiation of its relationship to white masculine supremacy transferred the problem inherent in the disjunction between masculine sameness and racial difference to the site of gender.

In couching this writing of race across the body of sexual difference as, simply, the black man's adoption of white masculine ideals—as opposed to "his own black-centered definition of manhood [where] his sense of himself was not endangered" (*Black Macho* 79)—Wallace inscribes an essential, natural black masculinity that even she, in the preface to the 1990 revised edition, has come to disavow. For the antagonism between black men and black women underlying nationalist rhetoric in the twentieth century is more than the black man's "choice" between a white perspective and a black one, between a seemingly destructive masculinity and a constructive counterpart (81). As Wallace rearticulates, "[t]oday I understand the problem as one of representation" (xix). In the context of both Wallace's refiguration and the analytic contours of *this* study, we might begin to understand the historical confluences through which Black Power's representation of

the African-American male was wrought. In its seemingly willful negation of the black woman and in its reiteration of patriarchy's privileging of
"manhood [as] more valuable than anything else" (79), Black Power demonstrates its place within—and not, as it may have hoped, against—the
structure of hierarchies among men.

Kobena Mercer and Isaac Julien's meditation on black masculinity is
an instructive gloss on the complexities of race and gender that underlie
the cultural contexts in which contestations between black and white men
emerge:

> Our social definitions of what it is to be a "man," about what consti-
> tutes "manliness," are not "natural" but are historically constructed.
> . . . The dominant definitions of masculinity, accepted as the social
> norm, are neither the products of a false consciousness imposed by
> patriarchal ideology. Patriarchal systems of male power and privi-
> lege constantly have to negotiate the meaning of gender roles with a
> variety of economic, social and political factors. . . . So, its [sic] not as
> if we could strip away the negative stereotypes of black men, created
> by western patriarchy, and discover some "natural" black masculinity
> which is good, pure and wholesome. ("True Confessions" 6)

As a construct within the discourse of patriarchy, black masculinity cannot
be posited as outside the historical nexus of gender relations, as something
essential awaiting the removal of white supremacy and patriarchy. Its content is contingent, as we have seen, on a negotiation between the various
categories of difference that structure U.S. culture.

In this sense, Black Power's writing of the black male across the body
of gender is no cultural anachronism, but is a broader representational
strategy that has operated with increasing force since the early nineteenth
century. While Wallace is indeed correct to see this writing as a highly mi-
sogynistic formation, such an articulation of black liberation struggle must
also be read in its historical challenge to the exclusionary logic of white
masculine power: that is, in rewriting the rape mythology in the 1960s,
black radical thinkers assaulted white supremacy's investment in patriarchal discriminations, redrawing the white beauty–black beast scenario and
making claims for a black masculine power that America in the late 1970s
and 1980s would spend much time, in both popular and political culture, disavowing. From the political perspective of the 1990s, of course, the
either/or nature of race/gender struggles have more than reached their impasses, and it is in the context of critical thinking about these impasses,
about their mutual and binary exclusions, that this study is itself engaged.

Another Willie

The enduring power of the black male rapist mythos is perhaps best witnessed in the contemporary era in the specter of Willie Horton, the convicted black male rapist used in George Bush's 1988 presidential campaign to signify the potential danger of Democratic party control. Through the figure of Willie Horton, Bush challenged the toughness of his opponent, Michael Dukakis, whose penal reform program in Massachusetts was reportedly responsible for putting a rapist back on the streets. Bush's get-tough discourse, deployed here in the context of a test of masculine strength between white men, functioned to align racism with the broader and perhaps more nebulous fear of national decline—that fear so well orchestrated by David Duke and other political spokesmen for white supremacy.[22] Bush's need to quickly disaffiliate himself from race baiting in the 1992 presidential campaign in light of both Duke's tactics and his popular support (which are not unconnected) has been one of the more enriching ironies of contemporary politics. But it also points to the historically aphasic conundrum in which we live, where the narrative scenario of black disempowerment following Reconstruction can be renewed as the fear-invoking context for organizing various levels of white supremacist activity.

In this sense, the image offered by Ralph Ellison in "The Birthmark"—where the body of that seemingly fictional Willie lies dismembered and suspended between white male legs—occupies a symbolic range quite arresting in its historical diversity. For Bush, in fact, the representation of the black male as sexual threat functioned as the phantasm of his own phallic potential, providing the framework for escaping the limitations of corpo-reality and thereby making possible his ascension into the highest position the disembodied abstraction of citizenry in U.S. culture can offer. More recently, of course, Clarence Thomas's Supreme Court confirmation hearings brought the contexts of disembodied abstraction, political ascendancy, and racial difference to the foreground, forging a political crisis quite stunning in its specular deployment. But where Willie Horton was cast as the new Bigger Thomas, Clarence Thomas was saved from this fate by the necessity implicit in certain aspects of post-segregationist relations of race. Here, Bush marshaled the specter of the black male to signify his seeming commitment to civil rights reform, the integrationist image of Clarence Thomas functioning to simulate America's transcendence of its history of race and racism and hence its achievement of that mythic, endlessly invoked possibility: democracy.

Even the integrationist text cannot dispel the history of the black male's sexualization, though it may serve as the context for seeming to overcome it. As my discussion in this and the previous chapter has suggested, the tension between corporeality (blackness) and citizenship's abstraction turns ultimately on the sexual. In the Clarence Thomas case, Anita Hill's accusations served to return the question of the black man's ascension to abstraction where it has routinely been: in the realm of the sexual. And once there, Thomas found himself invoking the very context of race that his legal and political affinities worked so thoroughly to renounce, citing the history of the black body and its symbolic and literal markings. In leveling his charge against the proceedings as a "high-tech lynching," Thomas placed himself within that history and sought to distance himself from it, simultaneously defining his corporealization within the logic and social organization of white supremacy, while establishing abstraction (to be a justice) as the only route for undoing the history that the lynch metaphor recalled. In the context of the hearings, the overwhelmingly white masculine gaze that served to define and arbitrate this racial/sexual conflict — that ludicrous panel of empowered white men — demonstrated once again the nexus of white dread and desire that oversees the representational field of black sexuality. From "long dong silver" to *The Exorcist*'s pubic hair to the rumors concerning Hill's antimale lesbianism, the white masculine gaze indulged its own powerful production of racial discourses at the intersection of sexuality and gender.

It is important to emphasize the shifting terrain of this production as part of the negotiation of power that marks and defines the realm of the social, for the contextual relationships that undergird the imbrication of differences are not transhistorically the same. For Clarence Thomas, the shifted locus of his sexual threat from white to black women (and his ultimate confirmation) indicate the post-segregationist context in which this political conflict itself dwelled. In an ironic reconfiguration of political passions, the conservative Republican party found itself defending as normative the sexual subjectivity of a black man wed to a white woman. Now the criminality of blackness as sexual perversity was constructed solely as the black woman's sexual and ethical infidelity, and the politics of the visible took another turn in the refiguring of bodies and identities within America's newly fashioned integrationist terrain. How we understand this reconfiguration is part of the challenge of defining both the political and political resistance in the contemporary era, and it moves us toward questions of integration and racial representation that will be explored in the following chapter. For much like George Bush's attempt to solidify his own civil rights investments through the nomination of Clarence Thomas, the black

male finds himself bound to recently fashioned integrationist representations that subtend, in decidedly pernicious ways, the reconstruction of a
white masculine vision. As we shall see, in forging through popular culture a new and frantically insistent image of interracial fraternity, American
memory turns the anatomy of lynching once again on its head.

In the prologue to the 1980 bestseller *The Lords of Discipline,* Will McLean, the white narrator, presents the purpose of his story: "I want to tell you how it was. I want precision. I want a murderous, stunning truthfulness. I want to find my own singular voice for the first time" (Conroy 6). The articulation of his own "singular voice," a voice which, by implication, has been denied, characterizes the recurrent representational gesture of the post–civil rights era, where a white masculine perspective poses as truth teller, origin of a solitary and seemingly marginal voice that must now provide the precision missing in *other* versions of the "story." This story, as the novel and its 1983 film version depict, is the story of "America," that infinitely rhetorical figure that secures itself through multiple historicizing narratives of geopolitical destiny and chosen peoples. But like every mythological text that functions to weld disparities together, "America" is tenuous, its mythic plan of liberation "a thousand points of light" above a gaping abyss.[1] That this abyss seems to be stretching out before us in more complicated, encompassing, and less easily resisted ways, bringing with it what many recognize as a political and philosophical crisis, constitutes the prevailing mark of the contemporary period. Such a crisis pressures both cultural critique and political organization, and has made it nearly impossible to continue articulating the contestatory nature of "America" along the lines of dissent used in the 1960s. As we head for the twenty-first century, it is the decade of the 1980s that has come to feel like the final subversion of the twentieth century's high hopes of radical politics, and it is to its various reconfigurations of race and gender that this chapter turns.

But why use "feel like" in the preceding sentence, instead of a visual metaphor to coincide with the broad contours of this project? Can we not say that the 1980s "looks like" a subversion of the political aims of civil rights and feminism, thereby understanding its representational field as a return to earlier, more conservative methods of deployment? The basic presupposition of my argument here is that we cannot, precisely because the subversion at work in the 1980s took place in the transformation of its visual terrain *toward* more clearly inclusive representational images, images that seemed to offer, indeed demand, recognition of an America where things, particularly in the wake of civil rights, had definitively changed. In the massive organization of the social gaze through visual technologies, most importantly film and television, in fact, U.S. culture in the 1980s began to answer more fully than ever before the critique of racial segregation. By locating such a critique as an ensemble of representative bodies in media production, the 1980s cannot also claim to have reshaped in politically progressive ways the status of these bodies in the economic and social spheres.[2] Instead, the decade marks a massive retrenchment of political gains for minoritized groups as an integrationist aesthetics (both political and representational) emerged as the strategic and contradictory means for reframing and securing the continuity of white racial supremacy. The disciplinary specularity of the lynching and castration scene traced in the previous chapter gave way (though not entirely) to other practices of surveillance and containment, and the long struggle for African-American representational inclusion in popular and political culture alike took center stage as the primary visible economy subtending the production of race.

This means that mass-mediated visual technologies increasingly became the primary locus for race's rhetorical (or performative) deployment, binding together the historical production of the body as a visible geography with the specular apparatuses of late-twentieth-century life. In the process, a proliferating inclusion of African-American characters and cultural contexts in mainstream film and television, at least from a 1950s perspective, could be heralded by some as evidence of a profound transformation of U.S. culture, an eclipse of its historical emphasis on segregationist exclusion. But, while such inclusion has been applauded as an advance toward the fulfillment of "America" and while we may welcome the transgression of segregatory logic, the modes and manners through which this inclusion has been achieved are certainly not without their own political problems, as Kobena Mercer and Isaac Julien, among others, have been concerned to point out.[3] In the frantic move toward representational integration, in both popular culture and the literary canon, the question of political power has been routinely displaced as a vapid fetishization of the visible has emerged to take its place. This fetishization attaches a heightened commodity value to blackness in the wake of civil rights, translating the difficult demands of Afrocentric political critique into strategies for expanding capital's consumer needs.

Such a commodity status is not without irony in the broad historical scope of race in this country, where the literal commodification of the body under enslavement is now simulated in representational circuits that produce and exchange subjectivities through the visible presence of multicultural skin.

By securing the visible, epidermal iconography of difference to the commodity tableau of contemporary technologies, the integrationist aesthetic works by apprehending political equality as coterminous with representational presence, thereby undermining political analyses that pivot on the exclusion, silence, or invisibility of various groups and their histories. Given the logic of white supremacy, very little presence is in fact required for the necessary threshold of difference to be achieved. Cinematic depictions of an integrated American landscape, for instance, typically rely on a multiplicity of Anglo-American players as the framework of difference, and racial transcendence is inscribed on the often singular bodies of African-American (or other non-Eurocentric) characters. While the integrationist narrative now current in U.S. culture makes claims toward equal representation, the marketing of inclusion is always implicitly bounded by this border-controlling logic, and white supremacy is able to continue its operation within a seemingly expanded but clearly restrictive social field.

A particularly powerful example of this, and the representational scenario on which this chapter dwells, is that offered by interracial male bonding narratives, whose massive deployment in popular U.S. culture in the decade of the 1980s is witnessed by this cursory list: the films *Stir Crazy* (1980), *Nighthawks* (1981), *48 Hours* (1982), *The Lords of Discipline* (1983), *Trading Places* (1983), *Enemy Mine* (1985), *White Nights* (1985), *Iron Eagle* (1986), *Running Scared* (1986), *Streets of Gold* (1986), *Big Shots* (1987), *Hamburger Hill* (1987), *Lethal Weapon* I (1987) and II (1989), *Cry Freedom* (1988), *Off Limits* (1988), *Shoot to Kill* (1988); the TV shows *Miami Vice, Sonny Spoon, The A Team, J.J. Starbuck* (the TV remake of the *Defiant Ones*) (all 1987), *Magnum P.I., Hill Street Blues,* and *In the Heat of the Night.*[4] While the male bonding structure can be used as the framework for ethical, physical, moral, sexual, or political struggle in all-male group arrangements, its primary figuration, as anyone familiar with contemporary Hollywood film can tell, focuses on a sole interracial couple, most often narrativized within the action genre, and featuring what Donald Bogle calls "huckfinn fixation," where "a trusty black . . . possess[es] the soul the white man searches for" (*Toms, Coons, Mulattoes, Mammies, and Bucks* 140). Implicit in this narrative scenario is the discourse of sexual difference, where the white male occupies the traditionally masculine position of rugged self-assertion, while the African-American male assumes the emotional, feminine sphere. Such an application of the binary grid of gender to the field of masculine relations continues to serve, as it has in the past, an important function in adjudicating racial differences among men.

It is significant that in a number of contemporary interracial male bonding narratives, the discourse of sexual difference does not simply reiterate the historical appointment of the African-American male as the feminine, but works instead to fully inculcate him into the province of the masculine, marking such a masculinization as the precise measurement of "America"'s democratic achievement. The fear of masculine sameness that underwrites the castration and lynching scenario of an earlier era thus emerges in a number of narrative scenarios of the late twentieth century as a positive and necessary cultural assertion. Such necessity can be read as a form of response to the phallicized discourse of Black Power, where the analysis of the specular project of lynching and castration was articulated, as I have previously remarked, as both a demand and a warning: "[w]e shall have our manhood . . . or the earth will be leveled by our attempts to gain it" (Cleaver, *Soul on Ice* 66). In their increasing appeal to the mutuality of masculine sameness, male bonding narratives of the 1980s became a crucial site for negotiating this threat of militant black masculinity, offering a particularly compelling revision of the U.S. cultural terrain.

Although this articulation of masculine relations most often forged the image of the African-American male within instead of opposed to the masculine, such a reconfiguration is not necessarily evidence for or part of the process of meaningful social change. That is, in aligning black men with the masculine, popular culture transforms the historical contestations between black and white men into the image of democratic fraternity, marking "America" as an exclusive masculine realm and further ensconcing the elisions at work in the popular phrase "blacks and women." Such elisions are, of course, crucial to the ongoing articulation of white supremacist and patriarchal logic in the contemporary era, as they work to fragment the realm of political opposition by reiterating the binary arrangements that underwrite the regimes of both bodily scripted hierarchies. In this regard, we might understand the use of the discourse of sexual difference to fashion the representational economy that governs African-American men, whether in terms of feminization or masculinization, as having the rhetorical effect in the twentieth century not only of homogenizing the complexities of their social positioning but also of reproducing the cleavage of gender within the category African-American itself.[5] Interracial male bonding narratives reinscribe this cleavage by routinely defining the representational world of female exclusion as the precondition for racism's transcendence. In such a narrative scenario, economic, social, and political differences among men are ultimately displaced by the prevailing framework of gender.

The Brotherhood of the Ring

The Lords of Discipline provides a telling portrait of the historical changes implicit in the shift from a segregationist to an integrationist representational mode by taking the military and its complicity with Jim Crow as the context in which the new "stunning truthfulness" of American culture can be born. To establish the tableau of masculine bonds that historically underwrite the mythology of military masculinity, the film presents the doctrinaire General Durrell (G. D. Spradlin), whose rhetoric explains, "America is fat . . . sloppy, immoral and she needs men of iron to set her on the right path again." Entrance into this "superior breed" that can right the effeminate ways of America is marked by the wearing of a ring, "the sacred symbol of the Institute and its ideals." The significance of this ring as the symbolic bond between men — fashioned across a discourse of masculinity, national identity, and power — displaces, even as it invokes, the heterosexual matrimonial union, marking relations among men as a privileged nonsexual domain. The seeming necessity for this privileged domain ("America is fat") and the racial conflicts within it point to a crisis within the cultural construction of the masculine, a crisis that evinces itself in the proliferation of interracial male bonding narratives in the 1980s.[6]

While the novel and its film version (dir. Frank Roddam) both explore this world of the "brotherhood of the ring, the fellowship of the line," the differences in their narrative structures highlight an increasing emphasis on race as a nodal point in exploring and articulating relations among men in the post–civil rights era. In the novel, the narrative of the sacred ring, of (white) honor and masculinity, is interwoven with the narrative of the ring's more traditional association, heterosexual matrimony. Here, Will McLean's struggle as a rebel in the institution and his subsequent role as the protector of the first black cadet, Tom Pearce, is juxtaposed with his affair with Annie Kate Gervais, a woman from a poor southern family who is impregnated by Tradd St. Croix, Will's best friend and academy roommate. Sexual difference, and the various trajectories of reproduction and responsibility through which masculinity is coded, thus takes a central role in the novel, becoming a primary means through which differences among white men, based on their ethical and moral responses to others, are crafted. In playing out these differences within a highly charged configuration of race and gender, the narrative emphasizes McLean's ethical regard for both poor white women and historically excluded black men.

But where the novel may foreground questions of the ethical within the hierarchies of both race and gender, it is significant that the film omits entirely the narrative of pregnancy and betrayal, focusing solely on the conflicts and tensions wrought by the presence of racial differences. This change is an interesting reconfiguration, suggesting that race has superseded sexual difference as a cultural priority, at least in the register of 1980s popular culture. But we can also read the film's narrative transformation as a consolidation of race and gender, since the elimination of Annie Gervais does not evacuate the symbolics of sexual difference altogether. Instead, it tellingly shifts such symbolics (through the matrimonial metaphor, for instance) from the white female to the black male, from heterosexual to homosocial bonds. Such a translation of the locus of sexual difference in this and other interracial male bonding scenarios inaugurates a narrative trajectory in which the black male, in being representationally condensed with the feminine, must subsequently be rescued from it. Such a complicated narrative symbolic — aligning the black male with the feminine in order to liberate him from it — clearly redraws the representational, not to mention disciplinary, practices of an earlier era. However, it does so in ways that disturbingly refigure, indeed recuperate white masculine hegemony in the post–civil rights years.

In *The Lords of Discipline,* set in Charleston, South Carolina, in 1964, the rescue of the black male from the feminine takes place in the context of an integrationist event: his entrance as the first African-American cadet into the institute. This entrance threatens the sacred circle of the ring by exposing how the institute's most prized ethos, masculinity, rests on an assumption of white racial superiority. Even Bear (Robert Prosky), the officer who assigns McLean (David Keith) to protect Pearce (Mark Breland) from racist attacks, admits, "Yeah, I'm a racist. I'd like nothing better than to see Mr. Pearce move his black ass right out of here . . . [but] Pearce is one of my lambs and all of my lambs get an even break." Bear's attitude paradoxically affirms racism at the same time it establishes a seemingly democratic perspective, one that promises fair treatment in the face of gross bigotry. This paradox governs the film, shaping as well the perspective of the central hero, McLean, whose rebellion against the corruption of the institute nonetheless becomes the means for fulfilling its goal of setting America "on the right path again." The contradictions embedded in McLean's heroic white masculinity are perhaps best revealed in his answer to the question, "Was it worth it . . . four years down the drain for a nigger?" "It wasn't for the nigger. It was never for the nigger." This phrase, reverberating not only throughout this film but across the many cultural texts that feature inter-racial male bonds, demonstrates how the integration of the black male into the sacred circle of the masculine — an integration that significantly rescues him from the historical elision with the feminine — is never "for the nigger," but for the white man so that, as Tradd St. Croix (Mitchell Lichtenstein) says to McLean, "*you* could be a hero."

The ideological project of *The Lords of Discipline,* its construction of an interracial male bond as the precondition for asserting the white male's heroic marginality, is evinced most strongly in the symbolic and narrative relations governing Pearce, the black cadet whose desire for "democratic" opportunity brings upon him the wrath of "The Ten," a secret group of cadets dedicated to preserving the white legacy of the institute. The Ten use a variety of means, including torture, to police and instantiate a normative masculinity among the new cadets, driving out those deemed weak and un-prepared for the rigors of military manhood. But the entrance of the first black cadet brings a new focus to the group, one through which blackness, as linked to sexual difference, is cast as equally excessive to the institute's ideal of masculinity.[7] In this context, it is not surprising that for the first half of the film, Pearce's masculinity is in question, and hence the various modes of harassment inflicted on him test the limits not simply of his convictions, but of his ability to survive the feminizing threat of castration. In an early scene, for instance, he is forced to perform pull-ups with a saber strategi-cally placed to pierce his crotch should his strength fail. Later, he finds a burning effigy in his room, hung lynch style and summoning the historic equation of lynching with castration. Then in the final torture scene, where he finally promises to leave the institute, gasoline has been poured over his genitals and The Ten stand poised to set him on fire.

But this is no narrative of the black man's defeat through corporeal dis-memberment, as castration is the symbolic figure belonging to the segrega-tionist, not integrationist era. And the crucial element of the integrationist narrative is the white man's intercession into the scene of genital mutila-tion, an intercession that preserves the black male's social and corporeal signification as male. In *The Lords of Discipline,* Pearce's struggle for racial equality is thus contingent on McLean's disruption of The Ten's torture, and it is significant that such disruption emerges through the invocation of his masculine bonds with a different group of white men: "I'm putting our friendship on the line," McLean tells his friends, "Now, how about it?" Thus pitting a renegade white male group against the Klan-like society of The Ten, the film posits racial equality as an issue between white men—and, more important, between a white supremacist cultural order and its reconstitution as democratic possibility. In this way, the integrationist rhetoric of the film reconstructs the historic injustices of segregation by fashioning a new tradition of action and authority through which white masculine power can exert itself. Indeed, the final words spoken by Pearce, addressed to McLean—"thank you, sir"—reinforce both the subserviency of his representation and the emergent and importantly reconfigured hegemony of the white male role.

The historical irony of this narrative turn is a powerful indication of the need to negotiate masculine relations in the contemporary era, a need inaugurated during radical decades of the twentieth century by moves away from segregationist toward integrationist representational and cultural practices. As I have detailed in chapter 3, the articulation of the African-American male as a threat to the white woman and white civilization and the transformation of this discursive tableau by black revolutionary politics have shifted the conditions under which the category black male is now culturally produced. To a great extent, as I will explore in the following pages, it is through the circulating specter of the African-American male that the white masculine renegotiates its own "singular voice," establishing a system in which the question of race and racial equality can only be answered through a struggle posed between and for white men. In the seeming equality of a post-1960s society, the "brotherhood of the ring" remains a white construct, one through which the historical struggle for racial equality as a hallmark of "America" was, and continues to be, "never for the nigger."

Negotiating the Masculine

Given the consequences of this production of "America," it is perhaps no surprise that the two "classic" bonding films—*The Defiant Ones* (dir. Stanley Kramer, 1958) and *In the Heat of the Night* (dir. Norman Jewison, 1967)—straddle some of the most turbulent years of racial protest and violence in U.S. history, interpreting that history in ways that say a great deal about the political investments of African-American male representation: on one hand, the darkly hopeful Huck Finn dream of two men on the run from white civilization (and white women) and, on the other, the integration narrative that links black and white across the discourse of cultural law and order. These two images of outlaw and officer are stock roles in interracial male bonding narration in the second half of the twentieth century, and in this they represent the mutually exclusive but ideologically conflated indexes of the African-American male's contradictory social position. Alternately aligned with margin and center, the African-American male traverses the boundaries of "difference," moving from criminal excess to central authority and thereby rearticulating his image in defiance of the segregationist codes to which he was heir.

In constructing African-American male representation within a framework that can accommodate his movement between margin and center — as outlaw and lawman, black and male — contemporary interracial male bonding narratives use his traversal of seemingly rigid categories of cultural (dis)empowerment as the vehicle for the white man's own rhetorical extrication from the role of "oppressor," making possible a rearticulation of the locus of cultural power and domination that seems to negate the historical supremacy ascribed to the white male. Through the representational framework of bonds with black men, the white masculine is cast as an oscillating and at times indeterminate formation, one marked by the relations of domination but no longer central to their articulation. As a consequence, the overdetermination of phallic authority within the interracial male bond can serve as the privileged emblem of nonhierarchical structures, reining black men into the ideological orbit of patriarchal relations while casting the white male as both victim of the social order and its potential hero. Through such narratives, the white masculine voice that has been attacked and silenced in the wake of black and feminist discourses can make claims for its own cultural exclusion, reasserting its "singular voice for the first time."

Such a representational strategy participates in the process of "remasculinization" that Susan Jeffords cites as central to contemporary modes of U.S. cultural production, where "[w]ith the advent of women's rights, civil rights, the 'generation gap,' and other alterations in social relations . . . the stability of the ground on which patriarchal power rests was challenged" (*The Remasculinization of America* xi–xii). This challenge resulted not in a complete negation of the patriarchal project but in large-scale renegotiations of structures of power in the 1970s and 1980s. As Jeffords defines it, the primary mechanism for this renegotiation is "a revival of the images, abilities, and evaluations of men and masculinity" — a remasculinization

most apparent, she contends, in contemporary filmic and televisual depictions of the Vietnam War where the masculine "place[s] itself . . . [as]
a social group in need of special consideration. No longer the oppressor,
men came to be seen, primarily through the image of the Vietnam veteran,
as themselves oppressed" (xii, 169). John Wheeler's summation of the war
is perhaps most telling: "the Vietnam veteran was the nigger of the 1970s"
(*Touched with Fire* 16), he writes, a formulation which, as Jeffords notes,
clears the space of cultural marginalization of its historical occupants and
reoccupies it with the seemingly decentered masculine voices that had once
held sway in U.S. culture. This articulation of the masculine as a category of
oppression elides the specificity of racial violence attendant to all African-
Americans, rejuvenating the masculine not simply in the context of, but
in the service of white supremacy as well.[8] In the figuration of the vet as
nigger, we witness the integrationist strategy in which the implicit feminization of race found throughout nineteenth- and twentieth-century U.S.
life is superseded by a supreme and supremely coveted masculinization.

The remasculinization project Jeffords describes emerges as one bound
to a double rhetorical move: by recasting the masculine as the newly marginalized position in U.S. culture and shifting the historically oppressed
toward the center, an image of social relations can be constructed that
posits the white masculine, in the guise of the veteran, "as emblematic of
the condition of all American men, not just those who went to war" (*The
Remasculinization of America* 135). According to Jeffords, this homogenization of the masculine as a newly defined category of difference, competing
in the cultural marketplace against other kinds of identity-based interests,
operates through the mythos of male bonding where the masculine "poses
survival—finally the survival of masculinity itself—as depending on the
exclusion of women and the feminine, a world in which men are not significantly different from each other and boundaries of race, class . . . and
ethnicity are [seemingly] overcome" (168). While the discourse of sexual
difference functions as the primary mechanism for regenerating the failure
of masculinity signified by Vietnam, the cultural crisis evinced by the war
and the recuperatory practices currently at work to negotiate its effects are
not limited solely to gender, but work across the various categories of difference that give shape and substance to U.S. hierarchical arrangements.[9]

For these reasons, we can read contemporary proliferations of interracial
male bonding narratives as equally powerful and often overlapping instances of the remasculinization process Jeffords sets forth, where the ideological investments of regenerating the masculine are done to rearticulate

dominant relations not just between men and women but, significantly, among men themselves. In such a process, the African-American male's inclusion in the separate world of the masculine is accomplished by detaching him from the historical context of race and installing him instead within the framework of gender. Here, the homosocial bond's assertion of a stridently undifferentiated masculine space can function to veil its simultaneous rejuvenation of racial hierarchies. Through these mechanizations, the African-American male's access to masculine power, contingent on his bodily presence as visible difference, disturbingly ignores contemporary modes of social and economic disempowerment. This diffusion of the hierarchical realms of race and gender demonstrates that it is the masculine that most strenuously (re)constructs the cultural status of the African-American male, making his greatest enemy not the feminine as the male bonding narrative often depicts but, through the brotherhood of the ring, the masculine itself.

The Lineage of Forefathers

The emphasis in bonding narratives on the rearticulation of the white masculine's "singular voice" constructs a new mythology of origins, one through which the white masculine perspective is cast as the originary term in the eradication of racism and hence as the potential site for democracy's achievement. In important ways, such a narrative strategy addresses the contemporary concerns about history, identity, and difference recently collected under the term "multiculturalism" by foregrounding the crisis attending the white masculine position, now pressured to relinquish its historical centrality to a diverse array of counternarratives. In the male bonding scenario, the multicultural comes to be figured in the contact between the white male and his racially different brother, and the narrative of their meeting, friendship, and most often tragic split offers a reconstructed conclusion to the painful history that Western imperialism has spawned. It is this reconstruction that addresses past conquests performed by and in the service of white men, simultaneously drawing global history as a drama, once again, that pivots on the actions of white men. The new mythology of origins, as we will see, is new only to the extent that it begins in the recognition of a national or global history of violence and disempowerment based on race. Its conclusion, as in *The Lords of Discipline,* establishes masculine sameness between men while consigning African-American male subjectivity to the contours of white masculinity.

In utilizing the narrative strategy of acknowledgment followed by negation-through-integration, *The Lords of Discipline* gave way in 1985 to *Enemy Mine* (dir. Wolfgang Petersen), a film overtly obsessed with the global history of imperialism and slavery that characterizes human activity on earth. Instead of forging its obsession as a critique of Western economic interests, the film narrates the imperialist's confrontation with cultural differences by offering the white male a new mythology of origins, one in which his historical position of privilege is exchanged for a heroic place alongside the oppressed. Here, the threat often attributed to multiculturalism of eradicating the history and achievements of white (and) masculine "civilization" is warded off by a glorious embrace of difference that preserves the centrality of the white male as it offers the specular assurance that race and gender have been represented and addressed. Such a strategy, akin in my mind to the political effectivity found in the quest to transform—through inclusion—the canon, maintains the emphasis on white and masculine sameness, forcing the historical relationship between margin and center to be leveled by a pervasive neocolonial ideology. In short, the white and Western foundation remains. This is not to say that multiculturalism has no radical pedagogical potential, but that its political effect is finally neither pure nor secure. Indeed, its claim to eradicate the systemic inadequacies of U.S. education may be another way for white Americans, in particular, to grasp difference in its most abstract and disembodied form, a grasping that has as its political consequence a further taming of those "differences" historically aligned with the margins.

It is just this kind of taming that seems to be at work in *Enemy Mine*, though the body of the other—if I can use a phrase so laced with imperial ideology—is anything but abstract. In fact, in refashioning the traditional interracial male bonding scenario as an intergalactic sci-fi story, *Enemy Mine* presents the dark buddy as quite literally an alien. A reptilian figure, Jerry (played by Louis Gossett Jr.) stands in stark contrast to Willis Davidge (Dennis Quaid), the alien's altogether human, white, and male counterpart. In casting the black actor as alien and his white bonding buddy as human, the film conjures up a long tradition of black stereotypes in U.S. culture, where African-Americans have been cast in the role of the white man's nonhuman other, the dark beast, the alien outsider who threatens the sanctity of the cultural order.[10] Such a representation repeats the now-classic structure of the colonial encounter: corporeal essence is defined and symbolized according to the logic of the visible, and hierarchical arrangements are naturalized in the dyadic relationship between identity and difference.

Within this structure, the alien body can only take its narrative place within an overarching contradiction, becoming the site for the nostalgic dream of bonding across incommensurate difference, while serving as the very signpost — the corporeal evidence — that sanctions, indeed reassures us, that the dream and its miscegenating potential remain impossibilities.

If the film presents difference along the lines of a human-alien contrast, what textual specificities underwrite my assumption that the film is in fact a racial allegory? Is Gossett's own racial categorization ample cause for reading nonhuman alterity as a symbol of blackness, thereby understanding the film as marking blackness as alien to humanity, indeed as alien to the "human" itself? The opening words of the film, spoken in voice-over by the white male, helps sort this out by shaping the narrative context, the latter part of the twenty-first century, as a neocolonial racial encounter. As Davidge, whose quest throughout the movie is the transformation of this "enemy" into "mine," tells us, "the nations of the Earth were finally at peace working together to explore and colonize the distant reaches of space. Unfortunately we weren't alone out there. A race of nonhuman aliens called the Dracs were claiming squatter's rights to some of the richest star systems in the galaxy. Well, they weren't going to get it without a fight." In positing the nonhuman as a difference of "race," Davidge's description simultaneously asserts Earth's transcendence of its violent imperialist struggles and defines space as the new arena for the exertion of colonial control — a representational scenario in which a "healed" human culture can disavow its historical inequities by reconstituting the imperialist tableau in an extraterrestrial domain. In the process, the casting of Gossett as the Drac (named Jerry by Davidge later in the film) must be viewed as hardly coincidental, for it is precisely his "blackness" that functions as the absent presence throughout the film.

While the film appears to offer a confrontation with new, unknown life — the fantasy of science fiction — its pursuit of the mythology of the interracial male bond, set now in the space world of the twenty-first century, is all pervasive. In this scripting of the bond, Davidge and Jerry become stranded on an uncolonized planet where they are forced to learn to overcome their "races'" untamed hostility toward one another for the sake of mutual survival and to articulate, as they say, a "love [that] might unite them." The overtones here of the matrimonial metaphor aptly mark the interplay of race and gender at work in the film and carry us into that now familiar discursive landscape where the black male figure is positioned vis-à-vis the white male within both the very space and symbolic locus of the feminine.

But this positioning is neither simple nor direct. Indeed, the film goes to great lengths to translate the alien's evocation of the feminine into a post-gender sphere. Like the difference of race that underlies the alien's alterity, however, the Drac's relation to the feminine is only initially veiled. This veiling takes its most overt form in the Drac's characterization as androgynous, but it is an androgyny that, as we will see, simultaneously invokes the feminine and presents it as the very difference from which the human must finally rescue the alien.

The great rescue from the feminine takes place during a birthing scene, where the androgynous Drac (whose swelling belly the film has visually charted), encounters complications and must turn to Davidge for help. Here, as the alien lies groaning in the throes of childbirth, the process of birthing as a function of the feminine is simultaneously asserted and disavowed:

> DRAC: Something is wrong.
> HUMAN: Oh no . . . you're going to be all right. Women always get nervous before labor.
> DRAC: I AM NOT A WOMAN.

In Davidge's naming of the Drac as woman and in the Drac's adamant denial, this interracial bonding scene replays, albeit in the intergalactic register, the complex representational history governing black men in U.S. culture. Though the layers of narrative reframing make the race-gender axis the unspoken absence of this science fiction, it is in the disparity between the discursive negation of the feminine and the corporeal figuration of the Drac as pregnant that racial alterity is joined to gender. And while it is the white male who consigns the Drac to the feminine, the alien's translation of the film's pretense of androgyny to not-woman demonstrates in broad allegorical strokes the contestation framing black male representation in the post–civil rights years.

Ultimately, the ideological movement of the film is uninterested in the significance of the black male's disavowal, and it is to the white man's intercession in black male feminization that the narrative quickly turns. Before "Jerry" dies, with the child kicking beneath the scaly folds of the belly, Davidge is instructed: "You must open me. Don't be afraid, my friend." While Davidge is initially horrified at both the instructions and "Jerry's" death, he tears open the pregnant womb with his fingers, pulling the baby from the dead body. By birthing Zammis, Davidge appropriates the feminine activity of reproduction to himself without any question of gender confusion: the possibility of his "being woman" is eradicated in the construction of birth as a masculine activity of tearing. This intercession significantly rescues the alien from the potential castration implicit in birthing (remember, there was no disavowal that the Drac was not a man), and hence makes possible the symbolic interchange between and reduction of androgyny to the masculine. The category "women" has thus been superseded in this film by the white masculine, which overcomes, in a simultaneous move, the threats of racial and sexual difference by "occupying" through this reproductive scenario the alien position altogether.

Through this series of interchanges and the narrative's subsequent plotting, *Enemy Mine* reconstructs the colonial encounter by rendering the white man's intercession as the very means for saving the alien culture. Following Jerry's death, Davidge works to fulfill his "sacred vow" to raise the child, Zammis, and to eventually return it to its home planet. In this process, Davidge becomes embroiled with other humans who, through the labor of enslaved Dracs, begin colonizing the far side of the planet. By saving Zammis from colonization and enslavement—and liberating all the Dracs from the labor camp—Davidge eventually earns himself a place in the Draconian song of lineage. As the voice-over at the conclusion states: "[a]nd so Davidge brought Zammis and the Dracs home. He fulfilled his vow and recited the line of Zammis's *forefathers* [emphasis added] before the holy council on Dracon. And when, in the fullness of time, Zammis brought its own child before the Holy Council, the name of Willis Davidge was added to the line." In this resolution, the colonial relationship between human and Drac is thus seemingly undone when the human (read: white man) enters the alien (read: black man) discourse, making himself both its savior and forebear. If the narrative force of the androgynous as vehicle for white masculinization had not been clear before, its overt equation is now complete, as Draconian history and memory emerge as a lineage of "forefathers."

But what of Jerry? Significantly, his role in procreation has been eradicated, displaced by the primacy of white paternity. This narrative resolution quite stunningly recalls the slave economy of the Old South, where the black male's position in reproduction is denied as paternity is signified almost exclusively in the figure of the white male. But this is the Old South with all of its complicated twists, for this white father is also the quintessential abolitionist, and it is in the dream wish of abolition that the full eradication of the black male is achieved. In the era of integrationist aesthetics, this outcome—this redrawing of white masculine hegemony as the ethical commitment to end racist injustice—is part of the anxious quest to own the margins, even if the center is beginning to heave. In giving birth to the Other (Zammis), Davidge confirms, in a necessary recreation of white masculine hegemony, his own status as savior of alien discourses, while also confirming that those alien discourses are themselves not alien to the white masculine. In such a scenario, gender as an initially ambiguous and transitory state veils the underlying struggle *within* the broad contours of the masculine by positing difference in sexual terms and thereby obscuring the alien's affinity to the masculine itself.[11]

The narrative trajectory of *Enemy Mine* thus addresses the fear of masculine sameness through a complicated process of signification: in aligning difference—both racial and sexual—with the alien, the white male's quest for a reinvigorated place in history begins with his ability to dissociate the alien from the feminine before inserting himself into alien culture as its forefather. The integrationist narrative of the black male's defeminization (his adamant refusal of being woman) becomes, then, the very vehicle for the white male's new role as protector and historian of the cultural (and colonial) margins. The film's emphasis on the Drac's physical difference, his reptilian features and bisexual reproductive capacities, evokes the damning bestiality and femininity simultaneously inscribed in segregationist narratives—and it demands, for the final mutuality of the interracial male bond, a rescue of the alien from the body. In so doing, in intercepting Jerry from the castrating birth of his femininity, and in revealing, through his paternal relation to Zammis, the racial in-difference of this colonial relation, *Enemy Mine* achieves the full force of integration's effect: the reconstruction of the white masculine, which, appropriating cultural difference through the alien, can proceed to embody, without corporeal threat, all difference within itself. Where *The Lords of Discipline* fully disposes of the narrative of gender and inscribes the white man as the leader in the struggle for civil rights, *Enemy Mine* occupies all positions of difference, the white man "fulfill[ing] his vow" in a sweeping recuperation that is the mark of the contemporary period.

America

But why not read *Enemy Mine* as a critique of white masculine hegemony in which the white male's connection to "the Other" is rearticulated as an anti-colonial bond? After all, Davidge does heed the call to fight the colonial incursion through which Dracs are turned into slaves. Is there nothing politically portentous about a film that depicts the white male as recognizing his own imbrication in issues of racism and colonialism? Are there, in short, only recuperative strategies at work in cultural narratives of interracial male bonds? While it may be difficult, given my reading of *Enemy Mine*, to view these questions as something more than rhetorical dead ends, it would be problematical to entirely dismiss the utopianism that underlies the figuration of interracial bonding. For the dream of the post-colonial, post-segregationist moment, of the possibility of bonding across racial difference, is no politically insignificant wish. In a nation whose self-identity is so deeply formed around the democratic — around the inculcation of difference into the framework of a citizen "same" — the confrontation in which difference is articulated and some fundamental affinity or similarity affirmed has long been the political hope for hierarchical subversion.

The question on which my readings of these films turn, however, concerns the possibility of difference to maintain its autonomy, the possibility for a *mutuality of difference* to stand as the fundamentally ethical relationship, a moment of kinship, if you will, that does not settle back into the body of the same. This is a seemingly impossible hope in the context of mainstream cultural production, particularly Hollywood film, since its version of the relationship between identity and difference is so territorially tied in the contemporary era to the representational propulsion of integration. Not that African-American characters are populating filmic productions in any equitable way, but the marketing logic of film (like television) is at pains to negotiate the multiculturalism of U.S. culture and that culture's historic reliance on the ideological supremacy of everything white, heterosexual, and male. It is this negotiation and the theoretical apparatuses we employ to read, understand, and plot to subvert it that interest me, in both a pedagogical and a political vein. These films do function as scenes of instruction for the construction of this nation's most pervasive and contested ideology, "America." As such, the realm of the popular, of popular cinematic productions, cannot be dismissed as either simple or vulgar, as mere perversions of a truer consciousness that lies elsewhere. Instead, popular cinema, like the host of interracial buddy narratives it has spawned, partakes in the very meaning of "America": that rhetoric of nation, narrative of origin, and abstracted locus of supposedly equal entitlements.

Indeed, it is the inability of "America" to function as a transhistorical sign that necessitates its reiterative production. And it is at the site of interracial male bonds that popular culture in the 1980s most repetitively struggled to rehabilitate "America" from its segregationist as well as its imperialist

past. In the bond's quest for a self-enclosed, racially undifferentiated masculine space, cultural production casts its net around a reconfiguration of
"America," providing narrative trajectories that pivot on the confrontation
with difference and its ultimate shimmering transcendence. This confrontation and transcendence is itself the narrative trope of "America," its most
prized and evoked ontology. But in the need for its representational replay, we witness one of the ways the contemporary crisis of the masculine
expresses itself: caught in its most complex contradiction—between the assertion of masculine sameness and the (re)construction of difference in the
face of that sameness—the interracial male bonding narrative embodies the
oscillation of "America," constructing on one hand the ideological dream
of cohesion, of an essential, uniform masculine identity, while forging, on
the other, discriminations that qualify and specify the boundaries of that
identity.

In the broad terrain of "America," the tension produced through this
contradiction allows for various discourses to gain visibility in U.S. culture—the inculcation of seemingly marginalized voices acting as the necessary proof of "America's" democratic possibility. In this process, where
the materiality of cultural relations are superseded by the dreamscape of
"America's" production, we encounter what Sacvan Bercovitch calls the
"American form," that transformation of "what might have been a confrontation of alternatives into an alternation of opposites" ("Afterword"
438). Bercovitch's description characterizes, to a certain scary extent, the
dynamic of U.S. cultural production, where the conflation of identity and
history into binary oppositions—in Bercovitch's terms, fusion or fragmentation, myth or material existence—enables the apparent opposition to be
absorbed by and set to work for its antithesis. As such, heterogenous elements can be homogenized in the enunciation of a seemingly larger cultural identity, one that incorporates the radical multiplicity inherent in the
disparate cultural identities that have converged on the Native Indian soil
of North America. As Bercovitch writes, "[t]echnology and religion, individualism and social progress, spiritual, political and economic values—all
the fragmented aspects of life and thought . . . flowed into 'America,' the
symbol of cultural consensus" ("The Rites of Ascent" 27). In this process, of
course, consensus is radically displaced by its symbolic production, which
in turn functions as the simulacra of consensus.

"America," in other words, becomes the repository for its own ideological and rhetorical ideals, the means for the reification of "nation." But it is
not only so-called dominant discourses that partake in this reification, for

appeal in which, as the title song by Lionel Richie proclaims, "Say you, say me, say it together naturally." As an audio counter to Greenwood's own complaints about U.S. culture—"they don't even think you're human and they want you to die for them"—the sound track reinforces Rodchenko's assertion: "Things have changed . . . it's a wonderful country."

Importantly, it is the Russian defector, the man who has cast away his citizenship in the Communist regime in favor of capitalism and its "freedoms," who acts as the voice of change, establishing the perspective against which the black man's alienation will be measured. In a long monologue, Greenwood describes this alienation to Rodchenko:

> I used to feel the way you do about America. I was a patriot . . . [a] cute little colored kid tapping away. . . . [B]y the time I grew up it was a different story. He's an adult black man now. . . . Give him a broom. . . . My mother says . . . "don't worry . . . something good's coming." . . . [S]he was right. Somebody did want me. Uncle Sam. Uncle Sam wanted the whole ghetto. . . . I said, "Ma, this is it . . . I'm going to get myself a real career . . . defend my country against communism." But . . . nobody said you gonna become a murderer . . . a rapist, you gonna maim and rob people. . . . This little voice in my head said, Ray, you're being used. They're trying to kill you. They don't even think you're human and they want you to die for them, make them richer. It was all very clear.

Greenwood's reading of U.S. culture's use of African-American men in Vietnam connects his narrative to the larger cultural disillusionment presented by that war.[13] But in setting his critique in the context of the film's Cold War politics, even the obviously racist procedures of the government and military—"Uncle Sam wanted the whole ghetto"—and the implicit betrayal of the black male by a system ostensibly fighting for democracy become an ironic simulation of the more deadly Soviet system, a system that similarly sacrifices people for ideals, using and discarding individuals in a maniacal quest for domination. Where the United States' betrayal is local and historically specific—"It's different there now"—the film presents the Soviet betrayal of its people and of Greenwood as the universal condition of communism, the underlying reason for the black man's need to return home. As Greenwood says to Rodchenko, "I was big news while they needed me," but now "[w]e're like rats in a cage. . . . We can't live like this."

The representation of the Soviet system as inherently corrupt, worse even than the racist policies of a pre–civil rights United States, reaches its zenith in the characterization of the KGB agent, Colonel Chaiko, from whose mouth the classic word of U.S. racism, "nigger," is formed. In this speech act, Chaiko embodies the very racism that initially forced Greenwood to seek solace in another country, foregrounding Greenwood's error and making way for the signification of "America" as the only place where the "the baby . . . [can] be free."[14] This idea of freedom ironically displaces the historical legacy underwriting interracial heterosexuality, where the very image of the black man and white woman (and the specter of their "mixed" progeny) served as precursor to mutilation and death. But here, in a post-segregationist interface with the Cold War, the interracial child's only hope of freedom is contingent on the black man's embrace of America as home. Significantly, Chaiko's use of "nigger" emerges in a conversation about sexual relations between Greenwood and his wife, thereby connecting the racism of communism to the figure of interracial sexuality and miscegenation. In the process, "America" is ostensibly cleansed of its historical legacy and signified as a new site for both intra- and transnational freedoms.

In an important refiguration of black masculinity, *White Nights* links the racism of communism to an anxiety over the black male's sexuality and impending fatherhood, and thereby it equates U.S. political transformation with the possibilities of African-American paternity. Such an image of "America" is a startling revision of the contemporary crisis of black male life, where cultural discourses berate the black male for his supposed disinterest in fatherhood, while institutional and economic relations make his fulfillment of paternity a difficult prospect indeed. At the same time, however, the image of the black male embracing fatherhood does counter his traditional U.S. stereotype as a renegade man and deserter of the family, providing a "positive image" of the black male on the side of family (and hence cultural law and order). But, as I will explore in the next section, the use of the positive image can have an insidious effect in the integrationist narrative, and we cannot dismiss the way the image of the black father maintains both the law of the masculine and of heterosexuality, often serving in the end as the specular representation of an integrated America.

In restoring the black male to the role of the father, which in *White Nights* takes place not in America but elsewhere, the film can offer a level of narrative assurance against the threat of homosexuality, that threat that routinely hovers around male bonding configurations (whether in cinema, sport, or politics), but which is perhaps even more tangible in a film that features dance duets between men. Here, the embeddedness of Greenwood's fatherhood in heterosexual romance functions to direct the desire attendant to male bodies on display away from a potential homosexual entanglement. As various dance productions between Greenwood and Rodchenko demonstrate, it is the athleticism and artistry of their bodies that negotiate the camera's voyeuristic gaze, highlighting their masculine contours—"[t]he 'naturalness' of muscles," as Richard Dyer writes, "legitimises male power and domination" ("Don't Look Now" 71). And yet, as Steve Neale contends, "male homosexuality is constantly present as an undercurrent . . . but one that is dealt with obliquely, symptomatically, and that has to be repressed" ("Masculinity as Spectacle" 15). The camera's perspective on Greenwood and Rodchenko is designed for this repression, as it continually disrupts their look at one another, lingers over their bodies as separate images, and frames both bodies only in a shot from the distance. This individualization of the dance isolates the erotic, warding off the possibility of desire between the men. The dance scenes thus privilege the male body as the narrative site of strength and specular appeal, but it is precisely the dangerous possibility inherent in that appeal that necessitates the subplot of heterosexual romance and paternity. As the concluding scene of the film indicates, with Greenwood first embracing his wife and then the camera freezing on his embrace of Rodchenko, the heterosexual is imposed, inserted, between the two men, all homosexual desire repressed in the affirmation of a "deeper" masculine bond.

In this movement within the bounds of heterosexuality, the interracial male bonding narrative establishes paternity, for Greenwood and America, as the determining feature of precisely how much "[t]hings have changed." In the process, Rodchenko, as neither a biological father nor a U.S. citizen by birth, can claim the status of cultural hero by rescuing the African-American male from the prison of his own alienation and fear, thereby suggesting that the oppressed "victims" of communism are themselves potential sons of the "American" ideal. Through the Russian defector, the expatriate son (even his name, Greenwood, symbolizes innocence) can reclaim and be reclaimed by America where, "for better or for worse," as he says at film's end, he can return home. In this symbolic marriage to America, a marriage that enables him to claim the positions of both father and son, Greenwood's homecoming repairs the cultural fragmentation wrought by racial segregation, oppression, and the Vietnam war. And through this image of the black male returning home, cleansed of anger, "America" is reconstituted, its sacred vow of democratic harmony upheld in a representation of cultural wholeness that takes place not on U.S. but Soviet soil. There in the land of Cold War fears, the film transforms, in the imagery of its title, America's own horrific moments into an unending spectacle of white.

The Positive Image

The shift in *White Nights* from the image of the black male as cultural traitor and outsider to citizen and father is obviously not a new narrative strategy within scenarios of the interracial male bond. Its more traditional configuration—the black male as cop, symbolic father of the cultural order—is a major trope in popular U.S. narration of the past twenty years. In what was perhaps the first of its kind, *In the Heat of the Night* (1967), for instance, the African-American male is a homicide detective, his knowledge and training essential to the restoration of order in a small Mississippi town.[15] Such a construction of the black officer as fighting not with brawn but with intelligence helps to settle that era's fear of racial violence by locating black masculinity on the side of cultural law and order. In the contemporary era, the black cop figure functions in much the same way, establishing masculinity as the necessary force for the protection of U.S. culture and containing, in the process, the specter of open black rebellion. By extending a strenuous masculinity to black men, the black cop figure can work to transform his potential subversion of U.S. culture into affirmation, protection, and appeal—through presence and visibility—to democratic enunciations. This transformation is remarkably facilitated within configurations of the interracial male bond in which the loyalty between black and white men can outweigh the cultural power imbalances between them, where "the love [that] might unite them" can evince an America where "things have changed."

As guardian of law and order, the black police figure plays out the role of cultural father, a role crucial to the remasculinization project of contemporary decades in which, in the face of a cultural economy that had been radically disrupted, the resurrection of the father in his many cultural guises is essential to the reestablishment of the masculine as the site for healing and wholeness. Through the black father figure, dominant discourses provide images of individual African-American males that offer the appearance of a reconfigured U.S. culture. While this reconfiguration can be witnessed in material practices as strategies of inclusion (affirmative action and the often tokenistic use of African-Americans as visible presences in otherwise all-white institutions), white supremacy is not necessarily dislodged but rather disguised and repressed. Most disturbing is the fact that while images of the interracial male bond and its rhetoric of democracy allow greater visibility for some black male actors and politicians, the same is not true for African-American women whose representational visibility has in fact decreased in the cultural obsession with narrations of differences among men. Indeed, as the threat of racial difference is worked through the remasculinization project, the political, economic, legal, and social status of African-American women will pay the heaviest price in the cultural rehabilitation of the white masculine.

Where her exiled image haunts most interracial bonding narratives — *The Defiant Ones, In the Heat of the Night, Shoot to Kill* — it is significant that the popular 1987 film, *Lethal Weapon* (dir. Richard Donner), manipulates the image of the black woman as evidence of U.S. cultural achievement; no longer the traditional stereotypes of mammy or whore, here, in a film featuring the black male as both father and police officer, she is offered the seemingly egalitarian roles of wife and daughter. In a grand reversal of cultural stereotypes, the African-American woman now occupies the traditional images of the white woman: tied completely to the bourgeois family, she exists both as the housewife Trish Murtaugh (Darlene Love) whose "bad cooking" becomes a joke between men and as the virginal daughter Rianne Murtaugh (Traci Wolfe) who must be saved by them. While for some readers the representation of black women in the more traditional roles of wife, mother, and virginal daughter might signal a positive representational shift, offering as it does black access to the realm of bourgeois culture widely denied until the civil rights era, it would be a mistake to view such representation as evidence of the black woman's real advancement in the struggle for race and gender equality. Indeed, as Robert Stam and Louise Spence write, "[t]he insistence on 'positive images' . . . obscures the fact that 'nice' images might at times be as pernicious as overtly degrading ones, providing a bourgeois facade for paternalism, a more pervasive racism" ("Colonialism, Racism and Representation" 3). The bourgeois facade of *Lethal Weapon* operates, in fact, to tie the black woman to a heterosexual economy in which her body functions not only, in the role of wife, as the plot space for the establishment of a normative (hetero)sexuality but also, in the role of virginal daughter, as the landscape across which interracial masculine bonds can be both formed and maintained.

Most specifically, by focusing its action on the interracial relation of Roger Murtaugh (Danny Glover) and Martin Riggs (Mel Gibson), *Lethal Weapon* seeks to override the potential disruption caused by race by establishing bourgeois culture as the signifier of racial *in*difference while constructing gender as the only significant, and seemingly natural, category of differentiation. All notions of historically constructed differences among black and white are thus recast as a function of capitalist attainment, and the spectacle of middle-class life provides the representation of America with an embodiment of its own democratic ideals. While the alignment of the black female with the representational space most often reserved for white women inculcates her into this democratic ethos, it is the relationship between black and white men that functions as the film's pivotal site for democratic wholeness: the black woman achieves her status only through the black male's connection to, and reaffirmation of, hegemonic power itself. Thus, in *Lethal Weapon,* the image of the black woman circulates in an economy of masculine power where racial differences among men are seemingly eradicated and the democratic rhetoric that has often histori-cally accompanied U.S. patriarchal power is reinscribed.

Like other interracial cop scenarios, *Lethal Weapon* is constructed on a basic pattern. By initially depicting the contrary lives of Murtaugh and Riggs, who are thrown together as partners against their wishes, the film charts their growing respect and affection for one another. Displacing racial difference into less volatile forms such as age, lifestyle, and mental health, *Lethal Weapon* begins in contrast: while Murtaugh enjoys a bath in his well-decorated home with his wife and children singing happy birthday to him, Riggs is shown lying in bed smoking a cigarette, his mobile home wracked by debris. Suicidal because of the recent death of his wife, Riggs is psychi-cally lost, the squalor of his environment indicative of his alienation from the commodified heterosexual norm that the black family represents. In an interesting reversal of paternalistic ideology, it is the white male who, de-bilitated by grief, can be restored to life only through the aid of the black "father"—the figure responsible, in the film's resolution, for drawing the alienated white male back into the folds of sanity and the bourgeois family. Earlier cinematic versions of African-Americans as alienated outsiders are refused in the narrative economy of *Lethal Weapon,* which provides a rep-resentation that shifts the terms of U.S. racial structures: the white male is both victimized—by fate (his wife's death), by his peers (who think he's crazy), and by himself (his suicidal tendencies)—and significantly rehabili-tated from such victimization with the help of a black man. At its deepest level, *Lethal Weapon*'s evocation of a world beyond race enables the white male to regain identity and power across a seemingly egalitarian represen-tation of the black bourgeoisie.

We Do This My Way

Most important perhaps, it is Riggs, a martial arts specialist, who emerges as central in the duo's quest to unravel a suspicious suicide. When Murtaugh's daughter, Rianne, is abducted by the men who orchestrated the suicide, Riggs goes on the offensive: "We do this my way," he tells Murtaugh. "You shoot, you shoot to kill. You get as many as you can." In the process, the white male body becomes the privileged emblem of masculinity in the film, a privileging that begins in the initial scenes where, in contrast to Murtaugh in a bubble bath, the camera follows Riggs's naked figure from his bedroom to the kitchen. In viewing the male body from behind, the camera avoids not simply an X rating, but the castration implicit in the voyeuristic look at male genitalia outside a scene of sexual activity, that is, outside erection and the displacement of desire onto the presence of the female body. In denying the sight of the penis, the film both represses the construction of the spectator's gaze within a homosexual economy of desire and reinscribes the penis as the phallus: Riggs's entire body, in its muscularity and strength, continually evokes the absent penis. Because, as Neale writes, "there is no cultural or cinematic convention which would allow the male body to be presented," the penis itself becomes unrepresentable except as the phallus ("Masculinity as Spectacle" 14).

In this representational process, "male" sexuality—the sighting of sex/genitalia—is transformed into a culturally constructed "masculine" sexuality in which the white male body achieves power and privilege in its reconstruction as stand-in for the absent penis. White masculine sexuality thus presents itself within an economy of desire greater than its parts, a desire through which the overdetermined evocation of parts (the phallus that proliferates in the absence of the penis) wards off castration by reconstructing itself everywhere. The film's various moments of looking at Riggs reclining, running, falling, fighting, shooting are affirmations that the threat of castration has not simply been averted but that the body has now become the phallus, literalizing itself in various displays of phallic authority as the "lethal weapon." In a key scene, Riggs, tortured until he becomes unconscious, hangs by rope from the ceiling when suddenly he springs back to life, attacking his captor and strangling the man with his legs. In a symbolic denouncement of castration, Riggs's body evinces its own phallicism, the villain's neck being literally snapped in the powerful crotch of the hero.

The construction of the white masculine body thus pivots on an exchange from its presentation in the opening scene as the site of the voyeuristic gaze to this later evocation of phallic activity and mastery. To deny our contemplation of Riggs's body in a scene of passive nudity or symbolic castration, in other words, enables the masculine body and its power before the gaze of the camera to not simply remain intact, but to exceed itself. This denial of the gaze stands in contrast to the film's articulation of the sexualized female body, which is overwhelmingly white. In the film's opening sequence, against which the credits are run, the white female body is established as the primary object of the voyeuristic gaze, providing the arena of visible difference across which interracial relations will be formed. From an aerial view of downtown San Francisco, the camera slowly focuses on Amanda Hunsaker (Jackie Swanson) who, clad in lace stockings, lingerie, and high heels, moves to the balcony, teeters briefly on its railing, and jumps. As her body crashes on top of a parked car, the voyeuristic gaze is so insistent that we look at it exposed, spread out *facing* the camera, her femininity—and hence her castration—open to view.

The look at Amanda's purely sexualized body, combined with the later narrative of Murtaugh's daughter, Rianne, whose chastity is threatened, establish what Teresa de Lauretis calls "female-obstacle-boundary-space," that "landscape, stage, or portion of plot-space [where] the female character . . . represent[s] and literally mark[s] out the place (to) which the hero will cross" (*Alice Doesn't* 121, 139). These women's bodies—as virgin (Rianne) and, as we find out later, as whore (Amanda)—evoke the classic construction of female sexuality, even as they invert the racial stereotypes that govern representational economies in U.S. culture. This inversion is crucial to the integrationist narrative, where the sanitary normativity of all the sexual roles within the black family is a necessary precondition for its function as the emotional and moral rehabilitative center for the white male.

To complete the film's emphasis on normative sexuality, Amanda is revealed not only as whore but as lesbian, a revelation that displaces all homosexual tension between the closely bonded men onto white female sexuality. Significantly, the assertion of Amanda's lesbianism is made during a conversation between Riggs and Murtaugh at the police firing range, the woman's lesbianism being framed by images of the men firing their weapons. In this overdetermined phallic setting, Amanda's sexuality reaffirms the masculine as itself the site of heterosexual wholeness; in this way, white female sexuality, while initially charting a heterosexual space, is fully negated as the masculine comes to stand for all culturally accepted sexuality. The narrative of Amanda's sexuality and the images of her body thus function in two ways and, importantly, in this order: first to assert heterosexuality at the film's beginning so that the ensuing scenes of Riggs and Murtaugh naked are read as heterosexual and not homosexual,[16] and, second, to assume the sexual tensions between the men entirely to herself, to the white female and not the male or black female body. In her dual function, the representational paradigm governing the white female is resexualized and racially inverted from virgin/mother to lesbian/whore, so that all sites in this film of unproductive female sexuality leave the space of production entirely to the masculine.

In establishing this racially dichotomized paradigm of sexual difference as the frame of the film, masculine sexuality can appear to be constructed rather homogeneously, with no internal hierarchies or imbalances of power. This illusion is provided by the text of sexual difference, which diffuses and renders secondary the bond's reconstruction of racial difference; through the discourse of sexual difference, the interracial male bond can seal over the frisson of its own construction, enabling all differences among men to be subsumed in the seemingly natural realm of gender. In addition, differences among black and white women can be strengthened, as it is the white woman's death (and her sexually illicit lifestyle) that initiates the narrative drama that threatens both the sanctity and the individual lives of the black family.

While these configurations of race and gender enable the masculine to assume the appearance of homogeneity (and conversely to posit the feminine as the site of disunity and fragmentation), the relations of "looking" established in the film's final scene demonstrate the symbolic significance of the white masculine body as the lethal weapon and the consequent passive position assigned to the black male. Here, in the final confrontation, it is Riggs who does battle with the most hardened criminal, Joshua, while Murtaugh looks on. In his exclusion from the scene of phallic activity, Murtaugh's passive looking confirms his displacement within the field of the masculine, situating Murtaugh in league with the camera's phallicizing of the white male body and marking the black male as physically impotent. Such a construction of the white body as spectacle and the black male as spectator, activator of the look that empowers the white body, demonstrates the underlying representational paradigm of the interracial male bond. In this construction, the white masculine body retains its privilege as the primary site of power while the black masculine role is forced to the margins of the scene; Murtaugh's plea, "Let me take him," and Riggs's response, "No, back off," evince the narrative's inflection of this economy, where the lethal weapon of the white masculine body articulates itself as the central term.

While such a hierarchicalized articulation poses a threat to the democratic enunciations of the interracial bond, it is significant that in this scene the black male is allowed to symbolically take on the power of the white phallus, to appropriate its evocation of masculine sexuality and power. In a configuration of bodies recalling, through inversion, Ralph Ellison's "The Birthmark," the white male, at the conclusion of the fight, leans against Murtaugh, constructing them as one: the white male poses in front of Murtaugh, functioning as his symbolic phallus. When Joshua wrests a weapon from another officer and prepares to shoot, Murtaugh and Riggs respond by drawing their guns. Positioned together, the black male sheltering the white with his raincoat and his body, they shoot Joshua simultaneously. In this way, the scene charts the mastery of the white male body (its ultimate phallic authority) while displacing it in the fusion of an interracial configuration. Ellison's image of the castrated black male functioning as the phallus of his white assailant is thus reconstructed in the cultural production of the 1980s as the black male drawing his own phallic power through the appropriation of the white phallus, an inversion that is symptomatic of contemporary strategies of racial recuperation in U.S. culture.

In characterizing the white male body as the lethal weapon, the film renegotiates its presentation of a world beyond racial difference, evincing within the remasculinization project that marks *Lethal Weapon* a subtle internal hierarchy. Indeed, Riggs's rehabilitation within the space of the black family is countered by his numerous acts of preserving it. In an early scene in the film, it is Riggs who saves Murtaugh's life, forcing the black male to apologize: "[l]ook, sorry about all that shit I said out there. You saved my life. Thank you." The privileging of Riggs is inscribed again when he is the first to escape from his captor, breaking into Murtaugh's torture chamber where the criminals are threatening to rape Rianne. Seconds before Riggs's entrance, the leader tries to silence the irate Murtaugh: "[s]pare me, son. There're no more heroes in the world." But, of course, there are heroes again, as Riggs's immediate appearance evinces, and it is no accident that the hero who comes bursting through the door, the hero who throws the body of his captor on top of an onrushing villain, the hero whose body is the lethal weapon that restores order to this post-1960s world, is white.[17]

An Endangered Species

In positing a racially healed America, *Lethal Weapon* and similar male bonding narratives of the 1980s demonstrate the rhetorical practices of contemporary U.S. cultural production, practices that incorporate the images of black men in popular representation even as those who live under its categorical sign are increasingly displaced by social, political, and economic processes of exclusion. While the visibility of the African-American player in a narrative offering egalitarian possibility seemingly redistributes masculine power, its primary political effect is not only a reaffirmation of the masculine as the basis of cultural power but also a confirmation of the centrality of white supremacy. The remasculinization process functions, in other words, to disrupt *racial* challenges to white supremacy by negotiating that difference through an appeal to masculinity and gender solidarity, thereby making race itself appear to be a settled site on the cultural "frontier." Most crucially, in presenting this story of post–civil rights egalitarianism, the "singular voice" that emerges is that of the white masculine, which has spoken itself not "for the nigger" but for himself, so that he "could be [the] hero."[18]

While configurations of the interracial male bond seem obsessively drawn to these narrative typologies—routinely inverting the historical relationships between identity and cultural marginality—their repetitions are significant not as details of contemporary Hollywood film, but in their circulation within broader negotiatory mechanisms in U.S. culture. David Duke, founder of the National Association for the Advancement of White People and contender for governor of Louisiana in 1991, demonstrates the extreme moment in cultural articulations of white masculine disenfranchisements in the post–civil rights years, articulations that have resulted in increasing support for his (and other similar) political aspirations. Regardless of the extent to which the Republican party wished to dismiss Duke as eccentric to its overall agenda during the early stages of the presidential election in 1992, the significance of his inclusion in mainstream politics and the effectiveness of his inversion of the discourse of civil rights demonstrate the contextual parameters within which images of interracial male bonds currently play. Through this nexus, Duke's fusion of white supremacist logic with the rhetoric of cultural marginality serves as the far-right position of insecurity that interracial male bonds, in a more liberally configured public sphere, can subsequently heal. The bourgeois black male, supporter and defender of the family, ensconced in heterosexuality, and in debt (psychically, if not financially) to the heroic white male offers a scenario of cultural acceptance that not only reinscribes the supremacy of father/family/capital/heterosexuality but also implicitly criminalizes the categories of opposition on which these images of cultural centrality and normativity dwell.

In this regard, the gleaming positivity of black men in interracial male configurations serves as both the precondition for and symbolic achievement of integration's possibility, a possibility articulated within the normative categories instantiating the subject in U.S. culture: masculinity, heterosexuality, and Anglo-American ethnicity. In the ascendancy of these normative positions and in the black male's representational inculcation into their systemic logic, integration entails a process of subjective identification, inscribing the black male within an economy of desire and prohibition that finally and paradoxically depends on the disavowal of differences. Such disavowal necessarily invites psychic violence, as the social subject is asked to identify, seemingly against himself, with a tableau of normativity that links race, in a complex and reinforcing pattern, to class, gender, and sexual hegemonies as well.[19] It is this link across categories of difference that binds the integrationist narrative to social determinations seemingly outside the scope of racial discourse. These representations of interracial male bonding level the threat of black male challenge to white supremacist power by reasserting, through the specter of bourgeois and heterosexual conformity, the patriarchal preconditions that have historically structured the illusion of coherence underwriting modern "man."

As this last comment suggests, what we make of the cultural fascination with interracial male bonding narratives is ultimately indicative of more than the integrationist aesthetic and its recuperation of the threat posed by twentieth-century social protest. It points as well to the enduring—and rapidly transforming—problem of vision and modernity, where the incorporation of the subject into visually coded corporeal identities takes center stage as the defining emblem of the public sphere. That these corporealities are predicated on asymmetries between bodies and their seeming ontologies is part of the racism that wends its way in various registers and modes of deployment through the U.S. social formation, making the challenge of social protest not simply difficult—because uncertain—but often quite painful as well. In our seduction into the visual realm of culture, in our desire to find the visible liberating, in our subjective need to reclaim bodies from their abjection and recuperation, we encounter both the threat and the utopic possibility of contemporary social critique. To forge this critique as part of undoing the illusion of "man," of refusing the myth of masculinity's completion in an interracial domain devoid of women, is to expose the continuing rift within whiteness, that materially violent abstraction that perversely gathers strength by offering itself now as a struggling, innocent, and singular voice.

White Mythologies

5 Canonical Architecture

When Leslie Fiedler's explosive reading of the American literary tradition as a drama "in which a white and a colored American male flee from civilization into each other's arms" appeared in 1960, Stanley Kramer's black and white classic, *The Defiant Ones* (1958), was the only cinematic version of interracial fraternity available to U.S. moviegoers (*Love and Death in the American Novel* 12). For the reader of Fiedler in the 1990s, this paucity of popular images is rather striking in the context of my previous discussion, which analyzed how the decade of the 1980s witnessed one box office film after another modeled on the symbolic marriage among men: from *Stir Crazy* (1980) in the decade's opening year to *Lethal Weapon* II (1989) in its last. For some observers of U.S. culture, such a proliferation might confirm Fiedler's assertion of interracial male bonding as "the central myth of our culture . . . the most deeply underlying image of ourselves," providing as it does a now generic narrativity in which dark male and white confront and overcome the tableau of differences among them (182).

But rather than simply positing the reiteration of buddy images in the popular culture of the 1980s as definitive evidence of the literary critic's profoundly truthful rendering, Fiedler's turn in the early 1960s to interracial male bonding figurations can be understood instead as a prototypical instance of the shift in the production of masculinities that characterizes the second half of the twentieth century more generally. The scene of racial differences among men emerges not simply as a primary social problem, but as this culture's most potentially violent and disruptive internal crisis—a crisis, as I have argued, in which the tenuous interplay of race and gender is renegotiated in the broader transformation from segregation to integration. Where black feminists have critiqued the civil rights movement for its blindness to gender asymmetries, it is in the province of the popular that the final reduction of black liberation struggle to a kind of masculine quest narrative has been most effectively achieved.[1] In this province, the image of interracial fraternity comes to signify the post–civil rights era: the figure of the non-Eurocentric player serving to evince both multicultural differ-ence and its shimmering egalitarian transcendence. In this regard, Fiedler's challenge to the prevailing critical interpretation of the U.S. literary tra-dition as Adamic—his emphasis on Chingachgook, Queequeg, and Jim as key to the antisocial quests of Natty, Ishmael, and Huck—epitomizes the revisionist scenario finalized in the popular domain of the 1980s, as con-temporary bonding narrations likewise displace myths of American singu-larity by heralding interracial fraternity.[2]

From the vantage point of this century's earlier segregationist ideal, the interracial male bond's emphasis on the "mutuality of gender," to use Joseph A. Boone's phrase ("Male Independence and the American Quest Genre" 193), brings into powerful relief the antagonism that underlies the deployment of racial difference in U.S. culture, providing a means for incul-cating the African-American male into the cultural economy along the lines of a shared, "common" subjectivity. But as I have discussed in the last chap-ter, the bond's reliance on gender sameness as the grounds for fashioning the move toward integration is not unqualifiedly revolutionary, no matter how important the transgression of segregation may be. In the transition from the segregationist logic of incontrovertible racial difference to integra-tion's embrace of gender sameness, we encounter the continued, if histori-cally shifting, mechanism that negotiates the contradictions between white supremacist and patriarchal cultural economies: sexual difference. While we may understand the social position of women, of whatever ethnicity, to find its articulation within the framework of a disempowering economy of gender (access to the masculine being summarily denied at the level of the individual woman), the African-American male has been variously located in relation to gender, offered at specific historical moments the priority of masculinity that, at another period, would most strenuously be denied.[3]

Although it is important to recognize the binary representational grid of sexual difference through which African-American male images have been coded, the "either/or" nature of my description above can be misleading. No particular figuration works apart from an engagement with its oppo-sition, and the framework of the masculine does not emerge as unitarily coterminous with either material or representational empowerment, as the example of the mythos of the black male as rapist reveals. In the contem-porary era, in fact, the alignment of the African-American male with an overarching masculine sameness within the interracial bonding configura-tion betrays the cultural panic underwriting the move toward integration,

where the specter of black male equality threatens the racial supremacy ensconced in U.S. patriarchal formations. By negotiating cultural fears around
black male entitlement in the context of representational (as opposed to
economic or political) inclusion, the difficult demands of 1960s civil rights
discourses have been translated into strategies complicit not only with the
expansion of capital's consumer needs but also with a shifting formation of
white supremacy. In the deep disparity between the bond's image of loving
interracial affection, then, and the social, political, and economic displacement of black men in late-twentieth-century America, we encounter one
of the particularly problematical aspects attending integration and its rhetorical invocation as democracy's final achievement.

For Fiedler, the move away from definitive constructions of U.S. literature as coterminous with individual enhancement and solitary sojourning
makes possible a less negating integrationist aesthetic, one that hopes to
challenge white supremacy by offering images of collective political engagement across the divisive bounds of race. But his critical foregrounding of
the bond begins in a curious place, linking as he does in his early, flamboy-
ant piece, "Come Back to the Raft Ag'in, Huck Honey!" (1948), the "Negro
and the homosexual" as the stock themes of interracial male bondings. As
he writes, "the fact of homosexual passion contradicts a national myth of
masculine love, just as our real relationship with the Negro contradicts a
myth of that relationship; and those two myths with their betrayals are . . .
one" (143). Through the figure of interracial fraternity, Fiedler builds a case
for understanding the quintessential American myth as predicated on the
"mutual love of *a white man and a colored*" (146), and it is precisely its
homoerotic content, its love without lust, its disembodiment that constitutes its utopian telos. Why, if sexuality is repressed and denied, did Fiedler
nonetheless begin by linking the negro and the homosexual?

In the full-length treatment of this mythic American nexus, *Love and
Death in the American Novel* (1960), it is significant that Fiedler replaces
the "homosexual" with the concept of the "homoerotic." By 1966, in the
revised edition, Fiedler would explain the shift: "'Homoerotic' is a word of
which I was never very fond. . . . But I wanted it to be quite clear that I was
not attributing sodomy to certain literary characters or their authors, and
so I avoided when I could the more disturbing word 'homosexual'" (349n).
Clearly, the assumption of the homosexual as synonymous with sodomy is,
to use his word, disturbing, but even this shift, he tells us, "has done little
good" in garnering the "proper" reading of his text: "what I have to say
on this score has been at once the best remembered and most grossly mis-

understood section of my book" (ibid.). In his linking of the negro and the homosexual as crucially intertwined in the male bonding narrative, it is the phantasmatic homosexual that continues to haunt the text long after Fiedler's attempt to make him disappear. But in the contemporary era, gay scholars have sought to reclaim the homosexual in the context of the bond's figuration, arguing for his presence, however oblique, in the narrative of male love. In this vein, Robert K. Martin (*Hero, Captain, and Stranger*) reads *Moby-Dick* as an avowedly homosexual text, as is its author, though that homosexuality is spoken through symbolic and metaphoric articulations. For Joseph A. Boone, the homosexual possibilities of the interracial bond as radical political praxis counter the stifling conformities of compulsory heterosexuality.

And what of the negro? That is, as they say, a much different story. Neither Martin nor Boone pays much attention to the interracial aspect of the bonding configuration and, in this elision, they tend to repeat the asymmetries of race through which Fiedler reads the bond. Ultimately, the imbrication of sexuality and race in all of these critical texts is too crucial and too complex to characterize in such simple and potentially dismissive terms, and I certainly don't want to discount the political project of bringing the issue of the homosexual back into critical view in the literary study of closely bonded men. The argument over the specificities of the bond and the particular frameworks through which the bond is read carry their own political portent in the 1990s, drawing us further into questions about the cultural crisis of the masculine and the negotiatory mechanisms that crisis has brought into play. For the narrative of the interracial male bond, read through that early conceptual moment as the negro and the homosexual, begins to chart a history, however provisional, of the bond's lengthy critical appraisal. To that end, this chapter begins with Fiedler, whose reworking of D. H. Lawrence's *Studies in Classic American Literature* (1923) crucially shapes and offers important points of departure for the subsequent explorations of Martin and Boone.

In citing the interracial scene of men together as the essence of an "American" literary tradition, Fiedler's 1960 *Love and Death in the American Novel* challenged the prevailing understanding of the literary tradition by extending the vision of the American hero as, in the words of R. W. B. Lewis, "an individual emancipated from history, happily bereft of ancestry, untouched and undefiled by . . . inheritances of family and race; an individual standing alone, self-reliant and self-propelling" (*The American Adam* 5). Where

Lewis would appoint James Fenimore Cooper's Natty Bumppo as this quintessential "American Adam" — a "figure of heroic innocence and vast potentialities" (1) — Fiedler focuses on Natty's relationship with his Indian soulmate, Chingachgook, examining how the white male's heroic escape from culture (and from the feminine that represents the "domestication" of culture) carries with it a longing for reconciliation with a (simultaneously eroticized and deeroticized) dark brother. By exploring the psychological and racially interdependent dimensions that underlie the quest narratives of white masculine individualism, Fiedler would reject New Critical attempts to maintain separations between the aesthetic and the social, and instead he emphasizes, as he says, "the neglected contexts of American fiction, largely depth-psychological and anthropological, but sociological and formal as well" (*Love and Death* 10).

By reading the literary text as a psychic symptom, the expression of our "deepest communal fantasies" (*Love and Death* 14), Fiedler hypothesizes a cultural unconscious whose meanings emerge most fully not in the singular work but in patterns of repetition traced across a range of texts, patterns he links to the psychic drama of the "American" context itself: "a world which had left behind the terror of Europe not for the innocence it dreamed of, but for new and special guilts associated with the rape of nature and the exploitation of dark-skinned people; a world doomed to play out the imaginary childhood of Europe" (31). By structuring his inquiry around the figurations of love and death as they repeat themselves in sentimental fiction and its renegade offspring, the male bonding quest, Fiedler associates the guilt of betrayal with the psychic reversion to an imaginary innocence, a developmental inversion reflected in the fact that "the typical male protagonist of our fiction has been a man on the run, harried into the forest and out to sea, down the river or into combat — anywhere to avoid . . . the confrontation of a man and a woman which leads to the fall to sex, marriage, and responsibility" (26). In the rejection of the heterosexual world for the "mythic" reconnection to the lost and betrayed other, "the great works of American fiction," Fiedler observes, in a clear echo of Lawrence, constitute a literature for boys, and hence "are notoriously at home in the children's section of the library" (24).

In locating the tension of the literary tradition "between sentimental life in America and the archetypal image . . . in which a white and a colored American male flee from civilization into each other's arms" (*Love and Death* 12), Fiedler's language evokes the homosexual, suggesting that escape from the bonds of culture entails an unambiguous movement toward

homosexual commitment. But contrary to the language he often uses to describe it, this flight is no simple rejection of the heterosexual for the homosexual but, in his formula, the very path of sublimated and conflicted desire.
The systemic repression and overdetermination wrought by the myth of
innocence and its repetitious betrayal (the contradictions and complicities between conscious acts and unconscious motives) strand the protagonist between two seemingly irreconcilable alternatives: innocent homoerotic bonding on one hand and "adult heterosexual love" on the other
(ibid.). Such a formulation constructs a developmental narrative of sexual
desire that locates the homoerotic in an imaginary, pre-symbolic realm,
while casting the heterosexual on the side of uncontested "law," a formulation that reiterates the psychoanalytic compulsion toward maintaining
heterosexuality as a natural psychic achievement. In this understanding of
the structural relationship among sexualities, the homoerotic, as the pre-
symbolic, has the force of originary desire, unmediated and culturally uncontaminated, the site within which nothing is repressed but against which
all repression occurs.

In the Fiedlerian landscape of interracial male bonds, it is this framing
of the homoerotic that accounts for the bond's mythic innocence, its arti-
fice of cultural disarticulation, and its romanticized presentation of masculine relations. By reading the homoerotic as the sublimated origin of a
pure, pre-cultural, and preeminently pre-conscious desire, Fiedler shapes
the particular instance of Natty and Chingachgook into this archetypal
scene: "two lonely men, one dark-skinned, one white, bend together over a
carefully guarded fire in the virgin heart of the American wilderness; they
have forsaken all others for the sake of the austere, almost inarticulate,
but unquestioned love which binds them to each other and to the world
of nature which they have preferred to civilization" (*Love and Death* 192).
Here, the opposition between nature and culture forms the central allegory
for the sexual,[4] necessitating that the bonds linking red man and white be
forged literally in the wilderness where, in the absence of women and culture, differences of race and region can be rendered meaningless and the
lofty, spiritual stability of an unquestioned and nonsexual love affirmed. As
the constitutive element of the bond, "the purity of such unions, the fact
that they join soul to soul rather than body to body" enables an imaginative transgression of the social codes marked by race, denying not only its
cultural significance, but also the possibility of an interracial sociality that
"threatens always to end in miscegenation" (368).

In recognizing that the male bond displaces social fears around miscegenation, Fiedler inadvertently reveals the contradiction residing in the discourse of myth and archetype to which his readings are wed—that the homoerotic dream quest is not simply the manifestation of an essentialized mass imagination, but an active representational site for negotiating the nexus of gender, race, and nation on "new world" shores. It is here that a taboo marking a particularly violent figuration of the limits of cultural sanction and desire—that of an interracial, procreative, and nonpropertied heterosexuality—is displaced onto an image of "two lonely men, one dark-skinned, one white." While the chaste love of men does indeed, as Fiedler suggests, circumvent the threat of miscegenation, it does so in a representational circuit inscribed by, and not in excess of, social scriptings of race and gender. In her early feminist rereading of the U.S. critical canon, Nina Baym describes the inversion of social power relations that underwrite narratives of masculine escape: "[i]n these stories, the encroaching, constricting, destroying society is represented with particular urgency in the figure of one or more women. . . . [A]lthough women are not the source of power, they are experienced as such" ("Melodramas of Beset Manhood" 133). If we understand "woman" as a heterogeneous entity, Baym's interpretation can be extended to demonstrate that it is the white woman, as reproductive agent for a racially coded citizen body, who stands as emblem of the constricting forces of the social. At the same time, the non-Eurocentric female character is routinely evacuated from the scene, locatable only as the excess of binary gender relations that propel the mythic escape toward unadulterated union.

This fracturing of the feminine significantly replays, even as it reconfigures, the arrangement of bodies in the lynching and castration scene. Here, as I have discussed in earlier chapters, the potential association of the white feminine and the black masculine is disrupted through their symbolic embodiment as emblematic civilization threatened by monstrous black phallicity. Within the literary scenario of radical individualism and heroism, the white man's escape from culture to the virgin elsewhere transforms the white feminine, as the flower of civilization in need of protection, into the agent of alienation, thereby allowing the red, black, or brown man to assume the role of the white man's compassionate, nonconsummate lover. In both narrative situations—the lynch motif and the interracial male adventure—the mapping of the feminine in relation to the masculine establishes the contours for instantiating or alleviating racial hierarchies among men, demonstrating the profoundly overdetermined function of sexual difference to define and proscribe differences of "race" in U.S. culture. A crucial component of both narrative instances is the disaffiliation of the non-Eurocentric woman from the province of the feminine: her position within the lynch scenario emerges as significatory absence just as she is unfigured in the bond's representation of the constrictions of culture as feminine.

Contrary to Fiedler's sentimentalized notion of the bond as the "mutual love of *a white man and a colored*" ("Come Back to the Raft Ag'in" 146), then, the interracial male couple provides a framework through which tensions within hierarchical social arrangements can be mediated, a mediation in which racial equality is understood through the cultural repertoire of gender sameness. In the world of men together, the "Holy Marriage of Males" provides the contrast to "mere heterosexual passion," suggesting for Fiedler that at the base of U.S. literary traditions is "a general superiority of the love of man for man over the ignoble lust of man for woman" (*Love and Death* 382, 368, 369). But in positing the interracial male bond as the binary opposition to heterosexual passion, the complexities of the relationships between homoeroticism, homosexuality, and heterosexuality as they structure and are structured by patriarchal organization are obscured. By insisting on the nonsexual nature of the homoerotic bond, "a passionless passion, simple, utterly satisfying, yet immune to lust — physical only as a handshake is physical, this side of copulation" (368), the heterosexual can be maintained as a devalued but nonetheless institutionally compulsory configuration. Not only does this define female sexuality within the domain of reproduction, but it makes possible male gender identities and identifications "uncontaminated" by the castigating influences of the feminine. These dual trajectories mark the patriarchal economy as reliant simultaneously on the homoerotic (bonds among men) and on the heterosexual (compulsory reproduction), demonstrating not an opposition but a contiguity between Fiedler's innocent homosexuality and mature heterosexuality.

This contiguity can be expressed by the concept of the homosocial, a term used by Eve Kosofsky Sedgwick to identify the continuum of male bonding activities that comprise a social formation, activities which may, "as in our society, be characterized by intense homophobia, fear and hatred of homosexuality" (*Between Men* 1). As a term "obviously formed by analogy with 'homosexual,' and just as obviously meant to be distinguished from [it]" (1), the homosocial can locate the contradiction in patriarchal relations between the primacy accorded to relationships among men and the compulsory imperative of heterosexual reproduction. By reading both trajectories of social organization as mediated by the taboo against actual (as opposed to the culturally sanctioned innocent) homosexuality, Sedgwick reveals the path of heterosexual desire as deeply homosocial, for even within the heterosexual circuit, "we are here in the presence . . . of a desire to consolidate partnership with authoritative males in and through the bodies of females. . . . [M]en's heterosexual relationships . . . have as their raison d'être an ultimate bonding between men" (38, 50).[5] The heterosexual contract, contrary to Fiedler's representation, is not the source of a mature equality among men and women, nor is it the supersession of the homo-eroticism underlying the "innocence" of the bond. Instead, it needs to be understood as a particularly powerful contiguous mechanism for the subvention of patriarchal relations. By failing to read in the literature of male bonding the complexities and asymmetries on which their representations of gender rest, Fiedler ultimately mystifies the relationship between heterosexuality and the homoerotic. Instead, he produces a paradigm of desire and sexuality that falsely opposes male bonds to heterosexual normativity, and thereby he casts homosexuality as the immaturity of arrested psychosexual development.

But it is only in this way that Fiedler can simultaneously sanction the homoeroticism of the male bond (and the great works of "children's" literature it has spawned), ward off the threat of homosexuality, and justify the evacuation of the feminine as precursor to interracial achievement. Such critical moves are part of the construction of a mythic "American" unconsciousness, a construction that significantly takes place without defining the subjective determinations through which this unconscious has purportedly emerged. In the articulation of a literary tradition that obsessively narrates the European son's renegade flight to a land more myth than real, "America," we witness a cultural dream of guilt and expiation founded on the psychic dimensions of an equally mythic white masculine subjectivity. This mythic subjectivity, marked by a narrative of desire that transforms systems of exploitation and oppression into mutuality and originary sameness, romanticizes social hierarchy by exchanging the conflict of race and nation for a "literature for boys" where the white male "ends up lying in the arms of the colored man" (*Love and Death* 389). This is an old myth, Fiedler tells us, one that "sinks deeper and deeper into the national mind, intertwined with nostalgic memories of books that we have read as children, like our fathers before us and theirs before them" (ibid.). The patriarchal paternity at work in this genealogy reproduces the elision at the heart of the interracial male bond where the absence of women is rendered natural by the narrative's masculinization, and the possibility of delineating the contours of the dark man's subjectivity is eschewed for the nostalgia of Anglo-American males.

The old myth that "comes to seem truer than the reality of headlines," that finds "not Little Rock but Hannibal [as] the place where black and white confront each other" emerges as the ego investment of white masculine subjectivity, the "us" and "our" of Fiedler's discourse returning forever to the singularity of the mirror where, as even he realizes, "this is finally a very personal book, in which I attempt to say with my own voice out of my own face (all masks abandoned) what I have found to be some major meanings of our literature and culture" (*Love and Death* 389; 13). By couching this personal voice in the language of myth and archetype, the unequivocal and reciprocal love of "white man and colored" that Fiedler finds at the center of the U.S. tradition is barely questioned for its inability to recognize the dark man's subjectivity outside the scene of white male guilt and expiation. Indeed, the very fact that these narratives "dramatize compulsively . . . the colored man as . . . victim" signals the enduring function of the archetype, which "makes no attempt to deny the facts of outrage or guilt. . . . It merely portrays them as meaningless" in the face of the bond's sentimental passion (389, 390). While Fiedler would later challenge (to some extent) the white masculine inscriptions of canonical architecture, the continuity he ascribes to the U.S. tradition is here predicated on the psychological centrality of the white masculine figure, whose normative positionality in relation to race and gender is heightened within the bonding narrative, as well as within its critical discussion.[6]

While I do not discount the productive value of the interracial male bond to the psychodrama of white heterosexual masculinity, Fiedler's romanticization of its suffering guilt and necessary dream of expiation offers rather little in the way of historical understandings of race, gender, and nation. Only through the critical disarticulation of its mythic inscription of brotherhood can the various functions underlying its production be brought to bear since the seduction of the bonding scenario lies precisely in its ability to transcribe the hierarchical weight and significance of race into a further instance of the masculine same, a sameness unrelenting in its extrapolation of the white man's heroic alienation, compassion, and guilt. Such sameness becomes the cleared ground for definitions of "America," thereby investing the interracial male bond with reproductive responsibilities, not the miscegenating kind (the bond already disarms that), but the spiritual and symbolic procreations that engender "America" along an unambiguously masculine line. As Fiedler writes of his text: "it does not spring to life unbegotten, unaffiliated and unsponsored. In one sense, it has been essentially present from the moment that I read aloud to two of my sons (then five and seven) for their first time *Huckleberry Finn*" (*Love and*

Death 13). This textual and textualized insemination, issued from father to son, is part of the paternal legacy Fiedler has inherited, and it culminates in this equation: "the truth one tries to tell about the indignities and rewards of being the kind of man one is—an American, let's say, in the second half of the twentieth century, learning to read his country's books" (16).

To read his country's books is to be inscribed within a narrative of white paternity, a paternity devoid of the very differences among men that define the "America" of Fiedler's American tradition. This elision, I would say, is the essence of the interracial male bond in its most frequent incarnation, an essence indicative not of the mythic mass mind, but of the political, social, and economic tensions underwriting masculine relations in their various historical configurations. As such, it is no accident that we witness, over the course of the nineteenth century, the transformation of the bond from the friendship between white man and Indian to "the fugitive slave and the no-account boy" (*Love and Death* 368), a transformation that evinces the bond's relation to shifting tensions within the structure of white racial supremacy. It is in this sense, too, that Fiedler's own text, written in the late 1950s, can be read as mediating the historical conditions of its production, locating in the face of growing African-American protest against segregation, the Adamic escape from women as an originary, pre-cultural compulsion toward the brown or black man. Such a reading of the literary tradition, of "the most deeply underlying image of ourselves," hinges on disavowing the psychological terror of race violence by transfiguring Little Rock into Hannibal, that place where "our dark-skinned beloved will rescue us . . . [and] comfort us, as if he knew our offense against him were only symbolic—an offense against that in ourselves which he represents—never truly *real*" (182, 389). In Fiedler's critical universe, as in the bond's cultural deployment, the outrage against Jim Crow is recast as symbol of the white man's internal drama, where the image of "two lonely men, one dark-skinned, one white" replaces that specter of race war known as Little Rock.

In citing Natty, Ishmael, and Huck as sojourning not alone but in tandem with a dark brother, Fiedler's reinterpretation of the Adamic narrative of individual escape and alienation serves as one of the first integrationist responses to canonical literature and is, in that sense, a politically revisionary work. Its initial appearance as an essay in 1948 and its later reworking into *Love and Death in the American Novel* in 1960 straddle the most incendiary years of the McCarthy period, marking a relation to Cold War rhetoric (and hysteria) that cannot go unnoted. Here, in fact, is where we might locate the seemingly necessary terminological shift—that attempt by Fiedler to cleanse the bond even further of its potential homosexual implications, of the very fact that in his reading of male bonds the heterosexual is jettisoned and the homosocial is literally superimposed onto it. The move from Huck's childish affection to the constitution of a national masculine infatuation with the "negro" is anxiety-inducing to the extreme, and in the various productions of cultural panic around potential otherness in the 1950s, Fiedler's challenge, even in its seemingly purged form, carries a threat of social and symbolic ruin. If the fairy is among us in the misogynist flight from home, if the turn away from women dissolves into homosexual innuendo, what becomes of locker and board room, judicial and legislative chamber?

It is also the case that Fiedler's figuration of homosexuality was itself subtended by heterosexist assumptions and patriarchal ideologies, as I have demonstrated, and that the obsessive response to the question of the homosexual had the effect of negating the negro as anything other than white masculine meaning. In this regard, Fiedler's psychological universalism ironically reinscribes the centrality of the Adamic figure he seemed to argue against by defining literary encounters among racially differentiated men as both symbols and symptoms of the psychodrama of white masculinity. In founding this psychodrama on the betrayal of and longed-for reconciliation with other men, Fiedler's redefinition of the U.S. literary landscape simultaneously reads and encodes the transformation of the historic agency of African-American protest into a sentimental male bonding relation. That such sentimentalization emerges as the definitive mark of white masculine subjectivity is perhaps less disconcerting than the critical elision propelling Fiedler's interpretive paradigm: his use of myth and archetype to fashion a transhistorical Oedipal trauma that integrates the "Negro and the homosexual" as intertwining thematic concerns, negating their subjective positionalities as components of the categories "man" and "America." Fiedler's critical reading thus encodes the very specular feature that interracial male bonding in the cinema of the 1980s came to rely on: the use of the dark brother as vehicle for forging a singular and monolithic account of masculine subjectivity.

This effect is not achieved through sinister bad will, but according to the assumptions underlying myth criticism. As Philip Fisher has discussed in his introduction to *The New American Studies:*

> Myth is a fixed, satisfying, and stable story used again and again to normalize our account of social life. By means of myth, novelty is

tamed by being seen as the repetition or, at most, the variation, of a known and valued pattern. Even where actual historical situations are found to fall short of myth or to lie in its aftermath, the myth tames the variety of historical experience, giving it familiarity while using it to reaffirm the culture's long-standing interpretation of itself. (vii)

While myth may not be quite so trans- or anti-historical, the case of Fiedler demonstrates the normalizing, through the creation of a pattern of repetition, of historical experience to coincide with American culture's interpretation of itself as the renegade son whose quest away from the domination of Europe necessitates a radical abandoning of social conformity and an embrace of difference as the evidence for democratic transcendence. By its very practice, interpretation necessitates at each historical juncture a variety of negotiations through which material conditions can be brought within the ideological scope of a nationalist interpretation. Fiedler's *Love and Death in the American Novel* bears witness to the materialist pressure of the struggle against segregation by forging a mythic narrative of inclusion that reasserts the historical transcendence of America.

While the effects of Fiedler's reliance on myth and archetype make one skeptical of the political possibilities of this methodological emphasis (and of the politics of the male bond to sustain its challenge of social norms), it is interesting that recent critical readings of this literary configuration insist on the bond's subversive potential. Most important, these liberatory readings emerge from two of the leading gay studies scholars working in American literature and culture. For Robert K. Martin, whose comments are set in the context of a critical reevaluation of Melville's sea novels, the male bond's "democratic union of equals" is capable of achieving "feminist goals" (*Hero, Captain, and Stranger* 11, 94). Masculine friendship, in short, challenges the appropriative and hierarchical gender structure of heterosexual coupling, which is viewed not as the culmination of mature development — what Fiedler calls "adult heterosexual love" (*Love and Death* 12) — but as a social relation of domination "founded upon the inequality of partners" (Martin 7). By pointedly refashioning homosexuality as a political category of social identity *and* sexual practices, Martin critiques both Fiedler's linkage of homosexuality with "innocence" and his attention to "the sacred marriage [of males not] as an alternative to dominant social patterns but rather as an evasion of them" (9). In redrawing the political agenda around which images of masculine fraternity are critically approached, Martin's discussion is itself part of the growing emergence of lesbian and gay critical studies in the 1980s, an emergence that has produced broadscale rearticulations of the terrain of the sexual in U.S. culture.[7] Often in league with feminism, and in many ways made possible by it, lesbian and gay studies has furthered the understanding of sexuality as socially constructed, forging crucial distinctions between sexual identities, practices, and their differing relationships with social forms of power.

Martin contributes to this body of scholarship not only by refusing to dismiss the centrality of masculine fraternity to Melville's oeuvre but also by insisting that the celebratory phallicism of Ishmael and Queequeg in *Moby-Dick,* nonaggressive and uneconomic in its production, constitutes a homosexual textuality central in Melville's time and our own to challenging the politics of the sex/gender system. Therefore, Martin rejects Fiedler's ascription of the novel in America as conjoining the homosexual with the "Negro," finding instead that "the proper model for an analysis of the condition of the homosexual is not the racial one but the sexual one: the situation of homosexuals in contemporary society is related to the situation of women" (13). While this shift discounts how the racial is itself sexualized in U.S. culture (the way blackness, for instance, has been aligned with the feminine), the figuration of homosexuality within a sexual paradigm assures the theoretical centrality of the discourse of sexual difference to images of closely bonded men. And yet, it also, paradoxically, establishes a heterosexual gendered paradigm as the vehicle for reading the homosexual: "[a] man entering into a homosexual relationship abdicates, in part, his role in the economy of power; no longer controlling women, he must therefore 'become' a woman" (14). Such a strict and seemingly incontrovertible binary opposition between (feminine) margin and (masculine) center maintains the logic of heterosexual coupling, even as Martin goes on to describe the force and power of homosexuality in Melville's universe as a transgression of patriarchal assumptions and social organizations.[8] Through the "affirmation of the values of nonaggressive male-bonded couples," he contends, "the power of the patriarchy can be contested and even defeated" (70).

For Martin, the quintessential Melvillean response to the possessive, destructive impulses of dominant masculinity can be found in the bond between Ishmael and Queequeg, whose coupling acts as the egalitarian antithesis to heterosexuality's hierarchical inscriptions:

> The destruction of the *Pequod* and its crew is a sign of the social disaster that for Melville followed upon the imposition of exclusive white male power in its search for control over all that is nature or non-

self, while the survival of Ishmael is made possible only through the example, love, and self-sacrifice of Queequeg. Ishmael's return to the surface . . . is an indication, in one of the novel's symbolic patterns, of the . . . restoration of the feminine and maternal to a world that has forsworn all softness and affection. Ishmael survives the cataclysm of patriarchal aggression to be restored to the lost maternal principle from which he has been exiled. (70)

But what of the power relationship between dark man and white? After all, it is Queequeg's coffin, literally scripted with the signs borne on his body, that enables Ishmael's return from the depths of the sea—a sacrifice, as Martin says, but is it one that heralds a protofeminist, anti-patriarchal possibility? Why this desire to transform femininity (as a maternal, soft, affectionate, self-sacrificing, loving emblem) into a vehicle for and symbol of patriarchy's transgression? Why gender as gender's transcendence? And why, in the process, such an evacuation of the significance of race and racial hierarchies?

Part of the answer to these questions lies in Martin's attempt to link the political struggles of gay men with feminism as a way of forging a commonality of interests that can aid contemporary political struggle. But must gay men become the feminine in order for feminism to understand the need to form political alliances within and across differences of sexuality and sexual preferences? To be sure, Martin's use of gender to orchestrate gender's transcendence is a provocative counter to the essentialized understanding of bodies that underlies the script that heterosexuality offers.[9] But when he asserts that "Melville's work may be seen as a consistent appeal against the "feminization" or domestication of American culture" and that "male homosexuality is . . . a means of rejecting effeminacy" (*Hero, Captain, and Stranger* 15), the contradictions are arresting. If the homosexually bonded interracial couple in Melville's text functions on the side of the feminine (evoking it, restoring it), how can homosexuality also be an appeal against feminization? A similar paradox resides in the status of the phallus. On one hand, Martin claims that Melville's "insistence on the presence of the phallus" (15) was a way of challenging the incipient feminization of nineteenth-century culture, a response to the (perceived) domesticating features of (white) women's emergence into the public sphere. At the same time, Martin assures us that "the emphasis on the phallus of which I speak is directed toward the kind of celebration of its erotic potential that is characteristic of matriarchal cultures" (15–16). The primacy of the phallus as image and symbol is thus simultaneously an avenue for a masculine reinvigoration *and* a characteristic of matriarchal cultures, both a protest against feminization and an emblem of a female-centered world. And both of these significatory functions are found within narrative scenarios that take place at sea, in a context defined primarily by women's absence.

What is most striking here is the clear disjunction between the political agenda of a male homosexuality that can somehow be protofeminist and woman-centered, yet oppositional to feminization and situated in a world composed only of men. In one of his most stunning paradoxes, Martin thus envisions the exclusion of women from the symbolic social order of the ship as the radical and necessary precondition for the transformation of patriarchal relations. By "eliminating the role of women in these novels," Martin claims that Melville can contrast the oppositional undercurrents within masculine sexuality: the "democratic eros" found in male friendship that reflects "the celebration of a generalized seminal power not directed toward control or production; and a hierarchical eros expressed in social forms of male power as different as whaling, factory-owning, military conquest, and heterosexual marriage" (*Hero, Captain, and Stranger* 4). The binary inscribed here reiterates the oppositional relation between homosexuality and heterosexuality, marking the homo as the site of a purified, committed male love and the hetero as its degraded counterpart. In both cases, the phallus functions as the primary signifier of the sexual, demonstrating not a transgression of patriarchal logic—that would, for instance, allow female desire(s) to be represented—but an appropriation of all erotic alternatives in the name of seminal power.[10]

While it is not impossible to imagine the realization of "some important feminist goals" (*Hero, Captain, and Stranger* 94) in a world without women (precisely because sexual difference does not require the scene of woman for its enactment or subversion), the desire to transform a romanticized male homosexual textuality into the framework for democratic union asks us to believe that love between men, as opposed to conquest and aggression, is the essential counterpoint to patriarchal dominations. This is clear in Martin's description of the ending of *Moby-Dick*, where among the chaotic destruction forged by patriarchal excess there exists "a pastoral vision of a restored harmony that might be achieved if only men would learn to love each other (individually and socially)" (ibid.). While it would be deeply problematical to disparage relationships "based on the principles of equality, affection, and respect for the other" (ibid.), it is nonetheless unclear how a noncompetitive masculine love for one another can translate into the kind of broad social transformation necessary to the abatement of patriarchy. To transgress the order of compulsory heterosexuality is not in and of itself a transformation of the symbolic and cultural laws that encode and enforce its centrality as normative. Indeed, Martin's singular scripting of masculinity as either patriarchal or anti-patriarchal might finally obscure more than it reveals about masculinity, sexuality, and the social production of power in U.S. culture.

In this kind of oppositional logic, Martin forges an image of the social that depends not only on the spatial conceptions of margin and center but also on a privileging of the margin as inherent locus of subversion. In the wake of a variety of poststructuralist teachings and in the context of contemporary political crises, such a position has become nearly impossible to maintain, inscribing as it does a deterministic understanding of power and marking subjective positionalities as uncontradicted, nonconflicted domains. It is this that finally undermines Martin's interpretive strategy, for in the idealization of the margins, he both rigidifies relations of sexual domination and comes to equate all marginal positions (of gender, race, class, sexuality) as the same. In positing, for instance, that "[t]he marriage of Queequeg and Ishmael is a vision of a triumphant miscegenation that can overcome the racial and sexual structures of American society" (*Hero, Captain, and Stranger* 94), Martin suspends close scrutiny of the implications of this metaphoric miscegenation—its culmination in the dark man's sacrifice for the white man's rebirth—in favor of an elevated praise for the loving bond of undifferentiated and seemingly equal men. "[P]oor Ishmael survives alone," Martin laments, "only symbolically supported by Queequeg; even there, it seems, Melville was not able to imagine what it might have been like for two men to love each other *and survive*" (7). The clear repression of the significance of race as a determining factor in the narrative's solution is a striking reinscription of the asymmetrical power that structures relations among men.

But while I may challenge Martin's dismissal of race in an interpretive framework that overtly seeks feminist goals, it is finally some of feminist theory's own paradigmatic elisions that his critical perspective encodes.[11] In offering an understanding of the social positionality of "man" along lines marked primarily by the hierarchical relations of sexual difference, Martin seems stranded within that earlier moment in feminist theorizations of the social when female homosexuality served as the first wave of difference to question the monolithic sanctity of "woman." Martin's attempt to clear the ground of the masculine same by inserting sexuality as difference in relations among men rehearses this necessary gesture, but it too uniformly constructs the realm of social positionality within the sex/gender system, displacing other formations (here, most notably race) that not only condition the very shape and substance of sexual difference but also challenge its theoretical logic and stability. That there is no realm in which masculinity or femininity can be fractured off from their determination in relation to other axes of difference necessitates an approach to issues of interracial male bonding attentive not just to normative sexual and gendered dimensions, but importantly to those of race as well.

The kinds of issues I have raised in connection to Martin's exploration of masculine fraternity perhaps circulate most coherently within broader critical discussions about the political and theoretical relationship of men to feminism, discussions that are almost always difficult and antagonistically formed.[12] Certainly a great amount of this difficulty involves the pressure such issues impose on feminism's historical reliance on female identity as the founding framework for its political articulation. In the context of a growing number of men trained in feminist academic discourses, as well as the rise of lesbian and gay studies and other recent investigative turns toward masculinities within the sex/gender system, the epistemological assurance of feminism as a collective "voice" or identity forged in the name of women has begun to give way. Add to this feminism's own dawning emphasis on women's multiple and noncommensurate subjective figurations in terms of race, class, sexuality, and nation, and one recognizes the broad-scale internal critique and transformation around "identity" that feminism currently engages. The contemporary debate over men and/in feminism must thus be seen not as an issue imposed by men, but as a response to political arguments and challenges that feminism has elicited, a struggle that both encompasses and exceeds "men and feminism" by importantly challenging the very epistemological security of "women's" relationship to feminism itself.

Interracial male bonding narratives and their critical canon are particularly interesting from this perspective, where identities in crisis comprise not only the cultural context governing their deployments but also the political and theoretical problematic that feminism brings to bear. If it is true that feminism has in many ways drawn its organizational sustenance from a counteridentity formation (locating in "woman" and "women" that which is excluded from patriarchy and therefore, as the logic goes, that which can most effectively undermine it), it is equally true that the iden-

tity of "man" and "men" has provided feminism with the definitional relation underpinning its understanding of patriarchy: as the central locus of
the patriarchal, masculine identity has served as the cohesive term through
which feminism has mapped the psychological and political determinations of the social itself.

Under these conditions, it is not altogether bizarre to suggest that the mythology of masculine fraternity functions, in a way akin to feminist invoca-
tions of sisterhood and common oppression, as the instantiation of both a
complicitous and potentially resistant rhetoric. In the contemporary popular realm, as in canonical literary formations, interracial male bonding narration obsessively replays mythic male union as a counter to the fragmentation and historically shifting "nature" of masculine identities within the
social. While I have read various films and critical evaluations in terms of
their mutual ideological effects (the primacy of the white masculine figure,
for instance), the proliferation of these images attests to the ongoing crisis
of identity in U.S. culture and points to the incoherency that contemporary
representations of the masculine simultaneously foreground and allay. As
in feminist theory's current attention to the limitations of identity and in
the context of postmodern understandings of subjectivity as multiple and
contradictory, it is the significance of this incoherency that has emerged as
central to rethinking both the political as a category and its epistemological foundation for struggle.[13] Therefore, it is particularly interesting that
critical discussions of masculine fraternity, drawing on feminist theory and
its political commitment to patriarchal disruptions, would so forcefully insist on the achievement of cohesion within the interracial male bond, an
achievement that tends to recontain differences among men within a rather
singular and monolithic subjective function.

Joseph A. Boone's discussion of the male bond in *Tradition Counter Tradition* (1987) is most telling in this regard. While it offers a sophisticated
understanding of the theoretical issues involved with linking masculine relations to feminist goals, it curiously reinscribes the centrality of the white
male by defining his attainment of a coherent, self-affirming identity as the
culmination of a radical social critique. As we shall see, this possibility is
contingent on displacing power asymmetries between racially differentiated
men in a narrative focus on the male bond's encodement in quest literature
where "the outward voyage to confront the unknown . . . simultaneously
traces an inner journey toward a redefinition, a 'remaking' of self that defies, at least partially, social convention and sexual categorization" (228–
229). By ascribing the dynamics of this inner journey to the protagonists

of such classic bonding novels as *Moby-Dick* and *Huckleberry Finn,* Boone charts a "counter-tradition" to the "courtship and wedlock plotting" of the literature of sentimental romance (226). Here, in language that recalls, alternately, Lawrence, Lewis, Fiedler, and Martin, a "single or unattached protagonist existing outside the boundaries of matrimonial definition or familial expectation" is able to discover "an affirming, multiform self that has begun to break through the strictures traditionally imposed on male social identity" (226, 228).

Boone's emphasis on "self" and "identity" signals his critical paradigm's most foregrounded assumption — that the problematic of masculine domination necessitates the "reintegration of [men's] often fragmented identity, a leveling of the reductively constructed hierarchies of heart and mind as well as those severed "halves" of personality associated . . . with the two sexes" (*Tradition Counter Tradition* 229). Such reintegration heralds the complete and "true self" (ibid.), one that exceeds the bifurcation of masculine and feminine constituted in the social script of gender and reiterated by the traditional marital relation itself. In this process, the feminine as a category of personal qualities and attributions can be incorporated into the male quester's identity as a way of challenging "society's constitution of "the feminine" as a specifically female and hence "inferior" category" (239). Significantly, Boone recognizes the potential appropriative gesture inherent in notions of integrating the feminine into man where the feminine's incorporation can simply reinscribe the dualism of gender. Instead, he "envision[s] a male subjectivity for which the 'feminine' is never 'other' because it is already an intrinsic, integral aspect of a dynamically multiform self" (ibid.). And it is this vision that he charts in the work of Melville and Twain, where the traditional conflict between masculine and feminine subjective formations is unhinged from its biologized essentialism and explored in worlds that are devoid of women, but indebted to the expansive possibilities of the feminine nonetheless.

Even if we consider the linguistic straitjacket imposed by gender — the very difficulty of defining alternative modes of sexual "identities" that do not reiterate the oppositional logic of sexual difference — can feminism risk the assumption that the male incorporation of the feminine as a non-Other relation will necessarily lead to a transformation of women's economic, social, and political *positions* in U.S. culture? Is there not a difference, a deeply important political difference between the realms of the individual psychosexual and the structural relations of which patriarchal domination is only a part? Most important, what political effect do we imagine from the equation that occurs in Boone's discourse between male dis-identification with the masculine on the one hand, and male identification with the feminine on the other? These questions seem to me central to the kind of critical paradigm offered by Boone's analysis, where the individual drama of masculinity emerges as the landscape/seascape of potential revolutionary praxis and thereby inscribes a masculine quest toward subjective wholeness as the precondition for patriarchal transcendence. That this "wholeness" is defined not in antagonism to the feminine but as an embrace of its potentially threatening alterity signals for Boone its radical redefinition, but I am struck by the formulation of such a social vision where notions of "true self," "independent self," "fluid identity," "inclusive, unlimited identity," "complete sense of self," and "autonomous selfhood" circulate as the teleology of political struggle (*Tradition Counter Tradition* 229, 243, 247, 251, 253, 252). This replication of the individualism and mythology of self-definition that heralds capitalist subjective formations fails to register the complexities not only of the subject's relation to the social, but of the social itself.

Boone is able to chart this replication as an emancipatory agenda, in part, through the formalist aspect of his reading, where the relationship of the quest's narrative plot and textual structure to its protagonist's psychological struggle work are intertwined. Ishmael's rejection of socially restrictive roles, for instance, is formally cast as Melville's rejection of traditional textual organization and plotting. As in *Moby-Dick,* Boone contends, the quest novel eschews the symmetrical narrative models of romance literature—which typically feature conflict-separation-resolution—by moving toward open form, multifaceted textual voices, and disparate representational modes. In this way, "the reader gains the sense not merely of several types of narrative strung together, but of one mode after the other being left behind, traveled beyond, as the evolving quest carries both reader and protagonist into increasingly uncharted and heteroglossic realms of discourse and plot" (*Tradition Counter Tradition* 240). In defining the form of the quest as an intrinsic aspect of the quest itself, Boone locates a new narrative rhythm, "a counter-traditional geography of male desire in fictional form" (241). At the heart of such a countertradition is a revolutionary mode of characterization, one that defies the linear model of psychological development for a variated pattern. Here, "as 'voices' and subjects of their texts' ever-shifting registers, Ishmael and Huck . . . attest to a construction of personality that embraces the fullness of contradiction and difference" (ibid.). In the process, their individuality and self-definition are affirmed, as a wholeness of identity emerges through the confrontation and incorporation of contradiction and difference.

Unification through contradiction. Difference as the vehicle for an expansive, fluid self. It is at the level of these figurations of identity that my skepticism about the accumulative logic of subjective wholeness is particularly engaged, since it is here that the white masculine protagonist of the quest genre encounters the racially differentiated masculine "Other" and is most fully liberated from his struggle with self-division and internal chaos by moving toward "inclusive, unlimited identity" (*Tradition Counter Tradition* 251). Such inclusivity pivots on an unacknowledged transformation of all social differences into the protagonist's internalized order of completion, allowing him an inclusive, affirming, and socially transgressive identity that is significantly achieved by no one else. What does it mean, for instance, that Huck's "multiple roles, identities, and fabricated biographies . . . give him the figurative space within which to develop a more complete sense of self" (253), when the very framework of such figurative space is made possible by the social scripting of race and gender — of white masculinity — that he enjoys? For Boone, these movements into unknown identities are enabled by the protagonist's narrative positioning as outside the realm of culture. But it seems to me that very specific aspects of his cultural coding underwrite the possibilities of transgression from the outset, aspects of cultural coding that do not cease to function merely because the narrative takes us down river or out to sea. It is not a great surprise that the transgressive image of masculine completion resides within a textual body defined, implicitly if not altogether explicitly, by white skin.

The fact is: the multiform self that Boone heralds as evidence of a new rhythm of masculine desire is transgressive only when we remain within the narrative logic of a romantic countertradition, where the image of a socially nonconformist masculinity — nonaggressive, fluid, encompassing — can subvert the dynamic of domination linked to patriarchal manifestations.[14] By thinking only through the paradigm of sexual difference, and understanding it primarily as an oppositional relation between masculine and feminine/male and female, the presence of an interracial male bonding configuration in quest literature can become the primary vehicle for gender's transcendence.[15] As Boone writes:

> [T]he male bond opens the way to an undivided identity, once Ishmael learns to overcome his initial prejudices and recognize in this seemingly racial "other" a mutual companion, an equal spirit, and an equivalent, mirroring self. And because this bond ultimately rests on equality and a mutual recognition of independent identities, it encodes, as Baym has observed, a set of values directly "opposite . . . the

usual female-male association"; it affirms one's individuality without halving it. (*Tradition Counter Tradition* 245)

The language of "*one's* individuality" betrays the singular trajectory of identity's articulation, not just in Boone's criticism or the canonical literature from which he draws his observations, but in the contemporary deployment of interracial male bonds as well. The seeming equality and mutual recognition made possible by the bond constitutes the "racial 'other'" as a "mirroring self," a constitution that incorporates difference into the affirmation of a now singular (one's) individuality. This reinscribes, in ways that are quite familiar, the confrontation of differences into a rhetoric of cultural sameness where the "racial 'other'" (the term itself signifying the asymmetry I am examining) serves as the textual body across which the subversive recasting of "the usual female-male association" can play. "Above all else," Boone asserts, "it is Huck's loving relationship with the slave, Jim, that measures his status as a cultural misfit and his unretraceable deviation from a traditional standard of manhood" (253).

The slippage from the racial to the gendered, evident in the various quotes used in the preceding paragraph, occurs repeatedly in Boone's discussion, marking the status of the "racial 'other'" not only as stand-in for the feminine, but as the white male protagonist's symbolic transcendence of the logic of gender altogether. The "racial 'other'" thus exists as the definition of white masculine multiplicity, a definition that reads the male bond solely through an individualized white masculine perspective. When Boone writes that "[i]f Huck's identity cannot be fitted to one role, neither does this bond conform to a single need" (*Tradition Counter Tradition* 256), it is Huck's identity that founds the descriptive contours and political possibilities of the interracial male bond itself. The analytic refusal to recognize the narrative disparity between Huck and Jim (the recognition, for instance, that Jim does not have access to the multiplicity of roles available to Huck) is the precondition for crafting their relationship as "a mutuality of spirit that, over time, becomes genuine, reciprocal, and nonpossessive: as such it at least partially transcends the hierarchies defining the relation of man and wife, parent and child, white and black, in American society" (ibid.). By finding in the interracial male bond an image of fraternity seemingly devoid of the hierarchical consequences of the heterosexual contract, Boone marks the transgression of the sexual as simultaneously a transgression of all hierarchical relations. But while the discourse of sexual difference thus functions to negotiate differences among men by veiling internal hierarchies through an image of masculine mutuality and independent identity, Boone's "at least partially" evokes the disavowed but frequently returning suspicion that this critical paradigm, as Jim says to Huck, is just "too good for true" (*The Adventures of Huckleberry Finn* 88).

While the proliferation of interracial male bonding narratives in the popular arena is certainly unmatched, in number if not in philosophical scope, by their presence in canonical literature, critical discussions of the American tradition have nonetheless debated, for almost half a century, the meaning, centrality, and utopian possibilities inherent in the image of closely bonded men. But instead of locating the interracial male bond along the double axes of race and gender, we have seen how the critical heritage more frequently focuses on the radical displacement of heterosexual romance as precondition to (and symbolic enactment of) the nostalgic dream of racial transcendence. From this perspective, the bond's defiance of the history of enslavement, lynching, and segregation through narratives that posit the similarities and compatibilities among black and white men subverts the heterosexual model of social interaction by translating alienation and differentiation into mutuality and sameness. But too often, as I have shown, this reading of subversion belies the complexities of cultural productions of interracial male bonds, enabling the defiance of one historical nexus (gender) to symbolically mark the defiance of a number of others (race, class, sexuality) as well. In reading the social and psychosexual dynamics of gender through a binary figuration of masculine/feminine, not only does this critical discourse reinforce gender's meaning and mode of inscription, but also it suspends the significance of other formations of power in a limited account of social relations. That the scene of bonds among men can thus be heralded as democratic achievement on one hand, or the mythic national unconscious on the other, marks the evacuation of woman and of the historical significance of race as the prevailing sign of "America" itself.

In transmuting the narrative of racial difference into a scenario of the mutuality of gender, the critical discourse demonstrates, at its deepest level, the integrationist ideal in twentieth-century U.S. culture: the deployment of sexual difference in the scene of relations among men turns away from the imposition of a highly sexualized difference toward an incorporation based on the contours of a masculine sameness. Here, the powerful seduction (and historically shifting articulation) of the discourse of sexual difference functions as the primary means for framing and negotiating power relations among black and white men. By understanding the deployment of sexual difference as operating in those narrative and cultural scenarios devoid of the presence of woman, we approach once again a central assumption of *American Anatomies:* that the implication of sexual difference always exceeds the biologizing foundation of its discursive coding as woman, and functions instead *across* categories of identity to inscribe, reinforce, and overdetermine hierarchical arrangements, even (indeed especially) those among men. In its articulation as masculine mutuality, the discourse of sexual difference operates quite impressively to disavow the impact of racial difference in interracial male bonding narration, in both the contemporary popular realm and canonical architecture. As such, the interracial male bond's vision of gender and racial transcendence, heralded as emblem of equality, does not necessarily encode broad social transformation, no matter how evocative and seemingly innocuous the central image of men can be.

In rejecting the universalized vision of men together as symbol of cultural freedom, I hope not to negate the potential for interracial male configurations to challenge social arrangements, since antiracist struggle necessitates forging alliances across categories of identity. Various gay male political groups in this country, for instance, have articulated their critique of heterosexual and white supremacy from a nexus of interracial relations among men, providing an alternative way of thinking about masculine fraternity that does not necessarily reinscribe the hierarchical dimensions of patriarchal homosociality. To this extent, the image of interracial male bonds under examination here cannot be aligned, uncritically or essentially, with a particular political agenda since all male bonds do not constitute, as certain radical feminist understandings of patriarchy might lead us to presume, a transhistorically misogynist or antifeminist function. And yet, by calling into question the idealization of the bond and its relation to discursive and social relations of race and gender, I want to emphasize again the historical and locational productions of both interracial male bonding narratives and their critical discourse, productions bound together in the increasing cultural struggle over the content and contextual parameters that constitute "America." That this struggle is not simply a quest for a more real or true America (or even one more faithful to its purported ideals), but a contestation over the political and discursive grounds of its very existence, demonstrates that America is, above all, a rhetorical figure, defined by its excessive performance, and constituted by the logic that establishes not only its geographical but its metaphysical borders.[16]

As a discursive entity, "America" is deployed along lines of subjective engagement that recall the constitution of "race": both not only demand a social body on which relations of identity and difference can be mapped, but also they routinely anchor those relations to the positivity of the "real" through narratives of essential, transhistorical being. Most important perhaps, each claims a seemingly natural referentiality, simultaneously defying the productive processes that engender them, while reducing the heterogeneous into a homogenized definitional field. But where race emphasizes the polarity of difference as its reigning epistemic logic, "America" offers the singularity of identity as its triumphant resolution, a resolution that incorporates the fragmented excesses of social scripting into a narrative of continuity and unification. Cultural productions of interracial male bonds work the tension between these two deployments, fashioning a transhistorical referent that serves as both conflictual origin and emancipatory telos, the great challenge of difference and its shimmering, revolutionary transcendence. In the image of two men — either outcast and adrift from civilization or battling in the midst of its decadent throes — the text of visible bodily difference works to convert the opposition of (racial) difference into the grounds for a universal (masculine) sameness. In this process, fragmentation is transformed into fusion, and "America" emerges as the integrating sign for a more encompassing identification.

That such incorporation is always contradictory, contestatory, and partial perhaps goes without saying. What seems most important in the context of the 1980s popular explosion of interracial male bonding configurations is how their repetition contributes to the performance of "America," marking its incessant productivity and underscoring the logic of specular integration that informs contemporary narration. Through this logic, the symbolic investment of "America" as locus of democratic achievements is rearticulated amid racial hierarchies, and its tenuousness under segregation is newly secured by representational circuits that not only posit inclusion but also equate that inclusion with social, political, and economic reform. Far from signifying the liberation and equality frequently attached to liberal humanist demands for presence and visibility, inclusion in the contemporary era often signals instead a translation of the demand for political representation into the fetishistic display of marginality as commodity. In such a translation, the visibility of presence stands in for, indeed simulates, historical and political subjectivity through a narrow and recuperated formulation of representation, one that integrates the commodified image of (racial) difference into the specular relations of contemporary cultural production. Such integration significantly draws on the categories of racial identity subtending segregation and social protest movements alike: here, the constitution of a collective black identity, secured under slavery and politicized by Black Power and civil rights, can be routinely exchanged for a hollow, historically vacated subjectivity, one simultaneously recognizable through categorical markings but denied the political force of collective engagement.

To some extent, critical debates within "American" literary studies (the term itself demonstrating the unification of a hemisphere into the geopolitics of U.S. domination) replay the fascination with difference as bodies of identity as articulated above. In this case, the inclusion of "women's literature" and "African-American literature," for instance, signals a contemporary accounting for specific historical exclusions by refiguring the canon through categories of identity. Many scholars who engage in these canonical debates reveal increasing resistance to such notions of political transformation and profound skepticism toward strategies that invert or reinscribe the dimensions of domination. Such a reinscription equates a political economy of race and gender with a disparagingly fetishized notion of representation, where mere incorporation — the circulation of texts, bodies, and images — becomes coterminous with the dissolution of the structural relations of racism and sexism themselves. To define the heterogeneity of the social as the presence of an eccentric body (whether that body be literal, as in department hiring practices, or textual, as in canonical reassessments) is to collapse difference and identity by relying on the economy of visibility once again. And it is this economy, an economy in which the body is the primary, if not only, locus for thinking beyond sameness, that continues to underwrite race and gender in U.S. culture today.

To draw attention to the way visibility functions is not to dismiss canonical interventions or hiring practices that insist on transforming academia from its historical locus as bastion of white masculine privilege, but to insist that the logic of visibility is a bookkeeping move that translates differences into unitary and deceptively equivalent formulations, displaying bodies in a specular appeal to integration that remakes, without wholly subverting, the white privileges more uniformly connected to segregation. As this chapter has discussed, the interracial male configuration provides an important opportunity for such a translation. In the contemporary critical canon as in its popular filmic deployment, the image of interracial male bonds calls "America" back from its segregationist past to the new possibilities attending integration, where it can be hailed in the context of "democratic possibility," its founding narrative and ideological trope. As Houston A. Baker Jr.

writes, it is the very idea of America (in his text, AMERICA[17]) that provides the unification through which the shifting and contentious identities within the United States can be yoked to a seemingly stable and inclusive governing sign:

> Black and white alike have sustained a literary-critical and literary-theoretical discourse that inscribes (and reinscribes) AMERICA as immanent idea of boundless, classless, raceless possibility in America. The great break with a Europe of aristocratic privilege and division has been filled by virtuoso rifts on AMERICA as egalitarian promise, trembling imminence in the New World. (*Blues, Ideology, and Afro-American Literature* 65)

While the context of Baker's discussion — "a literary-critical and literary-theoretical discourse" — points to a rather small enclave within the broader deployment of America, it is significant that the contextual parameters of discussions about the form, shape, and substance of the literary have historically revolved around the definition of America, finding within its scope the framework for appeals to canonical visibility and theoretical inclusion.

Baker's suspicious approach to such an inscription of integrationist logic hinges on the fact that the key players in literary-critical performances of America have been "founding (white) fathers, or black men who believe there are only a few more chords to be unnot(ted) before Afro-American paternity is secure" (*Blues, Ideology* 65). This is a telling figuration, not simply because it marks the domain of America's inscription as masculine, but more important because it recognizes the asymmetrical distribution of power among racially differentiated men that underwrites that masculine domain. The most stunning rhetorical aspect of Baker's figuration, however, is its deployment of the paternal metaphor to inscribe both the asymmetry among men and the "egalitarian promise" of its transcendence. Here, the founding white fathers can confer on the disinherited black sons the symbolic position of paternity, " 'initiat[ing]' [them] into American Democracy" for the first time as " 'contributors' to American civilization" (ibid.). In this integrationist (initiation) narrative, black men gain access to America's signification by providing symbolic proof of their issue (contribution), joining the white fathers in an interracial configuration that upholds both the idea of trembling imminence and its implicit logic of the white father's civilizing conquest. Significantly, national collective identity is thus constituted in a paternal relation, one in which the white father begets the black son who, in turn, can beget America as symbolic proof

and performative invocation of this patriarchal reproductive relation. Patriarchal paternity, negotiated across the body of racial difference, heralds "America" itself.

The focus on paternity as the metaphorical relation underpinning America's rhetorical enactment suggests the kind of anxieties attending reproduction that feminists have long linked to patriarchal productions. And it is in the context of the reproductive anxieties propelling America's obsessive desire for repetition that we are ushered, once again, into the symbolic heart of closely bonded men, where the generative stakes involved in collecting differences into a unified, autonomous, undivided whole are revealed. Boone's descriptive terminology for the quest protagonist's self-defining internal goal returns as the rhetorical topos of America, depicting a logic of paternal creation that, contrary to Boone's contention, seems quite far from revolutionary, feminist ideals. But where Baker describes a birthing process in which white man generates black, it is important that the narrative structure Fiedler, Martin, and Boone describe is marked by an inversion: the black male serves as the enabling figure for the white male's traumatic rebirth. As in the narrative scenarios offered by contemporary filmic production, this critical inversion bears the mark of integration's ideological subversion, allowing the white masculine figure to be healed, in his painful voyage through the psychological or physical domain of the social margins, by the now-loving black male he has misjudged, hated, or feared. In the process of this reconfiguration of hierarchical arrangements, a voice of authority and integrated wholeness emerges — a voice now both singular and multiple — that can narrate past, present, and future for an America, trembling beacon of democratic ideals.

This reconfiguration is contingent, as I have demonstrated, on the incipient reduction of the African-American male to a highly commodified construction, captured in an economy of visibility defined and specified by the specular relations of late-twentieth-century technological production. Academic discourse replays, in various ways, the specularity of the popular domain through its rhetorical pretense toward visibility and inclusion, where the circulation of an eccentric, "different" body is heralded as the prevailing sign of its emancipatory, post-segregationist appeal. But while we may applaud the stretch toward a new and different signification, both popular and academic discourse converge at a point of critical, nontransgressive return, not lighting out toward an unknown territory but ensconcing us perhaps more fully within the complexities and asymmetries the theoretical escape was to have healed. And it is here, as well, that my own discourse, reading the returns and elisions of the interracial male bonding configuration, cannot wholly transcend its consumptive logic of specular appeal. While the white masculine is called back from trying to tell its story, from finding his "own singular voice for the first time" (Conroy, *The Lords of Discipline* 6), the bond's other male figure is offered, in the end, no narrative, theoretical, or social release. Even in critique, some meaningful presence, some subjective weight, is inadvertently suspended, as the bond's powerful inscription of sameness and difference continues its work along the fault line of race and gender tensions.

6 The Alchemy of Disloyalty

reinscribed
in 'sisterhood'.

If the last chapter ends in self-conscious awareness of its own methodological crisis, my concluding remarks here will not rescue us from theoretical compromise. In fact, I can promise only to move us further into
the complicities of contemporary thinking on race and gender by turning toward feminism's own myth of integration—that phantom collectivity,
sisterhood. After all, the violences, both material and symbolic, that attend patriarchal narratives of transracial masculine bonding have been reinscribed in this, feminism's most famous counterfigure. But it is perhaps
one of the characteristics of the contemporary situation that feminists cannot escape the necessity of critiquing this figure—cannot escape questioning the referent in whose name we politically speak or the assumptions we
have historically made about the relations of (dis)empowerment that organize the social. In this regard, the *why* of political disenfranchisement and
oppression is, as Toni Morrison says, difficult to handle, both because of
the startling reiteration of human cruelty and greed that racism and sexism
signify and because political resistance entails a struggle against reconstituting, among and between us, that which has and continues to systemically
destroy us. The impossibility of a pure politics thus encounters the psychic
and material costs of our cultural epistemologies, and feminism (among
other political discourses) must confront its own inescapably damaging history as well as its contemporary historicity.

How we narrate this history is, of course, a primary arena of debate
within feminism, and it is in the contestations and incommensurabilities
between two main currents of conversation that this study has often elliptically dwelled: the critique, on one hand, of feminism's historically white
female subject and the postmodern suspicion, on the other, concerning the
constitution and centrality of the subject altogether.[1] *American Anatomies*
has negotiated these "framing terms" by moving in a number of directions. In the earliest chapters, I turned to the political and scientific con-

texts in which modern social identities began to emerge as corporeal and ontological categories, tracing not just the historical shape of race, but its epistemic link to discourses of sexual difference. By investigating the most taken-for-granted assumption of Western racial discourse—that the body is the visible domain of difference—I excavated the disciplinary production of just such a body, critiquing as others have done the corporeal logics of race and gender that underlie the "universal" status of the Enlightened subject. In this way, I offered a reading of the historical contours through which race and gender have been specified in American culture as "blacks and women."

The political consequences of this specification are far reaching, and it has been one of the major projects of this book to tease out the rhetorical and organizational dynamics of twentieth-century social struggle in the context of this formation of identity and modern discipline. But rather than move, as feminist theorists have more routinely done, to the figure abandoned in the race and gender conflation—the black woman—the middle section of this book traced the underside (or other side) of feminism's current emphasis on the heterogeneity of "woman." I did this not to claim for the masculine some kind of equal fracturing that would discount the hierarchical power of patriarchy, but to locate the myth of masculine *sameness* that functions as feminism's most intense reinscription of patriarchy's own illusory logic. I assumed, in other words, that the demystification of woman's common oppression was inextricable from a critique of man's totalized hegemony. I thus explored how "blacks and women" as a coupled configuration tied sexual difference to the bodies of black men in order to contribute to critical discussions concerning identity politics, white supremacy, patriarchy, masculinity, and male bonding. Such discussions have been and continue to be central to any cultural critique.

At the same time, however, I have tried to resist the kind of methodological stance that presents what is always contingent knowledge as a "new" truth, no matter how invested I have been in producing a rigorous and nuanced theoretical analysis of the cultural and critical dynamics of race and gender. By meditating at various stages of this study on the limits of knowledge and the historical contours of my own speech, I have been pursuing what I take to be one of the most important strategies of contemporary feminist politics: the refusal to claim for ourselves a methodologically transcendent perspective, one that can provide a liberatory political guarantee. But how have I arrived at such an assessment of feminism and its contemporary practices? And what are the consequences of a feminist politics that begins where this study now purports to end, in the alchemy of political and methodological disloyalty?

Necessary Disloyalties

In defining feminism's affinity with postmodernism, Nancy Fraser and Linda J. Nicholson tell a familiar story about the contemporary development of feminist thought, one that can begin to delineate the feminist debates about difference and political strategy that this study has implicitly engaged. Citing a mutual interest in challenging modern disciplinarity, they posit that "[f]eminists, like postmodernists have . . . expos[ed] the contingent, partial, and historically situated character of what has passed in the mainstream for necessary, universal, and ahistorical truths" ("Social Criticism without Philosophy" 26). Indeed, the very formation of Women's Studies as an academic discourse proceeds from the assumption that universal knowledge claims are part of a modern masculinist enterprise, and feminists throughout the humanities and social sciences have unveiled the corporeal, cultural, and historical specificity of the masculine agents of universalist theories. In doing this, they have hoped to articulate a social position and political perspective from which women could both define their own disempowerments and argue for a variety of civil entitlements. Through the political framework of "situated knowledges," feminists have emphasized, in ways akin to postmodern critique, the historical and cultural contexts in which all knowledge is produced.[2]

But, while skepticism toward transcendental methodologies has exposed the myth of universal man and articulated ways in which the production of knowledge is linked to women's oppression, feminist theory has nonetheless remained tied to a variety of modernist methodologies. Chief among these has been an assumption of the universal status of "woman" which, in dueling with humanism's generic "man," was based, as feminists now routinely remark, on insufficient attention to the historical and cultural specificities that constitute women's differences from one another.[3] As Fraser and Nicholson explain, in the decade of the 1980s, many feminists became more actively engaged in both the political and the theoretical elaboration of women's differences, critiquing feminism's normative assumptions and thereby creating a more radical break from the hegemonic determinations of modernity. By recognizing the political, social, and experiential contingency of its own situated knowledges, feminist theory exposed its earlier scholarship "as false extrapolations from the experience of the white, middle-class, heterosexual women who dominated the beginnings of the [movement's] second wave ("Social Criticism" 33). In the process, it turned increasingly toward a political practice based on alliances rather than "unity around a universally shared interest or identity" (35), and it is here, Fraser and Nicholson assert, that feminism began to harness, consciously or not, the possibilities of the postmodern.

Even as they applaud the postmodern for contributing to feminism's theoretical elaboration of "complexly constructed conceptions of social identity" ("Social Criticism" 35), Fraser and Nicholson warn against going too far with its theoretical challenge.[4] In particular, they worry that post-modern skepticism toward "large historical narratives" (34) will negate the genres of social criticism that have been useful to feminism, genres that ex-plore "broad-based relations of dominance and subordination along lines like gender, race, and class" (23). Therefore, they call for a postmodern feminism that can mediate the Lyotardian critique of grand narratives by es-chewing the foundationalism of Western philosophies without abandoning attention "to large political problems" (34), a feminism that is "pragmatic and fallibilistic . . . using multiple categories when appropriate and for-swearing the metaphysical comfort of a single feminist method or feminist epistemology" (35). They want, in short, a feminism that resembles "a tap-estry composed of threads of many different hues [rather] than one woven in a single color" (ibid.). Such a feminism, they claim, would be "implicitly postmodern," undoing modern disciplinarity by recognizing "that the di-versity of women's needs and experiences means that no single solution . . . can be adequate for all" (ibid.).

Like others before them, Fraser and Nicholson offer a convincing argu-ment about the necessity of jettisoning universal renderings of woman and the rhetorics of sisterhood and common oppression that have often accom-panied these rhetorics. Further, they demonstrate how the fracturing of a monolithic gender identity shares an affinity with postmodern decenter-ings of the humanist subject. But their analysis carries an implicit nostal-gia for a politics of unity, one paradoxically articulated in a multiplication of terms and methodologies—"in the plural as the practice of feminisms" ("Social Criticism" 35)—and evinced most overtly by the metaphor of the tapestry, "interlaced with differences, even with conflicts" (ibid.), but orga-nized according to a singular object of study, "the subordination of women to and by men" (26). Does the shift of the object of study from "woman" to "the subordination of women by men" transform or undermine modern disciplinarity, particularly feminism's historical investment in its method as the locus of its political guarantee? Can this feminism, cast as "the theoretical counterpart of a broader, richer, more complex, and multilayered feminist solidarity" (35), embrace the political contingencies of feminism's partial knowledges and still remain wed to the priority of gender? After all, to jettison sisterhood for the complexity of political solidarity, to recognize that women's oppression is not always or exactly the same, does not necessarily undermine the modernist compulsion toward a system of knowledge, a methodological focus that can underwrite liberation as a guarantee. In fact, by staging the encounter between feminism and postmodernism as "the prospect of a perspective which integrates their respective strengths while eliminating their respective weaknesses" (20), Fraser and Nicholson might be said to forfeit the contradictions and contestations within feminism to a narrative of progress and integration, one that culminates in feminism's theoretical "maturity" (32). For this reason, we might read the tapestry of many hues as restaging the disciplinary gestures of modernity, displacing "woman" as the object of knowability with feminism itself and finding there the promise of a political guarantee.[5]

How might we imagine a feminism that no longer locates its own political practice, its own vision of and for women, as the truth of female emancipation, as the necessary and final alternative to cultural discriminations and dominations? A feminism, in short, that is not simply disloyal to patriarchal civilization, but disloyal to the assumptions of its modernist teleologies as well? This question, with its reinvention of Adrienne Rich's famous phrase, "disloyal to civilization"[6] and its echo of Patricia J. Williams's *The Alchemy of Race and Rights*,[7] is not meant to dismiss feminism or its political and historical importance, but to reframe the implicit assumptions of loyalty and alliance that so often accompany feminism's modern and postmodern deployments. This allegiance has in the past been pressed foward as a covert, at times overt, demand, and it has been this demand that many women, especially "women of color,"[8] have routinely resisted. Alice Walker's "womanist" rearticulation of feminism, for instance, stages a resistance to the totality of feminism's modern narrative of inclusion, given that narrative's deep philosophical and political tie to Western racisms,[9] and Wahneema Lubiano, like bell hooks and Michele Wallace, has explored the way postmodern theories reflect, refract, or recuperate the racial demarcations that underlie the modernist subject.[10] In such contradictory and contestatory feminist contexts, it is increasingly apparent that the conversation about the modern and the postmodern now taking place within feminism does so on especially charged racial (and racist) terrain.

If Fraser and Nicholson's language of hues and colors, not to mention their methodological tactic of "integration," fails to suggest the racial subtext of feminist-postmodern debates, more explicit evidence can be marshaled. Nancy Hartsock's often-cited lament against the postmodern, for instance, is couched in the context of a struggle for racial liberation. But unlike Fraser and Nicholson, Hartsock reads the postmodern as occluding the progressive social advancements wrought in the 1960s and 1970s, offering the death of the modern subject at the precise historical moment when those previously denied subjecthood—because of their race and/or gender status—have begun "to demand the right to name ourselves, to act as subjects rather than objects of history. . . . Just when we are forming our own theories about the world, uncertainty emerges about whether the world can be theorized" ("Foucault on Power" 163–164). By questioning all equations between knowledge, truth, and political transcendence, the postmodern thus reasserts Enlightenment exclusions and undermines the political gains of civil rights, black nationalism, and feminism in this century. As she writes, "[t]hose (simply) critical of modernity can call into question whether we ever really knew the world (and a good case can be made that 'they' at least did not). They . . . have not known the world as it is" (171).

But have "we" known the world "as it is"? Can "we" claim knowledge innocent of power, or is the minoritized subject also an agent of power, also capable of complicity with various forms of social discrimination? Jane Flax asserts so, and it is significant that her call for the "end of innocence" links postmodernism with an antiracist social critique.[11] By viewing the emergence of epistemological issues alongside critiques by women of color of feminism's internal biases, Flax argues that "the projects of postmodernism and women of color overlap" by simultaneously calling into question feminism's critical assumptions and "the relations of domination that are the conditions of possibility for the coherence of our own theorizing and category formation" ("The End of Innocence" 459). No longer the antithesis that Hartsock posits, the postmodern and antiracist critiques are here wedded to feminism's own deconstruction, revealing the repressions and exclusions on which its anti-patriarchal allegiances to "women" have been constructed. Most crucially, Flax interprets white women's hostility to the postmodern as a displacement of their own "guilt and anxieties about racism (and our anger at the 'others' for disturbing the initial pleasure and comfort of 'sisterhood')" (ibid.). But because any direct challenge to the way whiteness has been critiqued "would be politically unthinkable," Flax suggests that it is "easier and more acceptable for white women to express our discomfort with difference . . . and the politics of knowledge claims by categorically rejecting postmodernism" (ibid.). Such an interpretation calls into question the kind of universalizing "we" deployed by Hartsock, pointing toward the way a feminist postmodernism could work to dissolve the epistemological comfort of a universalized margin by rethinking relations of power and multiple subjectivities. But the racialization of whiteness — the making of whiteness a race in order to counter its status as universal — cannot be guaranteed by the postmodern. No discourse can script its own unitary political effect, and this is as true of the postmodern as it is of modernity or feminism itself.

Nevertheless, the desire for a subject who can control the politics of discourse, who can guarantee the effects of her enunciations, who can totally and finally *know*, is a powerful desire, one that betrays through the very quest for mastery the partialities and contingencies that frame cultural productions of both knowledge and subjectivity. The anxiety in this betrayal — the anxiety that knowledge is not truth, that truths are not innocent of power, that subjectivity is not the transcendent ground of either knowledge or truth — may, as Flax suggests, reflect the insecurities of a racial privilege no longer wholly invisible to contemporary feminist discourses. At the same time, the postmodern shifts the locus of the critique of feminism's historical white supremacy to potentially farther reaching ground. This shift involves calling into question beforehand all methodological moves that seek to settle the complexities of power and knowledge through prior claims to system and procedure. In this, even an integrationist strategy — adding black women to feminist histories, for instance — or an inclusivist gesture toward differences — the monosyllabic, infinitely appended gender-raceandclass — become suspicious elements of a modernist disciplinarity. To pose a feminism disloyal to itself: this would entail exploring the boundaries, limits, and excesses of feminism's own historicity — what it thinks it knows, how it knows it, why it wants to know it, and at what cost.

But what is suspicious about gender, race, and class or any of the various configurations of difference that have helped retrieve women from their modernist appointment with universal "woman"? Why be suspicious of the way feminism has sought to explain and explore the crisis of its own primary category of analysis? After all, even those hoping to identify with a postmodern feminism become uncomfortable when its cynicism about methodology and historical metanarrativity calls into question the way the categories of gender, race, and class have served as conceptual linchpins for analyzing global social order. Fraser and Nicholson, as you recall, cite the postmodern's emphasis on local formations as making difficult feminism's necessary "critique of broad-based relations of dominance and subordination along lines like gender, race, and class" ("Social Criticism" 23). But the underlying assumption here is that these categories are, in fact, *fully adequate* to the task of defining and critiquing relations of domination, that only within their conceptual field can the deep disparities among genders, races, and classes be understood and/or ameliorated. But speaking of race is not the same as speaking of or against racism. Indeed, it might be the case that the circulation of these categories in critical discourses has worked more to appease the political need to address difference than, in fact, to illuminate their contradictory and contingent productions.

This concern with the way that the conceptualization of difference as genderraceandclass occupies a privileged explanatory position in contemporary feminist theory does not discount the importance of studying categorical formations as mechanisms of social control, as this study of race and gender clearly suggests. But it does raise a series of questions that trouble some of feminist theory's most well known critical assumptions. For instance, can we assume that the contents of categories like race and class (indeed even gender) are already historically and culturally known? that their invocation is a sufficient methodological strategy for articulating broadscale social critique? that each category clarifies the structure and functioning of discrete aspects of the social formation? that a compound ordering of categories necessarily articulates their imbrications? that the task of political criticism is to define social organization within the rubric of these categorical relations? that, in fact, only through these categories can we produce the politics of political criticism? If we cannot assume these things, if categories are not finally transparent epistemologies, what, then, becomes of the necessary feminist demand for both heterogeneous women and a discourse committed to social critique?

The answer to these questions does not entail an end of feminism or politics, but it does require articulating the anxieties of contemporary feminism in ways less loyal to the historical and political assumptions and assurances of modern feminist thought. In this context, the debate about modernity and postmodernity that *American Anatomies* charts is less about the possibilities of political critique than a struggle over the assumptions about women, difference, power, history, and subjectivity that will both guide and condition that critique. If, in this struggle, the identity of feminism as we have known it is threatened (and I would agree with Hartsock that it is), we might recognize such a threat and its implicit disloyalty as a political

necessity, one born from both the successes and failures of feminism's constitution within modernity. "The end of innocence" that Flax heralds as the
necessary consequence of critiquing modernity thus points to the recognition that feminism itself is not outside power or hierarchy, is not the truth
to which power and domination must reconfigure themselves. Its innocence
lost, its loyalty unassured, feminism faces a future unwritten by a methodological guarantee.

Taking Refuge: Take Two

Or does it? What, after all, are the implications of my own staging of feminism's history? Have I not assumed a historical trajectory that functions
more to liberate the present than to demonstrate the specificities and contingencies of feminism's theoretical and political past? I ask these questions
in order to foreground the necessity of reading the simultaneously linked
and contradictory enterprises of antiracism and postmodernism against
the grain of contemporary feminism's rendition of the historical, against
the grain, that is, of some of my own overt assumptions about what constitutes feminism's history, especially its theoretical missteps and elisions.
This possibility gestures toward disloyalty in two important and overlapping ways: not simply toward a rethinking of the priority of gender we have
both pursued and, according to current histories, most recently begun to
challenge, but toward a disloyalty to that very narrative in which feminism's
complex and contentious past is shaped as an uninterrupted trajectory of
that priority as well. After all, the very emergence of a public feminist discourse from the abolition movement demonstrates a kind of originary, if
I can risk such a term, imbrication of questions of race and gender inequality. This imbrication was as much a reflection of the pressing contexts
of the quotidian as of the dilemma of corporeal visibility within modernity
and its discordant political theory more generally.[12]

   In this regard, the pressure today to create a political economy of race
and gender that can undo the logic of "blacks and women" signals more of
a retrieval or rejuvenation than a wholly new concern for such complexities, and in this we are faced with the possibility of a historicizing gesture
that might seek to locate the racial, racist, and antiracist subtext that com-
prises "feminism" since its earliest American inception. To do this would,
of course, radically reshape the contemporary deployment of feminism as
a categorical unity created by and for white women, fracturing that unity
in order to propose a taxonomy that exceeds the binarism now codified

in phrases such as black and white feminist thought. This is not to say that there is no useful, at times even powerful, effect to such categorizing gestures, as feminism has certainly reinscribed within many of its organizational and theoretical practices a white racial hegemony. Such racism, past and present tense, is beyond dispute. And yet, the familiar gesture in contemporary feminist writing, a gesture this study has in its own way engaged — in which the past is written as a definitive absence or injustice that a present thinking will fill — may not only abandon the contingencies of the historical for a mythically transcendent present but also produce a devoutly racist rendition of feminism by evacuating from view the noninstitutional or anti-institutional sites of activism through which various kinds of feminist politics have been waged. Such histories, some feminist historians may assert, are more commonly produced by those of us trained within the literary tradition who use poststructuralist theory, but no disciplinary practice can currently be said to move beyond the mantra logic at work in contemporary feminism, where a "historical inability" to address the compounded nature of female subjectivity and social position — of genderraceandclass — serves as the past against which the present struggles to (re)write itself.

But at what historical point were there no American feminist thinkers interested in the way women were (and are) differently positioned — interested, that is, in articulating the complexities of a social order that variously inscribed female inferiorities? We routinely raise the figure of Sojourner Truth to demonstrate the elision of racial difference and black female subjectivity seemingly paradigmatic of nineteenth-century feminism, but it is precisely in that very act that we condemn her to a certain passivity. She becomes, in short, the emblem of a historical erasure that her presence could, on the contrary, be read to defiantly deny.[13] To purport the past as the history of the black woman's erasure in feminist thought is to relinquish "feminism" to its most racist and institutionally complicit construction, a construction that seems to me to retrace, albeit in vague and asymmetrical ways, some of the integrationist impulses of contemporary U.S. culture.[14] For at the same time that we disavow the utopic rhetoric of female bonding implicit in notions of a commonality based on gender, at the same time that we unravel the falsities of our 1970s and 1980s "sisterhood," feminists often gesture nonetheless toward a truer version of such myths, toward transcending their fault lines in order to grasp, in politically progressive fashion, our own post-racist historicity. We dream, in other words, our own version of the late-twentieth-century integrationist dream.

This "we" carries, I know, the force of a white racial inscription, and it would be dangerous not to read how overtly white has been the authority of the integrationist narrative not simply, as I discussed in previous chapters, in American culture or criticism most broadly, but within the contours of feminist discourses as well. White feminists in increasing number have begun to turn with frequency to issues of race, in part because of the extensive critique launched by "women of color" against the theoretical and political inattentions of second-wave elaborations, in part because of the national anxieties and reconfigurations under which whiteness is itself being culturally "remade."[15] While I do not discount the significance of such work and while my own scholarly preoccupations are clearly part of this contemporary trajectory, I am nonetheless stunned by the ideological affinities (and their recuperatory potentials) between such preoccupations and the economy of visibility that structures the integrationist containment of "difference" in American culture itself. Too often, as many of us know, white women situate themselves as the moral guardians of "race," policing other white women for evidence of racist transgressions, as if locating such transgressions demonstrates our own willful noncomplicity.[16] The desire to get race—and the critique of feminism's racism—off of *us* reiterates the integrationist dream, casting in this case white women as the heroic interlopers into and reshapers of feminism's historical reinscriptions of white supremacy. Such a racist past must, of course, remain entirely hegemonically fashioned in order to be so strenuously and heroically denied.

The political currency attending antiracist work by white women in academia cannot, however, be viewed apart from the remapping of white hegemonies throughout American culture, and this means a certain suspicion toward what is undoubtedly a crucial reevaluation of feminist history in the context of white racial supremacy. Such a suspicion takes place for me not so much on corporeal as on methodological grounds. That is, it is not the whiteness of the investigator that implicitly undermines or renders complicit the antiracist critique, as it is never simply a matter of whether that body can and should (or even how it might) speak.[17] (Nor can it be the corporeality of the subject of minority that in any simple way authorizes its own analysis, as Clarence Thomas among others continues to demonstrate.[18]) But as with the integrationist gesture more generally, the paradigmatic shift through which the figure of the minoritized Other is moved, in bell hooks's terms, from margin to center does not in and of itself undo the terms of social (dis)empowerment. Nor does it, as I remarked earlier, necessarily explain the complicated means by which this figure came to be situated at the cultural periphery. Indeed, the methodological fix can be

deployed in a variety of potentially pernicious ways, seeming to redress
on one hand the elisions of feminism's institutional practices and epistemologies, while commodifying in late-twentieth-century "multicultural"
fashion bodies that have rarely escaped the myriad forms of propertied abstraction attending U.S. racial and racist significations.[19]

This is, at least, one of the ways in which I understand the political epistemology that propels this project, where the belief in translating one object of study for another cannot ultimately provide the kind of guarantee
that has more routinely accompanied the feminist demand for transformative methodologies (regardless of the extent to which I have excavated
the categorical exclusions attending "blacks and women").[20] The disloyalty
of this chapter's title thus takes on a third possibility, one that returns us
to the question of the postmodern and its disarticulation of modernity's
methodological—disciplinary as well as political—assumptions: a disloyalty, that is, to the contemporary scripting of feminism's emancipation from
its racist complicities that hinges on exchanging, as our primary object of
study, one identity category for another. Indeed, to question the possibility
that categories of identity—whether "woman" in general or its subsequent
specificities, "white woman," "black woman," "lesbian," and so on—are
finally the only constitutive ground on which feminism can base its production of counter-knowledges is to challenge the logic of modernity and
its methodological propulsion toward increasingly territorialized interpretations of social and subjective being. It is to question the disciplinarity
that has accompanied the human's emergence as both subject and object
of knowledge, an emergence through which bodies have been increasingly
anatomized, quite literally as I have demonstrated, but metaphorically as
well. Such questioning does not dismantle the epistemic force of modernity
that we engage in, that engages us, but it does offer a way of approaching
feminism, its relationship to modernity, and its imbrication with corporeal
visibilities in narratively different ways.

But let me be clear. I am not saying that the project of reconstructing
Western knowledges about minoritized people is not an important, indeed
vital, aspect of cultural struggle, nor am I suggesting that displacing white
women as the primary (regardless of how veiled) focus of feminist investigation carries no contemporary political urgency. But just as the initiatory
move from "male" to "female" in feminist interventions into knowledge
reconfigures as it simultaneously marks an epistemic limit of modernity,
so too does the movement from margin to center of the minoritized feminine subject mark an investment in modernity's primary myth of meth-

odological liberation. Such an investment simultaneously disciplines that subject into the conceptual framework of her own multiple disempowering positionalities and establishes a set of newly formed categorical exclusions. "Women of color," "black women," "third-world women," "lesbians" —these definitions, strategically deployed as interventions into the seeming unity of "woman," both move toward and deny the kind of inclusion that their rhetorical gesture implies. The slippages and seepages between such categories partake in their own displacements, not simply because of the terms of difference unsignified by each category's territorialization, but because such categorical constructions rely upon, even as they resist, the logic of the visible that underwrites the racist and ethnocentric discourses of the West.

If my reading here evinces the postmodernity that questions, as Nancy Hartsock laments, the emancipatory project defined by the rights and privileges of majority (with its rhetoric of ultimate inclusion), it also, crucially, challenges us to rethink the gestures that we have understood as the paths of resistance undertaken by those historically minoritized as well. For instance, the linkage of the feminist phrase "the personal is the political" with experientially based writing by minoritized women can be (and has been) read as resistance to contemporary poststructuralist theory, an assertion of the individual voice, a reclamation of the humanist tradition for those categorically denied subjectivity within modern political anatomies.[21] As Hartsock says, "[w]e who have not been allowed to be subjects of history, who have not been allowed to make our history, are beginning to reclaim our pasts and remake our futures on our own terms. One of our first tasks is the construction of the subjectivities of the Others" ("Foucault on Power" 163). But to claim a subjectivity within the disciplinary practice of modern subject formation is not to enter into history on one's own terms. In fact, such a formulation of the subject as authoring agent of modern political practices may deemphasize the most radical aspects of the critique of modernity that the minoritized claim to subjectivity entails: the retrieval, that is, of a complicated psychic interiority, of "being" irreducible to the subjective determinations wrought by the social scripting of race and gender as corporeal visibilities.

In other words, the challenge to modernity—which characterizes the tensions within and political stakes of feminism and other political discourses in the United States today—lies in a potential resignification, not of the body as such but of the relationship between its interior and exterior domains. As we have seen, it is this relationship that underlies the anatomization of human beings increasingly established in the transformation of natural history to comparative science and the more respectable discipline of biology where the visible regime that constructs the body as the locus of difference is turned inside out, so to speak, by the internalizing and organic discourses wrought by the study of "man." In Foucault's terms, the classical episteme gives way to a technologizing quest for the visible's internal corporeal meaning and "blackness" in particular becomes, as I have argued, not only more than skin deep, but epistemically linked to the articulation of other differences, most prominently gender. In this process, the possibilities of a kind of interior psychic complexity is overwritten by the determinations of the body's corporeal scripting, and the African(-American) is consigned to a psychological as well as a physical negativity of "being."[22] At the same time, whiteness achieves its priority as a visible absence, signifying a dis-corporated, universal, and psychically complicated humanity.

The language of psychic interiority stands, to some extent, against the reiteration of modernist logic found in contemporary social constructionist discourse where the scripting of the body as a racial or gendered visibility is often equated with the contours of subjectivity itself. For instance, when we talk, as I have here and elsewhere,[23] of the necessity of charting the race, class, gender, and sexual differences that position subjects within the social, it is often assumed that such charting can simultaneously account for, if not define, the dynamics of subjectivity, as if the processes of the unconscious and the subject's formation can be both predicated and rationalized by reference to the subject's categorical designations. But even as social constructionist discourses seek to historicize and particularize our understanding of human being in ways that challenge essentialist assumptions, the equation between subject position and subjectivity fortifies those disciplinary activities of modernity through which corporeal visibilities are relegated to the body's interior domain — activities, that is, in which subjectivity is cast as a "deeper" rendition of the body's social script. In Western racial discourses, it is precisely the collapse of an interior psychic complexity with the body's exterior significations that inaugurates the hierarchical and asymmetrical configurations under which both a racialized humanity and citizenship have taken and continue to take shape.

This is not to say that reading interiority as always in excess of those corporeal scripts that seek to discipline it can adequately settle the complexities of human embodiment, identity, and power that the conversation about interiors and exteriors deployed here tries to illuminate. The very framework of interiority and exteriority presupposes a dichotomy that the technologizing apparatuses of modern visibilities both establish and increasingly disavow, and it is in the incommensurability between (and theoretical fragility of) a socially scripted and decipherable "outside" of the body and its psychologically nuanced and potentially inexplicable "inside" that the political stakes of identity politics in the late twentieth century dwell. To consign subjectivity to the categories of identity by which every subject is socially disciplined, in both senses of the word, is not simply to approach human being as ultimately knowable (because taxonomic), but to determine such knowability according to modernity's methodological rendering of the body. In this process of equating either subjectivity with identity *or* identity with subject position, the political is waged within and not finally against the corporeal visibilities established by modern epistemologies.

Anxieties, Once Again

My response to the disciplinary mechanisms of identity as the framework of and for economies of visibility has directed me throughout this text to interrogate the asymmetries and instabilities of modernity's corporeal scripts, and it has been toward rethinking the theoretical and historical narrative of feminism in particular that I have read the way the African(-American) body has been made "black" and how that blackness became increasingly intertwined with discourses of sexual difference. But by understanding the political imperative of my project as a strategic disloyalty to many of feminism's disciplinary assumptions, I have risked reinscribing the same kind of historical rupture—of a liberating new that disavows the hegemonies of the old—that my suspicion toward feminism's modernity would seem to forswear. For this reason, I want to shape my disloyalties in the final stages of this study in a fourth way: as a suspension of my own desire to posit this text as transcending the contingencies of its production, not simply its reflection upon and reaction to contemporary feminist theories, but its relationship to current constructions of the past as well. To do this—to figure disloyalty as something more than renunciation (or mythic repair)— I want to turn, at least briefly, to the text that most haunts my own, Harriet Beecher Stowe's *Uncle Tom's Cabin* and its difficult and highly problematic figuration of the social structures and corporeal scripts of race and gender.

But why would a text that is so closely aligned with racist stereotyping and with our reading of the white supremacist articulations of nineteenth-century feminism be used here to shape my own relationship to feminism, past and present? Why trace a lineage of any kind to Stowe? It is, after all, far easier to condemn her depictions of Topsy, Uncle Tom, and Sambo, thereby defining a political distance between her world view and my own. But if disloyalty to current feminist assumptions entails something more than the modernist renewal embedded in a theoretical disavowal, if it in fact forces a recognition of those difficult affiliations and associations that our disciplinary structures might otherwise allow us to repress or dismiss, if it necessitates, in short, relinquishing the methodological "fix," then Stowe would seem a crucial figure for thinking about the inescapable complicities as well as utopic hopes of my own authorship. For in its attempt to fashion an argument against both slavery and patriarchy, *Uncle Tom's Cabin* is one of the few popular moments in the literary landscape of this nation in which a white woman has sought to grapple, however inadequately, with the social consequences of both Western notions of race and U.S. structures of racism. That her novel often stands as the paradigmatic emblem of betrayal of the political collaboration called feminist-abolitionism perhaps says less about Stowe than it does about the changing shape of discourses of political reform and of race and gender in the past century and a half. Certainly it says a great deal about those gestures of renunciation that attend white women's contemporary integrationist dreams.

Still, how does one read Stowe without turning, in methodological compulsion, to renunciation or even to its antithesis of rescue and repair? Didn't Stowe rely on the figure of the African(-American) slave—nineteenth-century American culture's most predominant and contested symbol of oppression—as the expression of her own (white female) disempowerment? And is this not, as I have discussed in earlier chapters, an expression that analogizes two incommensurate forms of social disenfranchisement, interchanging the inhumanity and propertied abstraction ascribed to the slave with the civic exclusions circumscribing the potential citizenship sought by white women? If the answers here are, as they seem to be, "yes," how can we not concentrate on disciplining Stowe for assimilating the distinctions between the legal disenfranchisements of marriage and slavery and thereby glossing crucial differences between free white women and both female and male slaves? After all, her reliance on the faulty analogy of "blacks and women" is one of the means by which *Uncle Tom's Cabin* seems to undo itself, subverting its most overt political agenda by dissuading political alliances among minoritized groups. But to rehearse the faulty logic of the analogy does not necessarily reveal the various questions about social power and the structural relationship between race and gender that the analogy was used to answer. That excavation requires a different kind of critical gaze, one perhaps less seduced by the structure of self-renewal embedded in our disciplinary methods of critique.

In "Bodily Bonds: The Intersecting Rhetorics of Feminism and Abolition," Karen Sanchez-Eppler establishes the cultural context in which Stowe articulated her system of bodily exchange, arguing that "the problems of having, representing, or interpreting a body structure both feminist and abolition discourses, since . . . for both women and blacks it is their physical difference from the cultural norms of white masculinity that obstructs their claim to personhood" (29). This physical difference, based on what I have called an economy of visibility, casts social subjectivity as constitutive of the flesh, bound to both popular and scientific discourses that construct and discipline the body. In such a relationship, the binary rendering of race as white/black and of gender as male/female sustains the visible's authority not only to confer and deny social and human subjectivity but also to render the body's race and gender determinations as indexes (or evacuations) of psychic interiority itself. In this context, categories of social negation arise as corporeal identities — women and blacks — and the visible serves as the signifying structure for evincing the body's seemingly evacuated interior domain. This is the radical negation produced by domination and becomes for Stowe the political and discursive condition for her narrative's quest to analogize the patriarchal effacement of white women as entitled social subjects to the slave system's negation of African(-Americans) as human subjects. The slippage encountered here between the categories of social and human subjectivity — what Sanchez-Eppler culls under the heading of "personhood" — underlies the analogy's production, making possible its doubly inflected protest against the dis-corporated privileges of white masculinity.

At the same time, of course, incommensurabilities abound as Stowe must somehow render to both "blacks and women" an interiority that transcends the negations imposed by identities wrought from corporeal scripts. This is where the generic formulations of sentimental narration become both crucial and problematic, heightening and propelling the quest for interiority by establishing tears as the narrative's central signification of subjectivity and its primary rhetorical goal.[24] As Sanchez-Eppler discusses, sentimental narration functions by drawing readers into identification with the pain and suffering of others, and it is precisely through the invocation of tears that the process of reading is cast as a physical act capable of achieving, in sentimental terms, political force. The "physicality of the reading experience," Sanchez-Eppler writes, "radically contracts the distance between narrated events and the moment of their reading, as the feelings in the story are made tangibly present in the flesh of the reader" ("Bodily Bonds" 36). By understanding the political imperative of abolitionism as contingent on a regime of sentiment, the sentimental form works to overcome not only the alienating distinction between the material and fictional realms, but the problem of difference itself.[25] For Stowe, the sentimental form is thus a highly utopian gesture, one invested with the task of undoing the subjective negations and mutual alienations that attend corporeal visibilities in order to found a political alliance between slaves and white women.

In foregrounding sentiment as the most crucial and revolutionary political capital, *Uncle Tom's Cabin* significantly questions the popular equation in nineteenth-century discourses between blackness and inhumanity,[26] allowing the slave a psychic reality that challenges paternalistic views of the peculiar institution as protection for those unable to survive the rigors and responsibilities of civic society (and civilization itself). That the method for signifying the slave's humanity is contingent on the response of the reader, on her tearful identification with the pain of enslavement, demonstrates, of course, the political limit embedded in the sentimental form. How else can we read the fact that the slave's interiority must be evinced by the emotion of the white reader (both those who read the book and those who, like Stowe's Mrs. Bird and Mrs. Shelby, "live" in the book as its exemplary readers)? For while *Uncle Tom's Cabin* tries to forge a political alliance between slaves and white women by figuring subjectivities irreducible to the determinations of bodies in modernity, the transformatory hope attached to the analogizing function fractures under the inescapable priority accorded to white racial being.

For Stowe, the political necessity lies precisely here: in finding a means both for Anglo-Americans to identify with a political project that challenges their own interests and for white women in particular to translate their racial privileges into a *form* or method for the slave's enfranchisement. The political asymmetries attending the differences between the slave's humanity and the white woman's social subjectivity—and the novel's attempt to both signify and rectify these incommensurabilities—demonstrates at one level the very problem of the political in both nineteenth- and twentieth-century American life. This problem, which is fundamentally about detaching political interests and activities from a politics defined solely by identity, always carries the threat of recuperation, as with all politics. Recently, however, we have begun to witness a reemphasis on coalitionism and collaborative affinities as the vehicle for articulating political consensus, practices that engage people in political struggle in ways that are more issue than identity bound.[27] While the fragmentation of the social that this seems to entail—along with the threat of relinquishing, in the case of feminism, the centrality of "women"—currently coagulate within debates about the postmodern, the tensions within the political between identity figurations and noncorporeally based collaborations is not new. These tensions accompany the disciplinary emergence of "man" and the dynamic of (dis)corporeality that underlies, in an extensive way, the rights and injustices that attend modern political subjectivity.

As a negotiation of the tensions between bodies and identities and their figuration of and for political (dis)empowerments, Stowe's analogic wedding of women and slaves moves in contrary ways. On one hand, she seeks a political affinity across the categorical anatomies that govern the social body, offering a regime of sentiment to derationalize the proslavery argument and to simultaneously redefine the private and personal as central formulations of the political itself. Like other sentimentalists, she intervenes in the implicit masculinization of modernity's publicly defined political realm, engaging women in a series of reforms intended to resignify both the nation and the corporeal assumptions that underwrite the national body.[28] But in turning to the sentimental feminine—cast overarchingly as a symbolic and literal mother and bound, as I have discussed, to the priority of white female flesh—Stowe must attend to a number of theoretical problems, not the least of which concerns the difference of gender that territorializes in incommensurate ways the bodies of the enslaved. For where the sentimental feminine offers a means for humanizing the African(-American) woman by establishing her within the ideology of maternity that centrally defines the political in the novel, the male slave lacks the easy assimilation of (female) corporeality to (maternal) interiority that is necessary to the production of such a feminine function. Instead, *Uncle Tom's Cabin* must struggle, quite overtly and quite unsatisfactorily, to undo the significatory structures that attend male bodies in order to feminize and hence humanize the male slave. As my earlier conversations in this book may indicate, in translating the slave's potential masculinity into a feminine interiority, Stowe works to reverse the structural relations of gender on which nineteenth-century discourses of humanity and citizenry dwell.

Take, for instance, the novel's central figure, Uncle Tom. On one hand, Stowe depicts him in language that evokes a kind of noble masculine corporeality, as "a large, broad-chested, powerfully-made man," but immediately she undercuts such characterization by alleviating its potentially threatening edge, referring instead to his "humble simplicity" and to a face of "grave and steady good sense, united with much kindliness and benevolence" (21). Interiority and exteriority are in this way conflicted, as Stowe seeks for Uncle Tom the characteristics of femininity that the corporeal delineations of a black masculinity might otherwise deny. In this she claims for him a "gentle, domestic heart" (91), marking his interiority within the discourse of the sentimental feminine that the novel most strenuously avows. As Leslie Fiedler has aptly described him, Uncle Tom is a suffering heroine, masked by blackface and drag. "Indeed," emphasizes Fiedler, "it is hard to miss the equation . . . Woman = Mother = Slave = Black; or simplifying, Woman = Black, Black = Woman. The final formulation represents most accurately perhaps [Stowe's] perception of the relationship between race and gender" (*What Was Literature?* 172).

The bodily exchange that Stowe effects here emerges, as we have seen, from two overlapping contexts: the visible economy that writes the African's "blackness" as inhumanity on one hand and the priority attributed to masculine bodies in patriarchal social and symbolic systems on the other. In the contest between these, Uncle Tom is simultaneously deracialized as a corporeal entity and subsequently endowed with the moral superiority, heavenly religiosity, and spiritual self-sacrifice associated with an interiorized and subtly conquering feminine. He is, in short, "released" from the confines of his black masculine body in order to be ushered into Stowe's humanizing agencies of the feminine. The overtness of this process can be witnessed in the final horrific scene where transcendence of the body is complete: "the blows fell now only on the outer man, and not, as before, on the heart" (391). Separating the body and the heart, the flesh from its interiority, the masculine from the feminine, Stowe's articulation of identification across difference relies on the transformation of the black masculine ("the outer man") into the white feminine ("the heart"), a transformation that both releases the white feminine from an essentialized bodily origin and reconfigures it as the framework of and for the political alliance. In anchoring the sign of her text's racial body to a seemingly deessentialized discourse of sexual difference, Stowe's sentimental strategy foregrounds the problem of racial hierarchies among men even as it ultimately reasserts the binary logic of gender, crafting the masculine as oppressor and the feminine as the figure for all difference and disempowerment.[29]

While this elision between the male slave and the feminine partakes of that more wide-ranging gesture in nineteenth-century discourses to feminize blackness, it is significant how clearly Stowe recognized the need to differentiate among men based on the economic and political disparities that slavery quite strenuously created. Where a kind of mythic sisterhood or shared maternal potential made possible the novel's shaping of social and political affinities among both free and enslaved women—and in this sense reinscribed the bourgeois ideal of reproduction as the corporeal logic of the feminine—the patriarchal institution of slavery was shorn of its discorporated illusions of masculine hegemony, not simply as such illusions were founded in nineteenth-century formations of marriage and paternity, but as they configured Stowe's political perspective as well. After all, it is the simultaneous totalization of patriarchy on one hand and the masculine's anatomized black body on the other that produces the tension within *Uncle Tom's Cabin* that propels Stowe first to disarticulate Uncle Tom from the masculine and then to reconstitute the masculine as the political locus of the slave system's corruption, a system that was for her an inherently and overarchingly patriarchal one. The contradictions that abound here demonstrate the difficulties not simply of the analogy as a political function, but of the project of articulating a politics that can overcome the narrowing that identity-based interests historically confer. For while Stowe sought to displace the equation between political interests and categorical designations, her signification of black humanity in the guise of white bourgeois femininity had the political effect, finally, of returning the white woman to herself. As Sanchez-Eppler writes, "[t]he difficulty of preventing moments of identification from becoming acts of appropriation constitutes the essential dilemma of feminist-abolitionist rhetoric" ("Bodily Bonds" 31).[30]

While gesturing toward a politics that can apprehend and do justice to difference, in other words, the structure of identification enacts a translation that ultimately threatens to undo the utopic projection of sentimental affection and connection between white women and slaves. In Stowe, we witness how the enslaved function as figures for the white woman's disempowerment and hence how the identificatory gesture dissembles into a disturbingly imperialist one. Uncle Tom, Eliza, Topsy—all become vehicles for the imaginative articulation of a pacific maternal ideology that reflects the revised centrality of the sentimental feminine, itself borne of a political culture bound to the gendered dimensions of public and private spheres. Such spheres, as feminist historians have now well discussed, were more mythic than universally real for women in the nineteenth century, inscribing only the social organization of the middle class and thus displacing the economic conditions of both enslaved and wage laboring women.[31] In recreating as a political reform tactic the domestic ideology of their own class, Stowe and other feminist-abolitionists ultimately identified with the constitutive conditions of their own subject positions, which demonstrates, in one way at least, the epistemic link between identity-based politics and the project of identification offered as its transcendence. But in her faith in the humanist and bourgeois practices of identification, Stowe also hoped that the regime of sentiment would resignify the slave body, granting it the humanity and maternal interiority that white women, while disenfranchised, were nonetheless granted. For Stowe, sentiment as political agency thus liberated the slave into the contrary humanizing ideology that both defined and constrained white women.

In the twentieth century, Stowe's deeply religious configuration of identification and sentiment becomes characteristic of a variety of women's organizations, feminist and nonfeminist, and the transformatory hope of identifying with the pain and suffering of others seems ever more bound to an imperialistic cast. But is this the only fate for identification—or for sentiment itself? Does sentiment inevitably lead to the complicities of sentimentality? Can we envision a politics without an economy of feeling, an economy bound not simply to our own social conditions, but reaching toward and hence working against structures of oppression that implicate us in empowerment as well? The problem of the political within feminism, as elsewhere, involves the difficulty that adheres to such questions and their necessary but unacceptable irresolvability. The final movement in *Uncle Tom's Cabin*—the missionary resituation of former American slaves in Africa—demonstrates in rather overt ways the dead end of identification and sentiment that was Stowe's historically contingent political horizon. After all, identification with the pain and suffering of the slave is not a significatory retrieval of a complex humanity denied by the discourse of property, nor does identification found a disaffiliation from a variety of forms of privilege underlying white supremacy. In the paradoxes of her political gestures, Stowe's protest against slavery does not necessarily entail a challenge to the structural asymmetries in which white supremacy defines and constrains interiority itself.

This does not mean, of course, that the hope that I have tacitly offered throughout this study for the political possibility of feminist disloyalty carries none of its own historically contingent fallibilities. To so overtly challenge the methodological practices that underwrite feminism's articulation within modernity in the name of a certain interest in postmodernity is simply to foreground the anxieties that feminism has routinely grappled with, though not finally allayed. It is to partake in a political project similar to the kind we witness in Stowe, though bound now to quite different material conditions—integration instead of enslavement—and to a feminist political culture invested more in anger than in tears as the regime of sentiment attending activism.[32] But we have not escaped the constitutive challenge and crisis of the political that the questions of race and gender raise, nor have we found a way, through either modernist retrieval of the identity-based subject or postmodern skepticism of identities altogether, to articulate the differences among women that have made solidarity among women both the goal of and the impediment to feminism. The shifting theoretical gaze employed in this study, written under the specter of our contemporary postulations of feminism's historical failures, can make claims for historical continuity only by pointing to the desire for the apprehension of differences. It is this desire that repeatedly struggles to fulfill itself under the weight of critical as well as literary authorship. In this context, it may be our most necessary political gesture to approach feminism's complicities and failures not simply as that which continually alienates us from it, but as the very conditions that return us to it once again.

Mediating Method(s)

It is obviously against the grain of feminist thought to posit its political possibility as connected to its historical and contemporary failures. Political faith is far more compelling when attached to the fantasy of transcendent historicity, and feminists including myself have often turned to the language of political purity—of a wholesale disarticulation of feminism from the contingencies and complicities of its cultural framework, critical authorship, and public consumptions—in order to try to settle our ambivalences about its epistemic limitations. We have sought new paradigms, new models, new identities, new critical postures, new languages, new figures, new modes of activism, new pedagogies, new images of the political—a panoply of the new to mediate not simply the consequences of being female in defiantly misogynist cultures, but those inequalities among women that most threaten feminism's theoretical and political ability to speak to and for "women." This desire to invest feminism with the possibility of a future that relinquishes it simultaneously from the present and the past is, of course, part of shaping a liberation from ourselves, as it posits a route into knowledge and futurity untarnished by or out maneuvering the embodied contexts of both our being and seeing. In this, it recreates the mythology of modernist methodologies, even as it points to the inextricable tensions that underlie and propel the move toward such paradigmatic guarantees.[33]

To approach feminism as always embroiled in the limitations and complicities of its quest for the paradigmatic guarantee means reading it as simultaneously driven and constituted by its own historically shifting inabilities. Every destination, in other words, becomes inadequate with our arrival, just as the historic shape of our arrival transforms the destination into an emblem of our own contingent historicity. From this perspective, the contemporary emphasis on analyzing "women" across a range of social positions cannot be assumed to be, in political terms, a final response to the way the category of woman has itself functioned as a kind of discipline, within feminism and outside it. While its necessity may be self-evident in the contexts of power and privilege that currently configure hierarchical relations among women, the categorical extension — the move from gender to race, sexuality, class, nationality, age, and so on as the means for apprehending differences among women — finally relies on a more detailed taxonomy as the methodological guarantee for interpreting the multiple, overdetermining, and contradictory practices of social hierarchy.

In a similar way, the analytic framework of race and gender cannot fulfill the political desire to render the historical force of the violences and injustices of the social relations in whose name these categories are asked to speak, and this is true not only in Stowe's case, but in my own. To recognize this failure is not to discount the political project that I have staged here, nor is it to abandon feminism to the impoverished contours of contemporary politics or to disregard the urgency of the conversation about "difference" and disempowerment altogether. It is to posit, indeed to emphasize, that feminism's political difference — which is, one wants to hope, a crucial difference after all — lies not in its object of study or its categorical recreations, not in its heroic self-fashioning or in its affirmative noncomplicities, most certainly not in its utopic claims to transcendent, truth-saying methodologies. Feminism's political difference lies instead in plotting within and against it our shifting, historically wrought disloyalties. To take refuge here where answers are always most incomplete — in the *how* that can never reveal the *why* it methodologically seeks — means, in the context of this study, suspending any gesture of arrival at its end.

Notes

Taking Refuge: An Introduction

1. Various thinkers working in the poststructuralist tradition have explored how the disciplinary structure of knowledge is itself one of the contingencies that condition any claim to know. In *Discipline and Punish,* Michel Foucault discusses disciplinarity in two registers: as a host of increasingly specified practices that discipline the body in the school, the military, and the penitentiary, and as the disciplines of knowledge known as the human and social sciences. For Foucault, these registers are linked in the broad transformation of the Western episteme from the classical age (the Enlightenment) to the modern, and pivot around the rise of the human being as the new object of "his" own investigation. In chapter 1, I will discuss these epistemic divisions more fully, especially in the context of understanding their relationship to race and gender as corporeal technologies. Also see Foucault's *The Order of Things* and *The Birth of the Clinic.* For a critical assessment of the implications of Foucault's conversation about disciplinarity on contemporary organizations of knowledge, see Jonathan Arac, ed., *After Foucault.*

   It should be noted that Foucault's critiques of methodology and the disciplinary organization of both knowledge and the social body are not without their own methodological investments, assumptions, and practices. For critical discussion of Foucault's own methodological entrapment, see Nancy Fraser, *Unruly Practices* 17–66; Jurgen Habermas, "Taking Aim at the Heart of the Present," "The Critique of Reason as an Unmasking of the Human Sciences," and "Some Questions Concerning the Theory of Power"; Rosemary Hennessy, *Materialist Feminism and the Politics of Discourse* 38–46; David Couzens Hoy, "Introduction" and "Power, Repression, Progress"; Richard Rorty, "Foucault and Epistemology"; G. S. Rousseau, "Foucault and Enlightenment"; Gayatri Chakravorty Spivak, "Can the Subaltern Speak?"; Charles Taylor, "Foucault on Freedom and Truth"; and Michael Walzer, "The Politics of Michel Foucault." For a broader introduction to the way poststructuralist theorists have affected questions of disciplinary study, see Robert Young's *White Mythologies.*

2. In this and other ways, *American Anatomies* evinces an affinity to the critical

project currently being outlined as "cultural studies." Lawrence Grossberg, Cary Nelson, and Paula A. Treichler describe this emerging field of transdisciplinary and antidisciplinary study as engaging the "new politics of difference" — of gender, race, class, nationality, sexuality — in ways once anathema to the traditional disciplines. Hence, critical focus turns to

> gender and sexuality, nationhood and national identity, colonialism and postcolonialism, race and ethnicity, popular culture and its audiences, science and ecology, identity politics, pedagogy, the politics of aesthetics, cultural institutions, the politics of disciplinarity, discourse and textuality, history, and global culture in a postmodern age. ("Cultural Studies" 1)

While I am unconvinced that understanding the postmodern as an "age" is ultimately useful, the refusal of cultural studies practitioners to codify the field through traditional routes — by fashioning a distinct methodology and a discrete object (or objects) of analysis — might be read as distinctively postmodern. For conversations about cultural studies and its challenge to traditional disciplinarity, see Patrick Brantlinger, *Crusoe's Footprints;* Simon During, ed., *The Cultural Studies Reader;* Lawrence Grossberg, "History, Politics and Postmodernism"; Stuart Hall, "Cultural Studies and Its Theoretical Legacies" and "The Emergence of Cultural Studies and the Crisis of the Humanities"; Angela McRobbie, "New Times in Cultural Studies"; Cary Nelson, "Always Already Cultural Studies"; Graeme Turner, *British Cultural Studies;* and Raymond Williams, "The Future of Cultural Studies." On feminism's relationship to this field, see Sarah Franklin, Celia Lury, and Jackie Stacey, eds., *Off-Centre.*

3. In the objectivist and rationalist modes of knowing that have attended modernity, investigative method has often served to guarantee the equation between knowledge and truth, and it is this reliance on methodological objectivity that has linked the panoply of investigative sites that form the academic disciplines in the humanities and social sciences, from literary study, history, sociology, anthropology, philosophy, and biology to the "hard" or natural sciences such as physics and mathematics. In such a linkage, the fundamental crisis underlying modernity — the end of both political and theological sovereignty — can be brought under control, so the hope goes, by a new system. Indeed, the very quest for order and subjective mastery that accompanies the emergence of "man" as the-being-who-knows and the-being-to-be-known demonstrates the anxiety that the disciplinary practices of modernity hope to allay. But we would be wrong to assume, as contemporary critics often do, that in the context of such anxiety, modernity *is* the final or transcendent achievement of an epistemological or methodological security. Instead, it is more useful to understand modernity as the desire to replace epistemological anxieties wrought by vast changes in Western cultures (political, economic, aesthetic, and technological) with systems and methods invested with the power to guarantee both truth and transcendence. Such an understanding allows us to approach contemporary de-

bates within and about disciplinary knowledges, often culled under the broad heading "the postmodern," as part of modernity's own disciplinary anxieties.

In saying this, I am understanding the relationship between the modern and the postmodern not in terms of historical lineage, aesthetic formulations, or economic systems, but as a tension and struggle within Western productions of knowledge that have in fact marked modernity since its unofficial rumblings in the late Renaissance. But postmodernity, as Jean-François Lyotard says in *The Postmodern Condition,* is not the sequential successor to modernity "is not modernism at its end but in the nascent state, and this state is constant" (79). Postmodernity, then, as Diane Elam glosses, "is a rewriting of modernity, which has already been active *within* modernity for a long time" (*Romancing the Postmodern* 9). It is, if I can be allowed the irony of a schematic definition, the anxiety within modernity that surrounds both the ability of the subject to know and the articulation of the object as fully knowable. By refusing to share with the modern the hope that this anxiety can be anything other than the condition and limit of all knowledge, the postmodern precedes the modern, rereading the excesses of unknowability and contingency that modernity strives to expel from its theoretical frame.

In "Postmodernism as Pseudohistory," Craig Calhoun argues similarly, though for different political and theoretical reasons. He says, "The apparent historicity of the opposition of modern to postmodern obscures the extent to which this debate is the latest working out of tensions basic to the whole modern era" (92). See also, Wendy Brown, "Feminist Hesitations, Postmodern Exposures"; Judith Butler, "Contingent Foundations"; Bill Readings, *Introducing Lyotard;* and Lyotard's "Re-writing Modernity."

4. See, in order, David Michael Levin, ed.; Bill Readings and Stephen Melville, eds.; Hal Foster, ed.; John Berger; John Ellis; Linda Williams; Tessa Boffin and Jean Fraser, eds.; Fredric Jameson; Griselda Pollack; and Martin Jay.

5. For various takes on the issue of identity and postmodern theory in feminism, see Linda Alcoff, "Cultural Feminism versus Post-Structuralism"; Judith Butler, *Gender Trouble;* Dympna Callaghan, "The Vicar and Virago"; Donna Haraway, "A Manifesto for Cyborgs"; Sandra G. Harding, "The Instability of the Analytical Categories of Feminist Theory"; Angela McRobbie, "Feminism, Postmodernism and the Real Me"; Chandra Talpade Mohanty, "Feminist Encounters"; and Shane Phelan, *Identity Politics.* In "Ethnic Identity and Post-Structuralist Differance," R. Radhakrishnan explores the relationship between ethnic identity and contemporary critical theory, while Homi K. Bhabha's "Interrogating Identity" turns to the question of identity and postcoloniality. See Henry Giroux, "Living Dangerously"; two essays by Stuart Hall, "Ethnicity" and "What Is This 'Black' in Black Popular Culture?"; Phillip Brian Harper, *Framing the Margins;* Kobena Mercer, "'1968'" and "Welcome to the Jungle"; and Jonathan Rutherford, ed., *Identity.*

6. The mass commercialization accompanying the authorization of Martin Luther

King Jr.'s birthday as a national holiday in 1987 is a case in point, as even McDon-
ald's used his image to align itself with the same community it has so masterfully
exploited as a low-wage employment pool. In the circulation of King as specular embodiment of "American" culture, the national holiday was disarticulated
from its historical struggle for political representation and attached instead to
the commodity aesthetic, signifying the fulfillment of one leader's famous dream
regardless of the very real loosening of black political and economic power
witnessed during that decade. In this translation of racial identity politics into
consumable specularity, "blackness" becomes both a market commodity and a
commodified market — a strategy that results not only in the greater representational inclusion of African-Americans in U.S. film, television, literature, and
critical theory but also in the material disparity between practices of representation and of the social "real." See Angela Y. Davis's take on the absorption of
black politics into commodity culture in the 1980s and 1990s in "Black Nationalism" and Michael Eric Dyson's reading of race and contemporary popular
culture in *Reflecting Black*. For an archival history, see Jan Nederveen Pieterse,
White on Black, and Sieglinde Lemke's critique of Pieterse in "White on White."

7. See especially Hazel Carby, *Reconstructing Womanhood;* Teresa de Lauretis, "The
Essence of the Triangle or, Taking the Risk of Essentialism Seriously"; Diana
Fuss, *Essentially Speaking;* Elspeth Probyn, "Technologizing the Self"; Denise
Riley, *"Am I That Name?";* Gayatri Chakravorty Spivak, "In a Word"; and Eliza-
beth Weed, "Introduction: Terms of Reference."

8. This means, for instance, that the cultural determinations of both whiteness
and masculinity have become specific categories of analysis, though it must
be remarked that masculinity as a critical problem still exceeds, in both vol-
ume and theoretical articulation, that of whiteness. For a sense of the terrain of
the new masculinity studies, see Harry Brod, ed., *The Making of Masculinities;*
Rowena Chapman and Jonathan Rutherford, eds., *Male Order;* Jeff Hearn and
David Morgan, eds., *Men, Masculinities and Social Theory;* Michael Kaufman,
ed., *Beyond Patriarchy;* Michael S. Kimmel, ed., *Changing Men;* and Jonathan
Rutherford, *Men's Silences*. On the relationship between masculinity studies and
feminism, see Caroline Ramazanoglu, "What Can You Do with a Man?" and
Robyn Wiegman, "Feminism and Its Mal(e)contents."

9. Contemporary scholarship on the black woman is too extensive to list com-
prehensively, but the following played a crucial role in the critical reclamation:
Roseann P. Bell, Bettye J. Parker, and Beverly Guy-Sheftall, eds., *Sturdy Black
Bridges;* Lorraine Bethel and Barbara Smith, eds., *Conditions;* Toni Cade, ed.,
The Black Woman; Barbara Christian, *Black Women Novelists;* Angela Y. Davis,
Women, Race, and Class; Paula Giddings, *When and Where I Enter;* bell hooks,
Ain't I a Woman and *Feminist Theory;* Gloria T. Hull, Patricia Bell Scott, and
Barbara Smith, eds., *All the Women Are White, All the Blacks Are Men, but Some
of Us Are Brave;* Joyce Ladner, *Tomorrow's Tomorrow;* Gerda Lerner, ed., *Black*

Women in White America; and Michele Wallace, *Black Macho and the Myth of the Superwoman.*

10. The proliferation of black women's historical projects provides a variety of case studies for rethinking the breadth and strength of a feminist tradition within black women's political organizing in the United States. Such investigations pressure the very meaning of feminism, both in terms of its political activities and theoretical conversations. As Deborah McDowell discusses in "Transferences":

> The belief that feminism and whiteness form a homogeneous unity has long persisted, along with the equally persistent directive to feminist theorists to "account" in their discourses for the experiences of women of color. The unexamined assumption that white feminist discourse bears a special responsibility to women of color helps to maintain the perception that feminism equates with whiteness. (52)

In rethinking this assumption, feminists will have to consider the way we have defined both feminist consciousness and political commitment as coterminous with issues narrowly posited as being "about women." See also Evelyn Brooks Higginbotham, "African-American Women's History and the Metalanguage of Race."

11. Deterritorialization of the binary structure of race can take several routes, from turning to other figurations of race to tackling the binary from within its own discursive and political logic. While I am taking the latter approach in this study, such an analysis of race by no means precludes the former. On a comparative note, see Thomas E. Skidmore, *Black into White.*

12. In thinking about the way that white supremacy pivots on the binary construction of race, it is significant how threatening "multiculturalism" — as an emblem of both educational reform and the rapidly changing U.S. demographic — has become in recent years. As the overt target of conservative attacks on "political correctness" in academia, multiculturalism has the potential to expose the mythology of race as a binary and hence to rethink the hegemony of "whiteness" as a social (and political) majority. In "Questions of Multiculturalism," Gayatri Chakravorty Spivak and Sneja Gunew debate the political consequences of multicultural discourses. See also Henry Giroux, "Post-Colonial Ruptures and Democratic Possibilities"; Chandra Talpade Mohanty, "On Race and Voice"; and Christopher Newfield, "What Was Political Correctness?"

13. Martin Jay's "In the Empire of the Gaze," begins by establishing Foucault's work in the context of twentieth-century French antivisual discourse, demonstrating the preoccupation by a number of intellectuals with questions of vision and visuality, from George Bataille and Jean-Paul Sartre to Christian Metz, Luce Irigaray, Louis Althusser, and Emmanuel Levinas. One might add to the list Guy DeBord, whose *Society of the Spectacle* underscores the significance of the

visual in commodity culture and presents a vastly different understanding of the concept of spectacle developed by Foucault in *Discipline and Punish*. In his voluminous consideration of vision, *Downcast Eyes*, Jay devotes a chapter to the relationship between Foucault and DeBord (381–434).

Various critics have begun to turn away from the question of the visual to explore the epistemological underpinnings of other senses. See in particular, Nancy Love, "Politics and Voice(s)"; Emily Martin, "Science and Women's Bodies"; Lee Clark Mitchell, "Face, Race, and Disfiguration in Stephen Crane's *The Monster*"; and Mohanty, "On Race and Voice."

14. Anglo-American feminist theoretical accounts of the overlay of patriarchy, capitalism, and white supremacy, in particular, often suffer from an eagerness to systematize and linearize the emergence of various forms of cultural oppressions. For instance, Gerda Lerner's *The Creation of Patriarchy*—while offering an important intervention into feminist assumptions of patriarchal formations as transhistorical—maintains that the articulation of gender is the primary or originary structure of difference on which other forms are subsequently inscribed. She posits not only that "[t]he oppression of women antedates slavery and makes it possible" but that "[b]y subordinating women of their own group and later captive women, men learned the symbolic power of sexual control over men and elaborated the symbolic language in which to express dominance" (77, 80). While we may recognize the ability of a discourse of sexual difference to articulate relations that seem, at their most surface level, to exclude women (class and race differences among men, for instance), the linear historical narrative of an originary cultural difference of gender onto which all other systems have been mapped may obscure rather than illuminate the complex overlay of patriarchy, capitalism, and white supremacy. Most crucially, as my discussion here suggests, the relationship between specific discourses of difference varies according to their articulatory locus and needs to be deciphered within and not simply across those domains. Both Sandra G. Harding (*The Science Question in Feminism*) and Elizabeth V. Spelman (*Inessential Woman*) try to counter this tendency in Anglo-American feminist thought by offering frameworks for examining race and gender that do not posit linear development. For a very insightful discussion of these issues, see Elisabeth Young-Bruehl, "Discriminations."

15. While my focus on race arises from its epistemological connection to modern notions of humanity and citizenry, I am not making a claim that race science is either the most important or the only discursive context for reading the emergence of race and gender hierarchies. See Paul Gilroy's *The Black Atlantic* for a quite different way of reading the relationship between race and modernity.

16. By using the hybrid phrase "African(-American)" throughout this book, I am pointing simultaneously toward the African slave and her American-born descendants.

17. With the circulation of these positive images, certain seemingly representative identities gain a visibility in U.S. culture, but the social hierarchies of race and gender are not dislodged, no matter how effectively rearticulated they may be by a new rhetoric of social equality. Those who achieve greater access to the benefits of a materialist culture—women and people of color who enter the middle classes as emblems of this social equality—are the token representatives of the new order, often the same people who view their successes as individually motivated and not the products of a culture negotiating internal dissent. The fallacy of a liberating cultural pluralism is evident everywhere: in the decline of black enrollment in colleges across the nation, the increase in nonwhite poverty and unemployment, the loss of social welfare programs for the poor, the burgeoning numbers of the homeless, the growing membership of white supremacist groups, and the increasing inaccessibility of health care, including abortion, for women.

But the strength and cultural attractiveness of the belief in a transcendent America is not simply that it veils the material relations at work in contemporary culture, allowing us the easy assumption that democracy has finally been achieved, but that through this posture the discourses of dissent, particularly those of black power and feminism, can be rendered obsolete, no longer pertinent to the needs of our society. As Allan Bloom asserts in *The Closing of the American Mind,* "[t]here is very little ideology or militant feminism in most of the women [in college today], because they do not need it . . . the battle here has been won" (107); and of black studies programs, he writes, "[they] largely failed because what was serious in them did not interest the students, and the rest was unprofitable hokum" (95). The myth that feminist and black discourses have been incorporated into the U.S. cultural consciousness as a belief in innate equality becomes, ironically, the vehicle for discarding the very discourses that struggled against the barriers of segregation and sexism. In this way, the reconstruction project of the contemporary era can have its cake, the satisfying belief in egalitarian achievement, and eat it too, cannibalizing the voices of dissent in a massive recuperation of the twentieth century's most radical period of social challenge.

1   Visual Modernity

1. Colette Guillaumin's "Race and Nature" offers a useful explication of the contradictions that attend Western formations of race. As she says, race is simultaneously "an aggregate of somatic and physiological characteristics" and "an aggregate of social characteristics that express a group" (25). It is inscribed as both a social and a natural taxonomy and hence its ideological basis is conceptually inconsistent, but nonetheless consistently strong.

2. Race, in short, must be scripted and most importantly incessantly performed.

Its performativity accounts in part for the many appearances in U.S. literary production of the "mulatto," a figure who literally embodies the cultural contradiction of "race" by marking its fictivity as a visible relation. Because even a preliminary listing of the many novels and short stories featuring the mulatto would run several pages, I suggest the following secondary sources for bibliographic information and critical discussion: Judith R. Berzon, *Neither White nor Black;* Hazel Carby, *Reconstructing Womanhood* 88–91, 171–175; Barbara Christian, *Black Women Novelists* 35–61; Mary V. Dearborn, "Miscegenation and the Mulatto, Inheritance and Incest"; and Henry Louis Gates Jr., "The Trope of the New Negro." F. James Davis's *Who Is Black?* provides a useful historical accounting of miscegenation laws in nineteenth- and twentieth-century U.S. life, as does John G. Mencke in *Mulattoes and Race Mixture.*

3. Under a slave economy, we can read this elision as producing various legal and political structures of repression and violence, from the complete negation of the African(-American) subject as human to the codification of the one-drop rule that displaced issues of kinship into the more socially manageable paradigm of property relations. In the twentieth century, the logic of race has been negotiated, rather ironically, through the rise of various nationalist ideologies and a series of legal reforms that pivot on recognizing the specificity of innate, though not naturally unequal, "color" differences. The panoptic violence of the slave system, its various practices of surveillance and observation, have in this century reconfigured in the disciplinary mechanisms of urban space, and as the century moves toward closure the right of the master's position atop the hierarchy of race is being asserted with a renewed and disparagingly overt vigor. On contemporary racial politics, see Eric Michael Dyson, *Reflecting Black;* Robert Gooding-Williams, ed., *Reading Rodney King, Reading Urban Uprising;* Toni Morrison, ed., *Race-ing Justice, En-gendering Power;* Michele Wallace, *Invisibility Blues;* and Patricia J. Williams, *The Alchemy of Race and Rights.*

4. See, for instance, Richard D. Alba, *Ethnic Identity;* Richard Dyer, "White"; Hal Foster, "'Primitive' Scenes"; Diane L. Fowles, *White Political Women;* Ruth Frankenberg, *White Women, Race Matters;* Eric Lott, *Love and Theft* and "White Like Me"; Lee Clark Mitchell, "Face, Race, and Disfiguration in Stephen Crane's *The Monster*"; Dana D. Nelson, *The Word in Black and White;* and David R. Roediger, *Towards the Abolition of Whiteness.*

5. In *Black Skin, White Masks,* Fanon devotes a chapter to "the fact of blackness," discussing the "corporeal schema" that serves as the primary mechanism for the black "man's" alienation from himself: "I am overdetermined from without. I am the slave not of the 'idea' that others have of me but of my own appearance. . . . I strive for anonymity, for invisibility" (116). Such invisibility becomes, as he calls it, an "amputation" (140). Both the symbolic overdetermination of skin as a visible difference and the subsequent subjective disidentification, wrought through the invisibility of the black *subject* to whites, underlie

"the fact of blackness" and its complicated nexus of identity, subjectivity, and (in)visibility. Significantly, Fanon speaks in dialogue with both Freudian and Lacanian psychoanalysis and, in this regard, might be viewed as a counterpoint to contemporary feminist debates about the usefulness of psychoanalysis for studying the forms and effects of race and racism. On such debates, see Elizabeth Abel, "Race, Class, and Psychoanalysis?," and Jane Gaines, "White Privilege and Looking Relations."

6. See Homi K. Bhabha, "'Race,' Time and the Revision of Modernity"; Paul Gilroy, *The Black Atlantic;* David Theo Goldberg, *Racist Culture;* and David Lloyd, "Race under Representation." For an interesting critique of Lloyd, see Laura Chrisman's "Theorizing 'Race,' Racism and Culture."

7. Of course, the debate about what constitutes modernity—or the methodological transcendence it is often said to inaugurate—is voluminous and highly contentious, and it underlies in varying degrees the preoccupations of contemporary continental philosophy. Some of the major pieces in these debates include Immanuel Kant's "What Is Enlightenment?," Michel Foucault's response, "What Is Enlightenment?," and Jurgen Habermas's subsequent critique, "Modernity—An Incomplete Project." A useful anthology of essays on modernity/postmodernity is Thomas Docherty's *Postmodernism: A Reader.* See also Diane Elam, *Romancing the Postmodern;* Jean-François Lyotard, *The Postmodern Condition* and "Re-writing Modernity"; Mark Poster, "Postmodernity and the Politics of Multiculturalism"; and Andrew Ross, ed., *Universal Abandon?* Feminist conversations about modernity have tended to focus on the political philosophy of democracy and its universalization of the citizen subject. See Michèle Barrett and Anne Phillips, eds., *Destabilizing Theory;* Michele Gisela Bock and Susan James, eds., *Beyond Equality and Difference;* Susan Bordo, "The Cartesian Masculinization of Thought"; Christine DiStefano, *Configurations of Masculinity;* Moira Gatens, *Feminism and Philosophy;* Elizabeth Grosz, "Bodies and Knowledges"; and Anne Phillips, *Democracy and Difference* and "Universal Pretensions in Political Thought."

8. For an analysis interested in tracing the origins of U.S. configurations of white supremacy, see Reginald Horsman, *Race and Manifest Destiny.* Alexander Saxon offers an overview of the critical frameworks often used to explain racial inequality in *The Rise and Fall of the White Republic* (1–20). See also Michael Banton, *The Idea of Race* and *Race Relations.*

9. While the Spanish and Portuguese were engaged in early explorations of the globe in the fifteenth century, I am reading the history of U.S. configurations of race as Winthrop D. Jordan does (*White over Black*) by beginning with the English's first interest in Africa in the sixteenth century when various descriptive accounts were published by explorers who visited the continent. Richard Hakluyt's 1589 *The Principal Navigations, Voyages, Traffiques and Discoveries of the English Nation* set the tone, becoming as Jordan says, "a national hymn,

a sermon, an adventure story, and a scientific treatise" (3) for the English at home. On social forms of race and racism in the early American colonies, see Nelson, *The Word in Black and White.*

10. The theoretical tack I am taking here purposely exceeds various Marxist analyses of the historical production of race, which have often elided the complexity of the visual apprehensions of difference by equating them, solely and uniformly, with the forces of imperialism and capitalist expansion. Oliver C. Cox's 1948 *Caste, Class, and Race* epitomizes one strand of thinking by arguing that while the deployments of race and racism are not constant, all modern forms must be understood within the analytical framework of labor. Michael Goldfield offers a more contemporary version of this argument in "The Color of Politics in the United States." I am not suggesting that the trans-Atlantic slave trade and the increasing articulation of slavery as coterminous with skin color were not significantly tied to the creation and expansion of capital. But the movement from skin to enslavement is not a simple trajectory made possible by a primary ideological need to rationalize modes of production; a cultural context must exist prior to and in excess of the narrative of explanation and closure we now read back onto the first centuries of contact between the African and Anglo cultures. To this degree, I want to suspend the construction of an overarching determination that homogenizes the historical field in order to carefully consider differences within the production of racial discourse, differences that might move us closer to approaching the present deployments of race and the multiple conditions that enhance, circumscribe, and compound their productions. For historical overviews of the Marxian analysis of race, see Philip S. Foner, *American Socialism and Black Americans;* Wilson Record, "The Development of the Communist Position on the Negro Question in the United States"; and Cedric J. Robinson, *Black Marxism.* Recent works that focus on economic explanations include Manning Marable, *How Capitalism Underdeveloped Black America;* John Rex and David Mason, eds., *Theories of Race and Ethnic Relations;* Cornel West, "Marxist Theory and the Specificity of Afro-American Oppression"; and William Julius Wilson, *The Declining Significance of Race.*

11. While a number of historians of race, including Winthrop Jordan and Christian Delacampagne, are most interested with tracing a lineage for race that connects ancient Greek cultures with the contemporary West in terms of racist logic, Lucius Outlaw's "Toward a Critical Theory of 'Race'" pays closer attention to the significatory structure surrounding the concept. Here, he notes that the word "race" does not even appear in English until 1508 (in a poem by William Dunbar) and argues along with Michael Omi and Howard Winant in their *Racial Formation in the United States* that as a concept, race is best understood as a "social formation," irreducible to capital, and historically transforming. St. Clair Drake's two-volume *Black Folks Here and There* provides the kind of historical documentation of early Judaic, Greek, Roman, Egyptian, Ethiopian, and

Muslim cultures to support the contention that before the sixteenth century, as he writes, "neither White Racism nor *racial slavery* existed, although *color prejudice* was present in places" (1:xxiii). For me, such a contention demonstrates the necessity of understanding the shifting economies of visibility that comprise the historical field of "race." See also Elisabeth Young-Bruehl, "Discriminations."

12. As in Jordan's account, many tracings of race in Western thought take the location of difference at the site of the body as a fact of natural differentiation, as though the difference the eye registers exists prior to its cultural mappings in the realm of a visible truth. Paradoxically, in the twentieth century, we dismiss as myth or ideology such documented instances of purported racial difference as that recounted in *Letters Writ by a Turkish Spy in Paris,* where a late-seventeenth-century medical dissection of a "Negro" discovers, "[b]etween the outward and inward skin of the corps . . . a kind of Vascular Plexus spread over the whole Body like a Web or Net, which was fill'd with a Juice as Black as Ink" (quoted in Richard H. Popkin, "Medicine, Racism, Anti-Semitism" 414). As evidence for the visible "fact" of blackness, this recourse to the body as offering its own observable legitimation importantly reveals the *production* that underlies even the seemingly neutral moment of visual decoding. As I argue in this chapter, the visible is never an uncomplicated production, whether in the seventeenth century or our own.

13. In tattooing, for instance, the sign of lowly status takes its form from an exterior branding, imposed at a precise point in time and performed by a disciplinary system readily available to the slave's immediate (however disempowered) return gaze. But in the application of disciplinary power to the entire surface of the body, in the manufacturing of a discourse of natural inferiority that resides, without physical imposition, on the skin—that application is the product of a different technology, one in which the processes of organization are similarly imposed but wholly veiled. In this dispersion of the locus of power, the body is made the productive agent, a sign wrapped in the visibility it cannot help but wear. This does not mean that the public branding will no longer occur, but that from now on it plays a secondary role to the primacy of the bodily mark, reinforcing that mark through the seeming natural relation between visible body and auction block, plantation whipping, or, later, lynch scene.

14. Stuart Hall is perhaps the most prolific contemporary critic to deal with the elaboration of blackness as a politically and culturally constructed category. See especially "What Is This 'Black' in Black Popular Culture?" and "Ethnicity." See also Cornel West, "The New Cultural Politics of Difference."

15. For further conversation about the politics of vision in linear perspective, see Norman Bryson, *Vision and Painting.*

16. See Thomas F. Gossett, *Race: The History of an Idea in America* 32–34, and Jordan, *White over Black* 217–218.

17. See Gossett, *Race* 32–53.

18. For more on Buffon, see Claude Blanckaert, "Buffon and the Natural History of Man"; Gossett, *Race* 35–36, 44–46; Stephen Jay Gould, *The Mismeasure of Man* 39–40; and Robert Wokler, "From *l'homme physique* to *l'homme moral* and Back." Significantly, Linnaeus had earlier argued for a common parent for all human beings, but in contrast to other natural historians, he believed this parent was black. See A. Owen Aldridge, "Feijoo and the Problem of Ethiopian Color" 273.

19. On Blumenbach, see Gossett, *Race* 37–39; Gould, *The Mismeasure of Man* 36–38; and William Stanton, *The Leopard's Spots* 29–33.

20. See Stanton, *The Leopard's Spots* 1–14. Of course, not all Americans shared Smith's optimism about the liberating possibilities of black enfranchisement. Thomas Jefferson, for instance, publicly argued for innate and irrevocable differences. In his *Notes on the State of Virginia* (1782), Jefferson marks difference through the visual aesthetic of skin, condemning the African to ugliness and asserting inferiority to whites "in the endowments both of body and mind" (138). While Jefferson's position lacks the scientific authority ascribed to the natural historian, his articulation of a vast and inseparable division between Africans and Anglo-Americans partakes in the scripting of the visible from which race was established as the observational detail of the skin.

21. See Peter Camper, *The Works of the Late Professor Camper*. For information on the facial angle and its influence on craniology in the United States, see Gould, *The Mismeasure of Man*. For further elaboration on the Great Chain theory, see Jordan, *White over Black* 219–228, 482–511, and Nancy Stepan, *The Idea of Race in Science* 6–19.

22. But unlike Camper, who defined and classified anthropological distinctions among humans through a framework primarily grounded in aesthetics—as Stanton notes in *The Leopard's Spots*, anthropology and painting for Camper went hand in hand (25)—Cuvier's work took its lead within a new understanding of the human body, one in which the nervous system achieved a position of eminent importance. In classifying human beings within the category of vertebrates, Cuvier would create three subspecies of *Homo sapiens*—Caucasian, Mongolian, and Ethiopian—defining each of these further on the basis of geographical, linguistic, and physical grounds (Banton, *The Idea of Race* 32). In doing so, the Caucasian emerges as distinctively superior: "[i]t is not for nothing," Cuvier notes, "that the Caucasian race has gained dominion over the world and made the most rapid progress in the sciences" (quoted in Banton 33). For a wider discussion of these branches of race science, see Gould, *The Mismeasure of Man;* Sandra G. Harding, ed., *The "Racial" Economy of Science;* and Stanton, *The Leopard's Spots*. And for a consideration of the way African-American physicians and intellectuals have responded to anatomical discourses of difference, see Nancy Stepan and Sander Gilman's "Appropriating the Idioms of Science."

23. For further conversation about the American school of craniology, see Banton,

The Idea of Race; George M. Fredrickson, *The Black Image in the White Mind;* Gould, *The Mismeasure of Man;* and Stanton, *The Leopard's Spots.*

24. While the recognition of this subjection overthrows the rationalism of the classical episteme, it does not suspend all attempts to fashion transcendence, as Foucault details in his discussion of Kant. As Hubert Dreyfus and Paul Rabinow explain, Kant and his followers did not lament the limitation presented by the dissolution of rational objectivity, "rather they tried to turn it to advantage, making it the basis of all factual . . . knowledge" (*Michel Foucault* 28). In various attempts to harness the finitude of human being, to fashion it into a foundation for knowledge, Foucault locates the recurring quest for mastery that underlies Western thought itself.

25. We can read the cultural hegemony of realist technologies of representation as the still functional hope for some kind of transcendent vision, a means whereby the subject can hold to a sense of the truth of what it sees. U.S. culture is deeply stranded between the implications of referential "loss" and the emancipatory appeal of a renewed, however technological, illusion. This is especially apparent as we begin to live more fully in the integrationist era, where the rhetorical and representational inclusion of "blacks and women," whether in popular culture, academia, or even the military, can now provide the necessary cultural illusion of a radically transformed, indeed visibly different, social body.

26. In this way, Foucault explicitly argues for a notion of power that is not bound to the binary grid of domination versus oppression. For him, power is not "the 'privilege,' acquired or preserved, of the dominant class, but the overall effect of its strategic positions—an effect that is manifested and sometimes extended by the position of those who are dominated" (*Discipline and Punish* 26–27). Foucault's seeming displacement of a class analysis in which power is owned by some and wholly denied to others is one of the areas that feminists in particular have been quick to critique, arguing that Foucault denies the actual existence of domination. For instance, in "Foucault on Power: A Theory for Women?" Nancy Hartsock contends that he makes it difficult to "locate domination," chiding him, as part of a "majority" who cannot see inequality, for emphasizing the participatory features of subjugation. "It is certainly true that dominated groups participate in their own domination," Hartsock writes. "But rather than stop with the fact of participation, we would learn a great deal more by focusing on the means by which this participation is exacted" (169). For many readers of Foucault, including myself, tracing the means through which participation is exacted is precisely what his analyses do. Both Judith Butler, *Gender Trouble* (93–111), and Nancy Fraser, *Unruly Practices* (17–66), offer more complicated readings of the political consequences for feminism of Foucault's analysis of power. See also Susan J. Hekman, *Gender and Knowledge,* and Rosemary Hennessy, *Materialist Feminism and the Politics of Discourse.*

27. Gates's "The Trope of the New Negro" is accompanied by reproductions of

various artifacts from popular culture of the early twentieth century, including a postcard featuring a scene of multiple lynching, cartoons with Samboesque characters, and frontispieces for sheet music adorned with smiling "coons." Marlon Riggs's film *Ethnic Notions* is a particularly powerful documentary of Americana that relies on the stereotyped images of the African-American. See also Jan Nederveen Pieterse, *White on Black,* and William L. Van Deburg, *Slavery and Race in American Popular Culture.*

28. See especially C. Vann Woodward's introduction to *The Strange Career of Jim Crow.*

29. In *Primate Visions,* Donna Haraway notes how whiteness is "a designation of a political space, not a biological 'race,'" offering the example of the Irish who "moved from being perceived as colored in the early nineteenth century in the United States to quite white in Boston's school busing struggles in the 1970s" (401, 402n15). In assessing the inadequacy of whiteness as a "marker of actual skin color," Haraway turns as well to the U.S. Jewish population, which has "been ascribed white status more or less stably after World War II, while Arabs continue to be written as colored in the daily news" (402n15). See June Howard's *Form and History in American Literary Naturalism* for an important look at the way immigrant populations were initially posited within the typographies of African-American racial designations, and Spike Lee's 1991 *Jungle Fever,* which offers a particularly interesting exploration of the tensions between U.S. ethnicities (most pointedly, African-American and Italian-American) as they have been articulated along the fault line of racial difference.

30. I'm drawing this idea of second reconstruction from the historical accounts of both Manning Marable (*Race, Reform and Rebellion*) and Woodward (*The Strange Career of Jim Crow*) who see a comparison between the aftermath of the Civil War era in the nineteenth century and the decades following World War II in the twentieth. The second reconstruction refers to the integrationist legal and political remedies — affirmative action, for instance — that accompanied the demise of segregation. The kind of neosegregated society we now encounter in the 1990s, along with the proliferation of white rights groups and growing Klan activity, marks an uncanny similarity to the post-Reconstruction era of a century ago, and hence demonstrates the saliency of those very recuperative strategies that undid the possibilities of that enfranchisement. See also Eric Foner, *Reconstruction,* and Joel Williamson, *The Crucible of Race.*

31. While the postulation of subjection as the key term for understanding how social subjects are situated might seem to homogenize or flatten the hierarchical consequences of the deployment of the discourse of race, it is necessary to distinguish between subjection and subjugation. This distinction is crucial in order to ward off contemporary cultural rhetoric concerning "white rights" or "reverse discrimination" — rhetoric that appropriates and inverts the processes and products of hierarchical arrangements by ascribing a subjugation based on the

seeming loss of supremacy accorded white skin. But while whiteness achieves its signifactory power through a process of subjection through which the body is invested with social meaning and a subjectivity subsequently inscribed, such subjection is not coterminous with the kind of subjugation governing the production of the "black" body I have extrapolated in my discussion here. Subjection as the framework for the emergent modern subject does not necessitate that those aligned under the categorical privilege of whiteness be figured as victims of racial discourse, but it does entail the recognition that whiteness is a cultural production devoid of a natural, secure, wholly epidermal or psychological referential domain.

2   Sexing the Difference

1. A great deal has been written on the cult of true womanhood. See in particular Catherine Clinton, *The Plantation Mistress;* Nancy F. Cott, *The Bonds of Womanhood;* Ann Firor Scott, *The Southern Lady;* and Barbara Welter, "The Cult of True Womanhood, 1820–1860." On the representational relationship between the white woman's idealization and the black woman's sexualized denigration, see also Hazel Carby, *Reconstructing Womanhood,* especially 20–40.

2. In this statement, I am distinguishing between two social formations of slavery: as a system of exportation of people from their native lands and as the imperialistic imposition of enslavement onto indigenous populations. Ideologies of family and familialism that overlay the U.S. slave system (and that underwrite its reproduction of African[-American]s as property) thus have a specificity that may not translate to all colonial relations. In *When the Mater Dolorosa Speaks,* Kyeong-Hee Choi explores differences and similarities within the cultural contexts of postcolonial structures and discourses. See also George M. Frederickson, *White Supremacy.*

3. In *L'Invention du racism,* Christian Delacampagne links the philosophical discourses of antiquity and the theological writings of the Middle Ages to demonstrate that, as he says later, "racist discourse, as we have known it in Europe since the nineteenth century, did not appear ex nihilo. It is the fruit—or the inheritor—of other, older discourses. . . . Ancient or Medieval, this premodern racism . . . developed hand in hand with the very foundations of Western rationalism" ("Racism and the West" 83). To take the Foucauldian perspective, as I have done, is not to discount the early formations of racist discourse that both Nancy Stepan and Delacampagne point to, but to argue that such a lineage is not epistemologically continuous, given the vastly different contexts— the radically shifting formations of knowledge—in which the ancients, medieval theologians, and Enlightenment rationalists each respectively moved.

4. For a more thorough conversation about the conflict between nineteenth-century Christian theological assumptions and investigations into human anat-

omy, see especially William Stanton, *The Leopard's Spots* 42–44, 69–81. As always, Winthrop D. Jordan provides important historical information about the symbolic and religious figuration of race in the United States prior to 1812 in *White over Black,* especially 342–374.

5. On Gliddon, see Stanton, *The Leopard's Spots* 45–53.

6. The notion of race as a mutable difference thus recedes as the ascendancy of anatomical investigation turns toward the body for a more definitive anchoring of hierarchical social organizations. Although they do not use such terms, both Londa Schiebinger (*Nature's Body*) and Nancy Stepan ("Race and Gender") acknowledge the supersession of natural history by comparative anatomy as an epistemic shift wrought by humanism and its determinative investment in the body's internal domains. Or as George W. Stocking Jr. explains in *Race, Culture, and Evolution,* "[g]iven the static, nonevolutionary, classificatory point of view of Cuverian comparative anatomy, polygenism followed quite easily for those sufficiently uninhibited by religious orthodoxy" (29).

7. As I discuss later in this chapter, Henry Louis Gates Jr. offers in "Literary Theory and the Black Tradition" a brief catalogue of the racialist positions of a variety of Enlightenment philosophers, including Kant, Hume, and Hegel. See also David Theo Goldberg, *Racist Culture* and "The Social Formation of Racist Discourse," and Richard H. Popkin, "The Philosophical Basis of Eighteenth-Century Racism."

8. There, as Stanton writes, it was understood that the brain was "the seat of the mind and that each of [its] various parts . . . ha[d] its own function. . . . [T]he size of the part determined the degree of the function and . . . since the brain [wa]s closely encased by the cranium, the size of the various parts could be determined by the contour of the skull" (*The Leopard's Spots* 35).

9. See Jordan, *White over Black* 216–259, and Schiebinger, *Nature's Body* 75–114.

10. For more on the link between the Hottentot and sexuality, see Sander Gilman, "Black Bodies, White Bodies"; Thomas F. Gossett, *Race: The History of an Idea* 380–381; Jordan, *White over Black* 491–497; and Schiebinger, *Nature's Body* 160–172.

11. If, as Foucault argues, the late nineteenth century demonstrates the rise of a variety of scientific and medical discourses aimed at procuring normative sexual practices and disciplinary structures, we might understand the investigation of racial sexuality as part of this broader articulation of surveillance. The voyeuristic productions of scientific investigations into black sexuality function to displace the illicit sexual practices of the (intra)colonies from the realm of a sanctioned and recognized heterosexuality. In this, heterosexuality as the compulsory form of gender sexual relations is revealed in its tie to the maintenance of the white body's racial purity as much as it reconvenes masculine privileges and sexual definitions.

12. See Gilman, "Black Bodies, White Bodies," and Schiebinger, *Nature's Body* 172.

13. Jordan, *White over Black* 33; see also 136–178 and 216–233. On contemporary configurations of black male sexuality, see Kobena Mercer, "Skin Head Sex Thing", and Mercer and Isaac Julien, "Race, Sexual Politics and Black Masculinity"; Robyn Wiegman, "Feminism, the *Boyz*, and Other Matters Regarding the Male"; and Thomas E. Yingling, "How the Eye Is Caste."

14. Schiebinger, *Nature's Body*, provides the most thorough documentation of this saturation. See 75–114.

15. John S. Haller and Robin M. Haller concur with this reading of sexual difference as grafted onto racial discourse in nineteenth-century science:

> A considerable portion of scientific opinion relating to the sexes originated in somatometric examinations carried out during the nineteenth century, which focused upon difference among the various races of man. Analyses of skull capacity, facial angle, and body dimensions provided weighty documentation to support the Caucasian's claim of racial superiority. These early examinations included statistics on women, and evidence amassed from the very beginning tended to relegate the female, with the Negro, to a subordinate position in race and sex development. (*The Physician and Sexuality in Victorian America* 48)

In addition, Schiebinger's discussion in *Nature's Body* about the gendering of modern science, while crafted around a claim for gender's originary centrality, nonetheless supports my argument here that the anatomical study of racial difference begets the turn to anatomizing sexual difference. Such a claim is significant only as a demonstration of the shifting relationship between race and gender in different historical contexts and discursive registers, *not* as a foundation for citing race as the origin or paradigm for all formations of gender.

16. See Schiebinger, *Nature's Body* 115.

17. See ibid. 156–158.

18. In "Bodily Bonds," Karen Sanchez-Eppler notes that the category "feminism-abolitionism" is a contemporary figuration, not a nineteenth-century one. While my comments here are drawing on the reader's awareness of the broad survey of the discursive collaboration she describes, I will delve further into these political conjunctions in chapter 6.

19. Gossett, *Race* 39.

20. In "Of National Characters," David Hume writes, for instance, that "[t]here never was a civilized nation of any other complexion than white. . . . No ingenious manufacturers among them, no arts, no sciences" (3:252n1). And of the Jamaican poet, Francis Williams, Hume assumes "'tis likely he is admired for very slender accomplishments, like a parrot who speaks a few words plainly" (3:252n1).

21. For feminist critiques of the masculinist biases of the Enlightenment's public sphere, see Mary P. Ryan, "Gender and Public Access" and *Women in Public;* and

Michael Warner, "The Mass Public and the Mass Subject." On the importance of rethinking the public/private dichotomy altogether, see Seyla Benhabib and Drucilla Cornell, eds., *Feminism as Critique;* Dorothy O. Helly and Susan M. Reverby, eds., *Gendered Domains;* and Janet Sharistanian, ed., *Beyond the Public/Domestic Dichotomy.*

22. See, for instance, Jacqueline Jones, *Labor of Love, Labor of Sorrow,* and Deborah Gray White, *Ar'n't I a Woman.*

23. The Moynihan report is, of course, the primary contemporary source for the popularization of the discourse of the black family's matriarchal failure. For critical commentary on this, see Angela Y. Davis, *Women, Race, and Class;* Jones, *Labor of Love, Labor of Sorrow;* Michele Wallace, *Black Macho and the Myth of the Superwoman;* and White, *Ar'n't I a Woman.* See also "Scapegoating the Black Family," a special issue of *The Nation.*

24. While a full bibliography of the texts adopting this strategy is impossible to provide here, some of the most critically important include Carby, *Reconstructing Womanhood;* Patricia Hill Collins, *Black Feminist Thought;* Davis, *Women, Race, and Class;* bell hooks, *Ain't I a Woman* and *Feminist Theory;* Stanlie M. James and Abena P. A. Busia, eds., *Theorizing Black Feminisms;* Jones, *Labor of Love, Labor of Sorrow;* Gerda Lerner, ed., *Black Women in White America;* Marjorie Pryse and Hortense J. Spillers, eds., *Conjuring;* Cheryl Wall, ed., *Changing Our Own Words;* and White, *Ar'n't I a Woman.*

25. The trope of bringing to voice and visibility the black woman has been routinely used as a way of framing contemporary calls for rethinking the historical erasure of black women from both feminist and patriarchal cultural narratives. While this study does not argue against such a project, it does explore the contradictions of visibility, being the vehicle for both the cultural inscription of a host of corporeal inferiorities and the methodological practice through which disciplinary knowledge has been linked to a liberating, democratic transcendence. While we might recognize the significance and imperative of retrieving the black woman from marginality, the metaphorical weight of making her "visible" carries with it the commodity's historically shifting, but racially coded, determinations.

3 The Anatomy of Lynching

1. In various theoretical registers, but most predominantly the psychoanalytic, sexual differences have been explored as corporeal. That is, the body's seeming visual differences establish the logic of feminine inferiority that underlies Western cultural productions. In feminist film theory, for instance, the female body as a visual icon has been posited as the "stake" of masculine subjectivities, and the circulation of this body—its fetishistic display—has been defined as one of the primary characteristics of Hollywood film. In philosophy and literary theory, feminists have investigated at some length the implications of the

body as the grounds of feminine difference, and a number of emergent cultural studies projects look to the corporeal as a kind of disciplinary terrain through which femininity has (and is) both socially and psychically scripted. While work in this area is prolific, see especially Susan Bordo, *Unbearable Weight;* Judith Butler, *Bodies That Matter;* Elizabeth Grosz, *Volatile Bodies;* Constance Penley, ed., *Feminism and Film Theory;* Linda Singer, *Erotic Warfare;* and Susan Rubin Suleiman, ed., *The Female Body in Western Culture.*

2. Contrary to the way the narrative history of feminism is currently being written by a variety of feminist scholars, the question of differences and of the impossibilities of commonality and sisterhood are not new issues on the theoretical or political horizon. As I discuss at length in chapter 6, feminism in the nineteenth century was an equally contested site for the consideration of differences among women, as analogies between free white women and African(-American) slave women fractiously reveal. Racial differences among women, in short, are currently the repressed content of American feminism in our readings of its origins in the early nineteenth century.

3. While the distinction between symbolic castration and its literal enactment is undoubtedly significant and in many ways incommensurate, I have located the two together here in order to understand how the circulation of the lynch narrative, in relation to *and* apart from actual acts of torture, nonetheless bear a similar disciplinary function. The ideological script of lynching *as* castration thus produces at the level of representation a psychic reality and material force that are equally weighty.

4. But while black women may be absent from the cultural narrative that defines and sanctions lynching, their intellectual and political work against mob violence during the late nineteenth and early twentieth centuries in particular was crucial to broadscale African-American communal resistance. On this, see Hazel Carby, "'On the Threshold of Woman's Era.'" On white women's anti-lynching struggle, see Jacquelyn Dowd Hall, *Revolt against Chivalry.* For a broader consideration of the cultural narratives that underwrite the black woman's excision from the myth of the black rapist, see Wahneema Lubiano, "Black Ladies, Welfare Queens, and State Minstrels." Lubiano's analysis is constructed in the context of Clarence Thomas's use of the lynch metaphor. In "Split Affinities," Valerie Smith considers the implications of these configurations for black women and their relationship to feminism.

5. During final revisions of this chapter, I encountered James R. McGovern's *Anatomy of a Lynching.* While similarly interested in the practice of lynching, McGovern's book focuses on the specificities of the Claude Neal case and is therefore more singularly focused than my discussion here and less wed to poststructuralist and feminist theoretical concepts. But it is significant—and certainly not coincidental—that the concept of anatomy figures centrally in his discussion as well.

6. See especially Judith Fetterley, *The Resisting Reader* 22–33.

7. On mob violence and the Ku Klux Klan, see Jessie Daniel Ames, *The Changing Character of Lynching;* Richard Maxwell Brown, *Strain of Violence* 185–235; James E. Cutler, *Lynch-Law;* National Association for the Advancement of Colored People, *Thirty Years of Lynching in the United States, 1889–1918;* Joel Williamson, *The Crucible of Race;* and C. Vann Woodward, *The Strange Career of Jim Crow.*

8. Much like statistics on rape, numerical accounts of lynching vary widely, most obviously because of the way the legal apparatus has ignored and continues to ignore white violence against African-Americans. Trudier Harris cites 4,951 lynchings in the United States between 1882 and 1927 (*Exorcizing Blackness* 7), using figures provided by Cutler's *Lynch-Law.* See also Brown, *Strain of Violence* 320–326, and Hall, *Revolt against Chivalry* 134–135.

9. The 1992 acquittals of the white Los Angeles police officers who beat a black male suspect, Rodney King, unconscious demonstrate that the figuration of the law that Ellison depicted in 1940 continues to function as the disciplinary mechanism for instantiating and perpetuating white supremacy. One might even venture to say that the decline of the lynch mob in the second half of the twentieth century has less to do with real advancements in white supremacy's abatement than with the incorporation of the mob's tenor and function within the legal and law enforcement systems themselves. See Robert Gooding-Williams, ed., *Reading Rodney King, Reading Urban Uprising.*

10. In *On Lynchings,* Ida B. Wells-Barnett presents her argument against lynching by repeated attention to newspaper accounts. See also Harris, *Exorcizing Blackness* 1–19.

11. D. W. Griffith's 1915 *The Birth of a Nation* is perhaps the classic example of the hysterical tie between the African-American's social participation and the discourse of the black rapist. Here, in a film that literally transformed the technical achievements of American filmmaking, the glory and order of the Old South are contrasted with the devastation and ruin wrought by the Civil War and its aftermath. The picturesque racial harmony of the slave system gives way to massive black corruption, as the seemingly innate bestiality of the ex-slave wends its way to the surface. As blacks descend into laziness and drunkenness, they seize the polls and disenfranchise white citizens before finally laying sexual claim to white women. In the film's finale, as Donald Bogle writes, "a group of good, upright Southern white males . . . wearing sheets and hoods . . . [defends] white womanhood, white honor, and white glory . . . restor[ing] to the South everything it has lost, including its white supremacy. Thus we have the birth of a nation" (*Toms, Coons, Mulattoes, Mammies, and Bucks* 12). See also Alan Casty, "The Films of D. W. Griffith," and Michael Rogin, "'The Sword Became a Flashing Vision.'"

12. The most famous name change, of course, is Malcolm Little's shift to X. On the significance of naming to the African-American literary tradition, see both Kimberly W. Benston, "I Yam What I Am," and Michael Cooke, "Naming, Being, and Black Experience."

13. See Harris, *Exorcizing Blackness* 6–7.

14. See also Hall, who writes that "the proportion of lynchings taking place in the South increased from 82 percent of the total [of executions] in the 1890s to 95 percent in the 1920s; over the same periods the proportion of lynch victims who were white decreased from 32 percent to 9 percent. Lynching had become virtually a Southern phenomenon and a racial one" (*Revolt against Chivalry* 133).

15. Because of the relationship between the public and private in the post-war years—and its contrast to gender roles within the slave community—Angela Y. Davis has argued that the "salient theme emerging from domestic life in the slave quarters is one of sexual equality" (*Women, Race, and Class* 18). Michele Wallace concurs with this, finding that through emancipation, black men were encouraged to adopt white patriarchal roles and practices (see *Black Macho and the Myth of the Superwoman* 17–33). On the particular impact on black family structure in the transition from slavery to sharecropping, see Susan A. Mann, "Slavery, Sharecropping, and Sexual Inequality."

16. As Hall writes in *Revolt against Chivalry,* "The ideology of racism reached a virulent crescendo, as the dominant image of blacks in the white mind shifted from inferior child to aggressive and dangerous animal" (133).

17. The inversion of the black male rape mythos is complete in *Native Son* with the burning and decapitation of Mary Dalton, which I read as a symbolic castration because of the way it foregrounds dismemberment on one hand, while demonstrating the sense of power that accrues to the agent of violence on the other. Of course, the critical force of Wright's novel is that Bigger does not have the power of the law behind him, which means that Mary's decapitation is not analogous to lynching and castration, no matter how overtly evocative it is of these disciplinary practices.

18. For a discussion of the role of black women in *Native Son,* see Trudier Harris, "Native Sons and Foreign Daughters."

19. Baraka [LeRoi Jones] has often portrayed the white man and, significantly, black men who are in his terms pro-white as effeminate or homosexual. See, for example, the white and black police in *Police,* the white father in *Home on the Range,* the white professor in *The Slave,* and Karolis and Foots in *The Toilet.*

20. The consequences of Baraka's reading of cultural sexualities is most apparent in *Madheart,* one of four black revolutionary plays published under the tribute, "All praises to the black man." This piece, featuring five players designated by symbolic association—BLACK MAN, BLACK WOMAN, MOTHER, SISTER, and DEVIL LADY—is organized around the exorcism of the white woman from the mind of BLACK MAN, which enables BLACK MAN to embrace both blackness and his inherent masculine power. Significantly, the white woman serves as the lone symbol of the white world, the emblem of BLACK MAN's emasculation and the source of a cosmic filth (imaged by her genitals as a "stale pussy" [69], "[a]n old punctured sore with the pus rolled out" [73]). By constructing white culture as devoid of the masculine, as significantly the realm of putrefied vaginas,

Baraka is able to claim the masculine wholly for BLACK MAN; as he says at play's end, "I am the new man of the earth" (84).

In opposition to the pollution of DEVIL LADY, BLACK WOMAN serves as the life force for black masculinity—"Touch me if you dare," she says. "I am your soul" (74). Transforming the Freudian question, "What does woman want?" into "What do you want, black man?" (75), BLACK WOMAN offers herself: "I'm real and whole. . . . And yours, only yours, but only as a man will you know that" (81). This "only as a man" is accomplished by a graphic display, as BLACK MAN "wheels and suddenly slaps her crosswise, back and forth across the face" (81). In the taking of his patriarchal rights, BLACK MAN orders: "I want you, woman, as a woman. Go down. (*He slaps again.*) Go down, submit, submit . . . to love . . . and to man, now, forever" (81). Her response: "I . . . I submit. . . . I am your woman, and you are the strongest of God. Fill me with your seed" (82–83). In his wielding of authority as a "man," BLACK MAN demands the traditional powers of domination over "his" woman. While this scene, as critic Charles D. Peavy explains, "might appear somewhat brutal," it is "the final phase in the achievement of BLACK MAN's identity. In the past, BLACK WOMAN has seen BLACK MAN humbled. . . . He could do nothing then, but . . . now . . . he must assert himself. . . . He must symbolically (and physically) dominate her so that he can become her man, and the strongest of God" ("Myth, Magic, and Manhood in LeRoi Jones' *Madheart*" 172).

21. Robert Staples's analysis of the slave economy epitomizes such a reading:

> The black man's only crucial function within the family was that of siring the children. The mother's role was far more important than the father's. . . . The husband was at most his wife's assistant, her companion and her sex partner. He was often thought of as her possession, as was the cabin in which they lived. It was common for a mother and her children to be considered a family without reference to the father. (Quoted in Wallace, *Black Macho* 18)

See also Nathan Hare, "The Frustrated Masculinity of the Negro Male," and Robert Staples, "The Myth of Black Matriarchy."

22. See Nina Burleigh, "David Duke."

4   Bonds of (In)Difference

1. Most people will recognize here my play on George Bush's presidential election theme in 1991—the thousand points of light connoting for him the volunteering program of self-sacrifice needed to replace government entitlements.
2. In its defiance of broad economic and political transformation, the integrationist strategy functions in contemporary visual culture within the realm of the spectacle, thereby displacing the question of multicultural participation in the

economic and productive aspects of film and television. To be sure, Hollywood remains in the hands of predominantly white producers, directors, and actors, even as the rhetoric of integration heralds a cultural visibility of multiplicity.

3. Kobena Mercer and Isaac Julien, like Robert Stam and Louise Spence in "Colonialism, Racism, and Representation," are skeptical about the practices of social integration that interpret the "positive" image as the sign of democratic inclusion (see "Introduction: De Margin and De Centre"). They emphasize instead how the terms of inclusion and exclusion or positive versus negative carry little political utility for describing and critiquing the various forms that white supremacy can take. Indeed, it is precisely through the use of inclusionary rhetoric and representational positivities that the current recuperative strategies of U.S. cultural production have gained their most damaging political force. See also Marlon Riggs's film *Color Adjustment* in which the history of African-Americans on television is traced from within the context of the problematics of the "positive" and "negative" image. From a slightly different perspective, Michele Wallace takes up these issues in *Invisibility Blues* 1–10.

4. In presenting this list, I am trying to make a case for the cultural "hegemony" of interracial male bonding narratives in the 1980s, even as I recognize that such narratives, as Leslie Fiedler has suggested in *Love and Death in the American Novel,* are traditional components of the literary canon—that is, nothing wholly new on the American representational scene. But I would place Fiedler, as I argue in the following chapter, within the integrationist strategy that these films for me evince, thereby understanding their proliferation in contemporary culture and their mapping in post-1960s cultural criticism as historically linked enterprises.

5. Michele Wallace's work on the implications of sexual difference within black power discourses and organizational structures in *Black Macho and the Myth of the Superwoman,* discussed in the previous chapter, demonstrates the difficulties of forging a political movement against white supremacy when the interconnections of sexism and racism are ignored.

6. Like others engaged in interpretations of contemporary popular culture, I am anxious about our critical methodologies, especially the conditions under which we choose texts as paradigmatic examples of broader cultural forces and meanings. Such anxieties, as I have suggested in earlier discussions in this book, are not new, though the realm of the popular, given its sheer proliferation of texts, renders insufficient the traditional practices of literary criticism where our faith in canonicity and author study, for instance, help to alleviate the epistemological questions that underwrite this particular discipline and its modern anxieties. Not that literary study can protect itself from such issues any longer, but it seems to me that a chapter such as this one particularly begs the question of how and for what political purposes the critic pursues a historicizing cultural narrative. Certainly the films that I discuss bear no intrinsic "value" as cultural objects,

and I am under no illusion that the narrative I am constructing from them is the only or even the most salient interpretative possibility attending their cultural production. Indeed, it seems to me that a likely alternative approach might look at the disparity between the recuperative politics of interracial male bonding scenarios and the reception of such narratives by minoritized viewers for whom representational presence is itself understood, in the context of the everyday, as politically enabling.

7. The association between blackness and the feminine is initially drawn through the film's mapping of social space, as Pearce shares a room with the most effeminate character, Poteete (Malcolm Danare), who will eventually be driven by The Ten to suicide. In his proximity to Pearce, the overweight, high-voiced, and routinely crying Poteete is a significant, if short-lived character, becoming both the representative of femininity and the measurement against which Pearce's masculinity will ultimately be drawn.

8. Several Supreme Court cases of the late 1980s evince this resurrection of the white male as the new victim of U.S. cultural practices. The June 1989 decision conferring the right of affirmative action appeal to white firefighters in Birmingham, Alabama, is only one indication of the New Right's efforts to abolish civil rights legislation by claiming it discriminates against white men.

9. It is no accident that numerous representations of the interracial male bond are linked to the image of the vet or that the actors in popular Vietnam movies reappear in other bonding films. For instance, the central actors of the "classic" Vietnam war movie *Platoon* (dir. Oliver Stone, 1986), Tom Berenger and William Defoe, are recycled into two later interracial bonding pictures, *Shoot to Kill* (dir. Robert Spottiswoode) and *Off Limits* (dir. Christopher Crowe) alongside two African-American actors who have appeared in a number of bonding films, Sidney Poitier and Gregory Hines.

10. See in particular Donald Bogle, *Toms, Coons, Mulattoes, Mammies, and Bucks;* Thomas Cripps, *Slow Fade to Black;* and Daniel J. Leab, *From Sambo to Superspade.*

11. At the same time, it allows the alien to speak the words that naturalize human reproduction through the romance of heterosexual union: "you humans have separated your sexes into two separate halves for the joy of that bridged union."

12. While my analysis of this strategy of "proving" U.S. cultural equality through the displacement of racism onto the Soviet system will focus on *White Nights, Streets of Gold* (dir. Joe Roth), emerging a year later, operates in a similar way. The story of two poor boxers — one black, the other white — *Streets of Gold* depicts their initial hostility toward one another and their subsequent friendship, which emerges through their mutual concern for their Russian-born coach, banned from international competition because he is a Jew. The racism of the Communist world is depicted as anti-Semitism, and the resolution of the narrative comes when the two American boxers make the national team and can fight

the Soviets, winning for their coach. But the film does not allow the African-American boxer, who is clearly presented as the best, to fight; being injured, he can only be an onlooker when the less-talented white male confronts the Soviets. In a three-round fight scene that evokes *Rocky* with its brutality and specularization of the male body in combat, the white boxer finally wins, bringing glory to his team, his coach, and his nation. The white male is thus cast as the cultural hero—even in the face of his obviously inferior physical strength. The title comes to represent the possibility of AMERICA, a possibility that—while seemingly extended to all—is nonetheless narratively embodied by the white fighter.

13. Susan Jeffords writes that the "association of the loss of the war with the government and the honor of the war with the soldier reconstitutes one of the principal thematics of U.S. culture, in which individual interests exist in tension with those of the society as a whole" (*The Remasculinization of America* 5). While Greenwood's analysis of U.S. *cultural* relations in the context of the Vietnam war does not rely on the image of the soldier as honorable, it casts his own intentions in such a way that the government becomes the primary force in the debacle of Vietnam, not the men who fought the war.

14. In the context of U.S. culture's taboo against miscegenation, the film's emphasis on Greenwood's fatherhood importantly establishes the interracial sexual configuration as a positive element in the rehabilitation of America. Here, it is communism and not U.S. racism that will finally subvert the fate of the interracial child. Such a narrative turn counters what, in the leftist movements of the 1930s and 1940s, was the classic Communist reading of U.S. culture: its predication not only on a class hierarchy but on race. Susan Brownmiller discusses the Communist party's response to cases of interracial rape and sexuality in *Against Our Will,* highlighting its strategic questioning of capitalism through the public hysteria surrounding such famous cases as Scottsboro. While Brownmiller focuses on the victimization of the white woman in interracial rape scenarios and thereby reinscribes the myth of the black rapist, as Angela Y. Davis points out (*Women, Race, and Class* 178–179), she demonstrates how the American Communist party strategically invested in public commentary on interracial sexuality. In light of *White Nights,* such an investment is overturned in the representation of the Soviet Union and of communism as racist entities.

15. In 1988, NBC produced a sequel to *In the Heat of the Night,* which inaugurated a mid-season series that ran throughout the early 1990s. The sequel depicts Virgil Tubbs returning to Sparta to serve as its detective. Quickly Tubbs becomes involved in the investigation of a white woman's murder, a murder conveniently—and stereotypically—pinned on a black male who is also conveniently and stereotypically lynched in his cell. In unraveling the murder, Tubbs must confront the racist echelon of the town as the murderer turns out to be the son of the oldest, finest, and wealthiest family. The major difference between this and the earlier version is not the depiction of Tubbs, but that of his

white counterpart who, in the ethos of the 1980s, is no longer a bigot but a man who himself picked cotton alongside blacks as a child—a man whose fondest war buddy is black. This "humanization" of the white southerner evinces the strategy under examination here where the interracial male bond is necessary to the recuperation of the white male who must see himself transformed from victimizer/oppressor to partner—even if hesitant—in cultural and racial change.

16. The importance of disaffiliating the male bond from the threat of homosexuality is inscribed overtly in *Shoot to Kill*, where the male protagonists, Warren Stantin (Sidney Poitier) and Jonathan Knox (Tom Berenger), become trapped on a snow-packed mountain at dusk. Knox creates an igloo in the snow and the men spend the night there. As Stantin starts to show signs of frostbite, Knox removes his own shirt and crawls on top of Stantin's body to generate heat; in doing so, he cracks a joke about "country boys," they laugh, and the threat of homosexuality is simultaneously foregrounded and averted.

17. This is no less true of the 1988 film *Cry Freedom*, which tells the story of the struggle against apartheid in South Africa by recounting white journalist Donald Woods's (Kevin Kline) relationship with black rebel Steve Biko (Denzel Washington). Although the film is set in South Africa and directed by the British-born Richard Attenborough, it is in every way an American movie, not simply because of its use of American actors but more importantly because of its reliance on the representational trope common to contemporary American cultural production, that of the interracial male bond. Here, as in *White Nights*, "the West" is upheld as the site of freedom and egalitarianism and reinforced through scenes depicting the terror of the South African regime. In a reenactment of all the films under discussion here, *Cry Freedom* casts the white male as the defender of black liberty who risks his life for the salvation of the other: it is Woods who must escape South Africa with the manuscript he has been writing about Biko's life and political leadership; it is the white family that remains intact soaring through billowing white clouds to freedom in the final scene, a scene that is followed by a list of names, dates, and official reasons for the deaths of blacks held in detention by South African officials. The disparity between the narrative resolution of the white family's odyssey and that of the real victims of apartheid ironically demonstrates the ideological politics governing the representation of the interracial bond. One can only wonder, in fact, why Biko's story was not considered sufficient enough for a film about apartheid.

18. My readings of contemporary interracial male bonding films as recuperative practices for the historically shifting dimensions of white supremacy is not meant to dismiss the importance of Anglo-American interest in subverting the cultural primacy of white skin. But it is to foreground the difference between narratives of white heroism, cast now within a defining framework of antiracism, and the kinds of difficult and necessary negotiations attending any white figure involved in the struggle against white supremacy. Interracial male bonding nar-

ratives too often recreate the imperialistic gesture by simply appropriating a visible economy of difference to refashion Anglo-American centricity.

19. The 1993 film *Philadelphia* (dir. Jonathan Demme) offers an interesting contrast to interracial male bonding films of the 1980s, foregrounding the interplay between homosexuality and African-American ethnicity that earlier Hollywood productions struggled so hard to veil. Here, of course, the African-American male acts as the normative sexual character, and it is from within his biases and prejudices that the film's liberal discourse of homosexuality is defined.

5 Canonical Architecture

1. See Michele Wallace's *Black Macho and the Myth of the Superwoman* for a cogent analysis of sexual difference within civil rights and Black Power discourses and organizations.

2. For the classic discussion of the Adamic tradition, see R. W. B. Lewis, *The American Adam.*

3. To recall earlier parts of my discussion, the Reconstruction era witnessed the articulation of voting rights for African-American men based on the masculinization of the category of citizenry in U.S. culture. In the years following Reconstruction, however, the rise of lynching and of its attendant discourse of the black male as rapist worked to summarily deny the masculine rights enacted during the post–Civil War years. We can also understand the history of African-American men in the armed forces as articulating both a denial of their abilities as men and subsequently conferring such abilities on them, as their inclusion in all services in the mid-twentieth century indicates. Clearly, economic, political, and social factors impact on this masculinization or its withholding, and it is one of the key points in my discussion here that the status of the masculine is historical and changing.

4. For a more extended discussion of the sexual mapping of the nature/culture binarism in U.S. literary production, see both Nina Baym, "Melodramas of Beset Manhood," and Annette Kolodny, *The Lay of the Land.*

5. Eve Kosofsky Sedgwick's reading of the homosocial nexus of masculine bonds provides an important rethinking of Luce Irigaray's rather transhistorical account of the homosexual economy underpinning patriarchal relations in *This Sex Which Is Not One.* For Sedgwick, Irigaray's transmutation of the homosocial into the homosexual displaces the force and power of the heterosexual imperative, and makes the understanding of homophobia and misogyny difficult to apprehend. See in particular *Between Men* 26–27.

6. Leslie Fiedler's interest in rethinking the canon is perhaps most apparent in his anthology, *English Literature: Opening Up the Canon,* coedited with Houston Baker Jr.

7. Diana Fuss's anthology *Inside/Out* offers a wide-ranging and useful bibliography to this important body of work.

8. This evacuation arises in part from the way Robert K. Martin interprets Fiedler's discussion of homosexuality in *Love and Death* as "the situation of homosexuals in contemporary society" (*Hero, Captain, and Stranger* 13). "[H]ow painful it has been," Martin writes, "to see homosexuals' lives and artistic creations so abused. . . . *Love and Death* was important for gay people. . . . it announced that we were there . . . [but] it instantly . . . said, in effect, that we must be cured" (9). In reading *Love and Death* as evoking the presence of "gay people," Martin credits Fiedler with a conceptualization of sexual *identity* virtually absent from Fiedler's discussion of the bond, thereby too neatly packaging homosexual tensions, homoerotic desires, and homosocial masculine relations.

9. For an important discussion of the political possibilities of this kind of subversion, see Judith Butler, *Gender Trouble.*

10. This revision of the closed economy of the phallic signifier is perhaps best demonstrated by Martin's graphic insistence that "[s]urely no one can read Melville without rejoicing in the verbal exuberance, in the sheer delight of handling words, of touching them, of rolling them around in the mouth, almost as if they were globules of sperm" (*Hero, Captain, and Stranger* 11–12). To contest patriarchal inscriptions of the phallus as instrument of domination and conquest is obviously a necessary political deployment, but Martin's equation of a benign masculinity with democracy's most radical potential, represented by the phallus as non(re)productive sexuality, offers a less aggressive but nonetheless wholly masculine representational body for the signification of America.

11. In an earlier piece on Melville, I take Martin to task for his "failure" to adequately articulate the male bond in relation to feminist goals. That reading now strikes me as not simply faulty, but overly committed to constructing the masculine as a homogeneous entity itself. Martin's desire to begin to isolate differences among men, while needing to be further textured, does indeed have important consequences for feminism — as my own text has set out to explore. My rethinking of this earlier critique of critical discussions of interracial male bonding extends, as well, to Joseph A. Boone, whom I discuss shortly. See Wiegman, "Melville's Geography of Gender."

12. While the relationship of men and feminism did not simply appear in 1987 with the publication of Alice Jardine and Paul Smith's (eds.) anthology, explosively titled *Men in Feminism,* this text has provided a focal point for many discussions in subsequent years. See Boone's response to this anthology, "Of Me(n) and Feminism," as well as the bibliography provided in *Engendering Men.* See also Bruce Robbins, "Men in Feminism."

13. In "Ethnicity," Stuart Hall reviews the various developments in Western intellectual thought that have provided important challenges to the logic of identity, with its pretense toward a true or autonomous self. From Marx, we under-

stand "that there are always *conditions* to identity which the subject cannot construct" (11); from Freud, that the unconscious "destabilizes the notion of the self, of identity, as a fully self-reflective entity" (ibid.); from Saussure, "that one is always inside a system of languages that partly speak us, which we are always positioned within and against" (12); and from Nietzsche, that "the end of the notion of truth" (ibid.) implicitly decenters the tradition of Western rationality, undermining the possibility of identity as the product of an essential, logical truth.

14. Christopher Newfield's "The Politics of Male Suffering" offers an important rethinking of the singular association between aggressivity and patriarchal domination by analyzing the masochistic passivity of masculinity in Hawthorne's *The Scarlet Letter*. Such masochism he reads as supportive of patriarchal structures.

15. In his subsequent work on men's relation to feminism and to anti-patriarchal politics, Boone overtly seeks out relations of power discrepancies among men as a way of circumventing the dire binary of sexual difference that underlies both his reading of quest literature and much feminist theory itself. In "Of Me(n) and Feminism," for instance, he critiques the ways in which "man" has been constituted "as a homogeneous entity" (18). While he makes no reference to his earlier work on the romantic countertradition, he does offer insights into the theorization of "man" that move in important new directions.

16. The preoccupation in this country with the definitional contours of a U.S. cultural or literary tradition in the past two hundred years attests to the ongoing struggle over the content of the sign that most invests us, as social subjects, with meaning. The assumption that this sign is a political as well as rhetorical production — and not simply a matter of essential being — underlies the theoretical framework governing recent debates in U.S. education around issues of multiculturalism. Here, the contestation over "America" is most vivid, as the debate pointedly questions the identifications and systems of economic and political alliance through which the narrative of America is being told. In a similar way, critical discussions about the literary canon pressure its historical point of view, questioning the subsumption of a variety of texts and cultural contexts under a unified and singular understanding of tradition. See especially Betty Jean Craige, ed., *Literature, Language, and Politics;* Henry Giroux, "Post-Colonial Ruptures and Democratic Possibilities"; and Gayatri Chakravorty Spivak and Sneja Gunew, "Questions of Multiculturalism."

17. "Writing AMERICA in capitals [*sic*]," as Baker explains, "enables one to distinguish between an *idea* and what Edmundo O'Gorman describes . . . as a 'lump of cosmic matter.' As an idea . . . the sign AMERICA is a willful act which always substitutes for a state description. The substitution imposes problematical unity and stasis on an ever-changing American scene" (*Blues, Ideology* 66).

6 *The Alchemy of Disloyalty*

1. There are of course other ways to posit the framing terms of contemporary feminist theory, ways that might refuse to settle for only two primary trajectories of investigation. As should be clear from my conversation about the contestations of historical narrative, feminism's rendering of itself, particularly its contemporary history, is now a serious and recurrent debate. See especially Nancie Caraway, *Segregated Sisterhood;* Diane Elam and Robyn Wiegman, eds., *Feminism Beside Itself;* and Jane Gallop, *Around 1981.*
2. For a more extensive discussion of "situated knowledges," see Donna Haraway, "Situated Knowledges"; Rosemary Hennessy, "Subjects, Knowledges . . . And All the Rest"; and Sandra G. Harding, "The Instability of the Analytical Categories of Feminist Theory" and "Subjectivity, Experience and Knowledge."
3. The conversation within feminism about its necessary critique of universal woman is extensive and might be best characterized as emerging out of diasporic liberation struggles and critical projects. See, for instance, Angela Y. Davis, *Women, Race, and Class;* Bonnie Thornton Dill, "Race, Class, and Gender"; bell hooks, *Ain't I a Woman?* and *Feminist Theory;* Chandra Talpade Mohanty, Ann Russo, and Lourdes Torres, eds., *Third World Women and the Politics of Feminism;* Cherríe Moraga and Gloria Anzaldúa, eds., *This Bridge Called My Back;* and Trinh T. Minh-ha, *Woman, Native, Other.*
4. In *Situating the Self,* Seyla Benhabib is likewise hesitant to take the postmodern critique into some of feminism's more sacred grounds, especially its assumptions about the necessity of experience, voice, and agency to any resistant politics. See also Linda Alcoff, "Cultural Feminism versus Post-Structuralism"; Christine DiStefano, "Dilemmas of Difference"; and Nancy Hartsock, "Postmodernism and Political Change."
5. Of course, more recent conversations about the possibilities of the postmodern for feminist thought have been less faithful to the political privilege feminism has inscribed for itself than is Nancy Fraser and Linda J. Nicholson's turn toward the postmodern in "Social Criticism without Philosophy." See, for instance, Wendy Brown, "Feminist Hesitations, Postmodern Exposures"; Judith Butler, "Contingent Foundations"; Jane Flax, "The End of Innocence"; and Jennifer Wicke and Margaret Ferguson, eds., *Feminism and Postmodernism.* In a more recent essay, "Feminism and the Politics of Postmodernism," Linda Nicholson answers various anti-postmodern arguments lodged against her by feminists.
6. Invoking Adrienne Rich's use of disloyalty also foregrounds the significance of race to the modern/postmodern debate, since it was precisely in the context of challenging white women to disidentify with their racial privileges that she used the phrase — a phrase drawn from white antiracist activist and writer Lillian Smith, for whom "disloyalty to civilization" describes the political work done by white women who "smelled death in the word 'segregation'" (quoted in Rich, "Disloyal to Civilization" 284). But of course, Rich is no champion of

the postmodern, and she certainly had no intention of suggesting that feminists become disloyal to the narrative of feminist liberation. In fact, for Rich, all hierarchical arrangements (race, class, heterosexism, and colonialism) are patriarchal products that can be overcome when women become loyal to one another. She writes, for instance, that

> I can easily comprehend that when black women have looked at the present-day feminist movement, particularly as caricatured in the male-dominated press (both black and white), and have seen blindness to, and ignorance of, the experience and needs of black women, they have labeled this "racism," undifferentiated from the racism endemic in patriarchy. But I hope that we can now begin to differentiate and to define further, drawing both on a deeper understanding of black and white women's history, and on an unflinching view of patriarchy itself. (290–291)

In *Gyn/Ecology,* Mary Daly also relies on a notion of patriarchy as the generating force for all other forms of social oppression and hierarchy. For a more critical view of the relationship between patriarchy and white supremacy — and white women's participation in each — see Marilyn Frye, "On Being White."

7. Patricia J. Williams is arguing in particular for a structure of law that is attentive to the rights of the minoritized by rejecting objective truth as the epistemological foundation of legal discourse.

8. The problems with the phrase "women of color" have been commented upon by a variety of activists and scholars. In "Black Women on Black Women Writers," for instance, Cheryl Clarke et al. point to the way it "seems to negate difference" (95), and Leslie Bow, in "'For Gesture of Loyalty, There Doesn't Have to Be a Betrayal,'" discusses the disturbing collapse of cultural and geopolitical distinctions in the phrase. See also Sabina Sawhney's "The Joke and the Hoax."

9. See Alice Walker, whose subtitle to *In Search of Our Mothers' Gardens* is *Womanist Prose;* Chikwenye Okonjo Ogunyemi's "Womanism"; and Sherley Anne Williams's "Some Implications of Womanist Theory." Laura E. Donaldson's *Decolonizing Feminisms* reads womanism as a critical method for thinking about colonialism and postcolonialism.

10. See in particular Wahneema Lubiano, "Shuckin Off the African-American Native Other"; hooks, *Yearning;* and two works by Wallace, *Invisibility Blues* (especially 77–90) and "Modernism, Postmodernism and the Problem of the Visual in Afro-American Culture." Barbara Christian's "The Race for Theory" is a rather forceful condemnation of postmodern theory as it is employed in contemporary literary criticism. See Michael Awkward's response in "Appropriative Gestures." A slightly different tack on the topic is taken by James Snead in "Racist Traces in Postmodernist Theory and Literature," which locates the way race serves as a prevailing, if rarely discussed, figure in postmodern theoretical discourse.

11. Flax is not alone in reading a commonality between the postmodern and anti-

racist critique. See especially Brown, "Feminist Hesitations, Postmodern Exposures"; Butler, "Contingent Foundations"; and Lubiano, "Shuckin Off the African-American Native Other."

12. For a rather positive reading of the feminist-abolitionist connection, see Blanche Glassman Hersh, *The Slavery of Sex*, and Ellen Carol DuBois, *Feminism and Suffrage*. While Karen Sanchez-Eppler offers a convincing discussion of the fusion of feminism and abolitionism in "Bodily Bonds," Barbara Berg argues against locating the origins of U.S. feminism in the abolitionist movement in *The Remembered Gate*.

13. For a compelling conversation about the way Sojourner Truth has been used as a symbol by white feminist theorists, see Deborah McDowell's "Transferences."

14. To a certain extent, Caraway's *Segregated Sisterhood* falls prey to this tack, reading the black woman's historical erasure as the history of feminism and thereby inscribing, even as she argues against it, a white feminist lineage.

15. While it has become a rather routine gesture for book-length historical or literary studies to take up issues of race by devoting a chapter or two to the contributions by black women, the most sustained inquiries by white women into race as a dynamic of power can be found in Caraway, *Segregated Sisterhood*; Zillah R. Eisenstein, *The Color of Gender*; Ruth Frankenberg, *White Women, Race Matters*; Donna Haraway, *Primate Visions*; Minnie Bruce Pratt, "Identity"; and Elizabeth V. Spelman, *Inessential Woman*.

16. Stories about white women engaging in vigorous and often vituperative critique of other white women for their theoretical racisms variously circulate, both inside and outside academia. Specific examples here would only repeat the compulsion to demonstrate my own desire to disarticulate myself from such racisms and would, moreover, rely on academic methodologies of intellectual "murder" to secure a transcendent position from which to speak. As my conversation in this chapter will demonstrate, such a move discounts the historicity in which we are all embroiled as it reinvests in the modern disciplinarity of academic discourse.

17. For various takes on the relationship between experience, embodiment, and critical authority, see Caren Kaplan, "Deterritorializations," and Judith Roof and Robyn Wiegman, eds., *Who Can Speak?*

18. The disturbance created by Clarence Thomas of U.S. understandings of party affections and political affiliations on both the Left and the Right demonstrates how wedded were our cultural associations between corporeal identity and political position in the segregationist era. Thomas represents, of course, a decided rupture of such civil rights and black nationalist sentiments, and it is this rupture that shapes a great deal of the intellectual conversation about the meaning of Thomas's "blackness" in the aftermath of the confirmation hearings. See Toni Morrison's (ed.) anthology, *Race-ing Justice, En-gendering Power*.

19. As my conversation in earlier chapters suggests, the emergence of multicultur-

alism cannot be understood as simply a transcendence of the white, Western, and imperialist formations of knowledge that have been shaped and perpetuated by the American educational system. It must also be viewed in relationship to contemporary reconfigurations of both national and global economics where the reigning hegemony of the commodity form can harness "difference" to the expansion of cultural, as opposed to militaristic, imperialism. Gayatri Chakravorty Spivak and Sneja Gunew debate this issue in "Questions of Multiculturalism."

20. Feminism, in short, has often assumed a subversion of patriarchal logic by transposing the figure of woman for the hegemony that "man" has held as the focus of humanist disciplinary inquiries. The object of study has, in this regard, defined the feminist intellectual enterprise, giving rise in the contemporary moment to the debate about how (or who) to constitute feminism's object of study. My comments in this chapter are shaped by my academic training within the historical moment of these debates, and they demonstrate in many ways the exhaustion of categorical reshapings as the means to do justice to human differences. By questioning the gesture to locate feminism's contestation of knowledge formations as contingent on its object of study, this chapter points toward a politics that refuses to settle the anxieties on which modern disciplinary strategies rest.

21. See especially Christian, "The Race for Theory."

22. In this context, it is interesting to note just how adamantly white supremacist and bourgeois have been the articulation and application of psychoanalytic discourse in the United States. As many readers may well know, one of the major feminist criticisms of psychoanalysis has been its supposed inapplicability to minoritized racial subjects (see for instance Jane Gaines, "White Privilege and Looking Relations"). Often cast within the essentialist-social constructionist debate, this critique opts for the language of social positionality, of a mechanistic subjectivity to counter the seemingly essentializing and homogenizing discourses of psychic development. More recently, however, a number of feminist theorists have begun to make claims for the reshaping of psychoanalytic discourse through its applicability to African-Americans in particular. See especially Elizabeth Abel, "Race, Class, and Psychoanalysis?"

23. In an earlier discussion of some of the issues being foregrounded in this chapter ("Toward a Political Economy of Race and Gender"), I invest too heavily in the ability of categories to articulate and define the contours not simply of social position, but of subjectivity itself. This slippage occurs, I think, in the unexplored contradictions between the understanding of the social that drives Athusserian ideology critique, with its implicit Marxian structuralism on one hand and psychoanalytic understandings of the subject as interiority on the other.

24. For further discussion of the sentimental form, see Leslie Fiedler, *Love and Death in the American Novel* and *What Was Literature?*; Philip Fisher, *Hard Facts*; and Jane Tompkins, *Sensational Designs*.

25. It is important to stress, as Eric Lott's work on nineteenth-century minstrelsy demonstrates, that the sentimental form is not inherently recuperative of racial difference. Rhetorical strategies and historical deployments are crucial aspects of any configuration of race and the melodramatic. See *Love and Theft*.

26. Other commentaries about the cultural context for Stowe's representational strategies include George M. Fredrickson, *The Black Image in the White Mind;* Thomas F. Gossett, *Uncle Tom's Cabin and American Culture;* Thomas Graham, "Harriet Beecher Stowe and the Question of Race"; Richard Yarborough, "Strategies of Black Characterization in *Uncle Tom's Cabin* and the Early Afro-American Novel"; and Jean Fagan Yellin, *The Intricate Knot* 121–153.

27. On coalitionism and affinity politics, see especially Caraway, *Segregated Sisterhood;* Donna Haraway, "A Manifesto for Cyborgs"; and Bernice Johnson Reagon, "Coalition Politics: Turning the Century."

28. Key essays that explore Stowe's figuration of the feminine include two by Elizabeth Ammons: "Heroines in *Uncle Tom's Cabin*" and "Stowe's Dream of the Mother-Savior." See also Dorothy Berkson, "Millennial Politics and the Feminine Fiction of Harriet Beecher Stowe"; Gillian Brown, "Getting into the Kitchen with Dinah"; Ann Douglas, *The Feminization of American Culture;* Severn Duvall, "*Uncle Tom's Cabin*"; Mary Kelley, *Private Woman, Public Stage;* Lora Romero, "Bio-Political Resistance in Domestic Ideology and *Uncle Tom's Cabin*"; Tompkins, *Sensational Designs;* and Jean Fagan Yellin, "Doing It Herself."

29. Yellin gestures toward this same point when she explains that through "[t]he primary distinctions . . . between non-Christians and Christians, Stowe assigns intellectual superiority and worldly power to the first group and spiritual superiority and otherworldly power — seen as infinitely more important — to the second. In the process, she conflates race and sex. Her first group consists primarily of white males. Her second group includes essentially white females and all nonwhites" ("Doing It Herself" 101).

30. The appropriative nature of these identifications is perhaps best revealed in the trajectory that the struggle for white women's enfranchisement would take in the post–Civil War period, when the analogy between woman and slave no longer operated within the politically charged field of antislavery crusade. Instead, for white feminists who viewed suffrage as a key marker in the struggle for legal equality for both slaves and women, the passage of the Fifteenth Amendment granting black men the vote seemed to signal a shift of cultural power that simultaneously betrayed their abolitionist sympathies and left patriarchy intact. Claiming that "the black man is still, in a political point of view, far above the educated white women of the country," Elizabeth Cady Stanton would assert, "it is better to be the slave of an educated white man, than of a degraded, ignorant black one" (quoted in Davis, *Women, Race, and Class* 70). In this way, Stanton simultaneously foregrounds the exclusions of social privilege that constrain black male entrance into "freedom," as she elides such a recognition by

casting enslavement as a metaphor for gender discriminations—a reading that articulates more overtly the priority of gender that underwrites *Uncle Tom's Cabin* as well. Noting how Stanton's strategy assumes that "[b]lack men [would gain] the full privileges of male supremacy," Angela Y. Davis has aptly characterized Stanton's understanding of the structural link between race and gender as "superficial," a charge that pressures not simply Stanton but the broader cultural discourse of white feminism and its often rigid devotion to reading racial oppression as coterminous with sexual difference (*Women, Race, and Class* 75, 71).

31. See especially Nancy F. Cott, *The Bonds of Womanhood;* Dorothy O. Helly and Susan M. Reverby, eds., *Gendered Domains;* Linda Kerber, "Separate Spheres, Female Worlds, Woman's Place"; Carole Pateman, "Feminist Critiques of the Public/Private Dichotomy"; Mary P. Ryan, *Women in Public;* Ann Firor Scott, *The Southern Lady;* and Barbara Welter, "The Cult of True Womanhood, 1820–1860."

32. There are, of course, other distinctions between Stowe's analysis of race and gender and my own. For instance, where she translates the masculine priority of the public sphere into an invigorated politics of the domestic and the feminine, I have reversed the priority of the terms, finding in the discourse of the "racial" body an increasing imbrication with the symbolic and social organization of sexual differences. Where she seeks the white woman's identification with the African-American, I have used, implicitly, a disidentification with the identity logic of "blacks and women," reading these not as material figures but as discursive categories constructed by modern anatomizations of "man." Where she invests in an ideology of women's common maternity that can ground a kind of feminist collaboration, I have repeatedly suspended the possibility of defining "women" outside of or apart from their reduction to disciplinary scripts. While I believe in the necessity of these theoretical shifts as part of defining the significance of race and gender hierarchies to contemporary contestations over knowledge and power, they are equally bound to the political failure they seek to explain.

33. The flip side of this scenario is the contemporary emphasis on personal writing, on the use of the experiential to forge a negotiation of the contradictions in feminism's use of objectivist methodologies. But to locate the truth of the subject in her rendition of experience, without explicating the representational and socially constructed practices in which any subject is disciplined into being able to speak, is to exist within the logic of modernity, of a subjectivity that is fully knowable.

Bibliography

Abel, Elizabeth. "Race, Class, and Psychoanalysis? Opening Questions." *Conflicts in Feminism.* Ed. Marianne Hirsch and Evelyn Fox Keller. New York and London: Routledge, 1990: 184–204.

Alba, Richard D. *Ethnic Identity: The Transformation of White America.* New Haven, Connecticut: Yale University Press, 1990.

Alcoff, Linda. "Cultural Feminism versus Post-Structuralism: The Identity Crisis in Feminist Theory." *Feminist Theory in Practice and Process.* Ed. Micheline R. Malson, Jean F. O'Barr, Sarah Westphal-Wihl, and Mary Wyer. Chicago: University of Chicago Press, 1989: 295–326.

Aldridge, A. Owen. "Feijoo and the Problem of Ethiopian Color." *Racism in the Eighteenth Century.* Ed. Harold E. Pagliaro. Cleveland and London: The Press of Case Western Reserve University, 1973: 263–277.

Ames, Jessie Daniel. *The Changing Character of Lynching.* 1942. Reprint, New York: AMS Press, 1973.

Ammons, Elizabeth. "Heroines in *Uncle Tom's Cabin.*" *American Literature* 49.2 (May 1977): 161–179.

———. "Stowe's Dream of the Mother-Savior: *Uncle Tom's Cabin* and American Women Writers before the 1920s." *New Essays on Uncle Tom's Cabin.* Ed. Eric Sundquist. New York and Cambridge: Cambridge University Press, 1986: 155–195.

Arac, Jonathan, ed. *After Foucault: Humanistic Knowledge, Postmodern Challenges.* New Brunswick, New Jersey: Rutgers University Press, 1988.

Awkward, Michael. "Appropriative Gestures: Theory and Afro-American Literary Criticism." *Gender and Theory: Dialogues on Feminist Criticism.* Ed. Linda Kaufman. Oxford and New York: Basil Blackwell, 1989: 238–246.

Baker, Houston A., Jr. *Blues, Ideology, and Afro-American Literature: A Vernacular Theory.* Chicago: University of Chicago Press, 1984.

Banton, Michael. *The Idea of Race.* London: Tavistock, 1977.

———. *Race Relations.* London: Tavistock, 1967.

Baraka, Imamu Amiri [LeRoi Jones]. *Home on the Range. Drama Review* 12.4 (Summer 1968): 106–111.

———. *Home: Social Essays.* New York: William Morrow, 1966.

———. *Madheart.* 1966. In *Four Black Revolutionary Plays.* Reprint, New York and Indianapolis: Bobbs-Merrill, 1969: 65–87.

———. *Police. Drama Review* 12.4 (Summer 1968): 112–115.

———. *The Slave.* In *Dutchman and the Slave: Two Plays.* New York: William Morrow, 1964: 40–88.

———. *The Toilet.* In *The Baptism and the Toilet.* New York: Grove, 1967: 33–62.

Barrett, Michèle, and Anne Phillips, eds. *Destabilizing Theory: Contemporary Feminist Debates.* Stanford, California: Stanford University Press, 1992.

Baym, Nina. "Melodramas of Beset Manhood: How Theories of American Fiction Exclude Women Authors." *American Quarterly* 33.2 (Summer 1981): 123–139.

Bell, Roseann P., Bettye J. Parker, and Beverly Guy-Sheftall, eds. *Sturdy Black Bridges: Visions of Black Women in Literature.* Garden City, New York: Anchor/Doubleday, 1979.

Benhabib, Seyla. *Situating the Self: Gender, Community and Postmodernism in Contemporary Ethics.* New York: Routledge, 1992.

———, and Drucilla Cornell, eds. *Feminism as Critique: On the Politics of Gender.* Minneapolis: University of Minnesota Press, 1988.

Benston, Kimberly W. "I Yam What I Am: The Topos of Un(naming) in Afro-American Literature." *Black Literature and Literary Theory.* Ed. Henry Louis Gates Jr. New York: Methuen, 1984: 151–172.

Bercovitch, Sacvan. "Afterword." *Ideology and Classic American Literature.* Ed. Bercovitch and Myra Jehlen. New York and Cambridge: Cambridge University Press, 1986: 418–442.

———. "The Rites of Ascent: Rhetoric, Ritual, and the Ideology of American Consensus." *The American Self: Myth, Ideology and Popular Culture.* Ed. Sam B. Girgus. Albuquerque: University of New Mexico Press, 1981: 5–42.

Berg, Barbara. *The Remembered Gate: Origins of American Feminism.* New York: Oxford University Press, 1978.

Berger, John. *Ways of Seeing.* London: British Broadcasting Company and Penguin, 1972.

Berkson, Dorothy. "Millennial Politics and the Feminine Fiction of Harriet Beecher Stowe." *Critical Essays on Harriet Beecher Stowe.* Ed. Elizabeth Ammons. Boston: G. K. Hall, 1980: 244–258.

Berlant, Lauren. "National Brands/National Body: *Imitation of Life.*" *Comparative American Identities: Race, Sex, and Nationality in the Modern Text.* Ed. Hortense J. Spillers. New York: Routledge, 1991: 110–140.

Berzon, Judith R. *Neither White nor Black: The Mulatto Character in American Fiction.* New York: New York University Press, 1978.

Bethel, Lorraine, and Barbara Smith, eds. *Conditions: Five—The Black Woman's Issue* (1979).

Bhabha, Homi K. "Interrogating Identity: The Postcolonial Prerogative." *The*

Anatomy of Racism. Ed. David Theo Goldberg. Minneapolis: University of Minnesota Press, 1990: 183–209.

———. "'Race,' Time and the Revision of Modernity." *Oxford Literary Review* 13.1–2 (1991): 193–219.

Birth of a Nation. Dir. D. W. Griffith. 1915.

Blanckaert, Claude. "Buffon and the Natural History of Man: Writing History and the 'Foundational Myth' of Anthropology." *History of the Human Sciences* 6.1 (Feb 1993): 13–50.

Bloom, Allan. *The Closing of the American Mind: How Higher Education Has Failed Democracy and Impoverished the Souls of Today's Students.* New York: Simon & Schuster, 1987.

Bock, Michele Gisela, and Susan James, eds. *Beyond Equality and Difference: Citizenship, Feminist Politics, and Female Subjectivity.* London and New York: Routledge, 1992.

Boffin, Tessa, and Jean Fraser, eds. *Stolen Glances: Lesbians Take Photographs.* London: Pandora, 1991.

Bogle, Donald. *Toms, Coons, Mulattoes, Mammies, and Bucks: An Interpretative History of Blacks in American Films.* Rev. ed. New York: Continuum, 1989.

Boone, Joseph A. "Male Independence and the American Quest Genre: Hidden Sexual Politics in the All-Male Worlds of Melville, Twain and London." *Gender Studies: New Directions in Feminist Criticism.* Ed. Judith Spector. Bowling Green, Ohio: Bowling Green State University Popular Press, 1986: 187–217.

———. "Of Me(n) and Feminism: Who(se) Is the Sex That Writes?" *Engendering Men: The Question of Male Feminist Criticism.* Ed. Boone and Michael Cadden. New York and London: Routledge, 1990: 11–25.

———. *Tradition Counter Tradition: Love and the Form of Fiction.* Chicago: University of Chicago Press, 1987.

Bordo, Susan. "The Cartesian Masculinization of Thought." *Signs* 11.3 (Spring 1986): 439–456.

———. *Unbearable Weight: Feminism, Western Culture, and the Body.* Berkeley: University of California Press, 1993.

Bow, Leslie. "'For Gesture of Loyalty, There Doesn't Have to Be a Betrayal': Asian American Feminist Criticism and the Politics of Locality." *Who Can Speak? Authority and Critical Identity.* Ed. Judith Roof and Robyn Wiegman. Urbana: University of Illinois Press, forthcoming.

Brantlinger, Patrick. *Crusoe's Footprints: Cultural Studies in Britain and America.* New York: Routledge, 1990.

Brod, Harry, ed. *The Making of Masculinities.* Boston: Allen & Unwin, 1987.

Brown, Gillian. "Getting into the Kitchen with Dinah: Domestic Politics in *Uncle Tom's Cabin.*" *American Quarterly* 36.4 (Fall 1984): 503–523.

Brown, Richard Maxwell. *Strain of Violence: Historical Studies in American Violence and Vigilantism.* New York: Oxford University Press, 1975.

Brown, Wendy. "Feminist Hesitations, Postmodern Exposures." *differences* 3.1 (Spring 1991): 63–84.

Brownmiller, Susan. *Against Our Will: Men, Women and Rape.* New York: Bantam, 1976.

Bryson, Norman. *Vision and Painting: The Logic of the Gaze.* New Haven, Connecticut: Yale University Press, 1983.

Burleigh, Nina. "David Duke." *Z Magazine* (Dec 1991): 47–51.

Butler, Judith. *Bodies That Matter: On the Discursive Limits of "Sex."* New York: Routledge, 1993.

———. "Contingent Foundations: Feminism and the Question of 'Postmodernism.'" *Feminists Theorize the Political.* Ed. Judith Butler and Joan W. Scott. New York: Routledge, 1992: 3–21.

———. *Gender Trouble: Feminism and the Subversion of Identity.* New York: Routledge, 1990.

Cade, Toni, ed. *The Black Woman: An Anthology.* New York: New American Library, 1970.

Caldwell, Charles. *Thoughts on the Original Unity of the Human Race.* New York: Lippincott, Grambo and Co., 1830.

Calhoun, Craig. "Postmodernism as Pseudohistory." *Theory, Culture & Society* 10.1 (Feb 1993): 75–96.

Callaghan, Dympna. "The Vicar and Virago: Feminism and the Problem of Identity." *Who Can Speak? Authority and Critical Identity.* Ed. Judith Roof and Robyn Wiegman. Urbana: University of Illinois Press, forthcoming.

Camper, Peter. *The Works of the Late Professor Camper, on the Connexion between the Science of Anatomy and the Arts of Drawing, Painting, Statuary, etc.* Trans. T. Cogan. London: C. Dilly, 1794.

Caraway, Nancie. *Segregated Sisterhood: Racism and the Politics of American Feminism.* Knoxville: University of Tennessee Press, 1991.

Carby, Hazel. "'On the Threshold of Woman's Era': Lynching, Empire, and Sexuality in Black Feminist Theory." *"Race," Writing, and Difference.* Ed. Henry Louis Gates Jr. Chicago: University of Chicago Press, 1986: 301–316.

———. *Reconstructing Womanhood: The Emergence of the Afro-American Woman Novelist.* New York and Oxford: Oxford University Press, 1987.

Casty, Alan. "The Films of D. W. Griffith: A Style for the Times." *Journal of Popular Film* 1.2 (Spring 1972): 67–79.

Chapman, Rowena, and Jonathan Rutherford, eds. *Male Order: Unwrapping Masculinity.* London: Lawrence & Wishart, 1988.

Choi, Kyeong-Hee. *When the Mater Dolorosa Speaks: Historical and Maternal Narratives of Buchi Emecheta, Pak Wanso, and Toni Morrison.* Dissertation, Indiana University, forthcoming.

Chrisman, Laura. "Theorizing 'Race,' Racism and Culture: Pitfalls of Idealist Tendencies." *Paragraph* 16.1 (1993): 78–90.

Christian, Barbara. *Black Women Novelists: The Development of a Tradition, 1892–1976.* Westport, Connecticut: Greenwood, 1980.

———. "The Race for Theory." *The Nature and Context of Minority Discourse.* Ed. Abdul R. JanMohamed and David Lloyd. New York and Oxford: Oxford University Press, 1990: 37–49.

Clarke, Cheryl, Jewelle Gomez, Evelynn Hammonds, Bonnie Johnson, and Linda Powell. "Black Women on Black Women Writers: Conversations and Questions." *Conditions: Nine* 3.3 (Spring 1983): 88–137.

Cleaver, Eldridge. *Soul on Ice.* New York: Dell, 1968.

Clinton, Catherine. *The Plantation Mistress: Woman's World in the Old South.* New York: Pantheon, 1982.

Collins, Patricia Hill. *Black Feminist Thought: Knowledge, Consciousness, and the Politics of Empowerment.* New York and London: Routledge, 1991.

Color Adjustment. Dir. Marlon T. Riggs. Signifyin' Works, 1991.

Conroy, Pat. *The Lords of Discipline.* 1980. New York and Toronto: Bantam, 1982.

Cooke, Michael. "Naming, Being, and Black Experience." *Yale Review* 68 (1978): 167–186.

Cott, Nancy F. *The Bonds of Womanhood: "Woman's Sphere" in New England, 1780–1835.* New Haven, Connecticut: Yale University Press, 1977.

Cox, Oliver C. *Caste, Class, and Race: A Study in Social Dynamics.* Garden City, New York: Doubleday, 1948.

Craige, Betty Jean, ed. *Literature, Language, and Politics.* Athens: University of Georgia Press, 1988.

Crary, Jonathan. "Modernizing Vision." *Vision and Visuality.* Ed. Hal Foster. Seattle: Bay Press, 1988: 29–44.

———. *Techniques of the Observer: On Vision and Modernity in the Nineteenth Century.* Cambridge, Massachusetts, and London: MIT Press, 1990.

Cripps, Thomas. *Slow Fade to Black: The Negro in American Film 1900–1942.* New York: Oxford University Press, 1977.

Cry Freedom. Dr. Richard Attenborough. Universal, 1988.

Cutler, James E. *Lynch-Law, An Investigation into the History of Lynching in the United States.* 1905. New York: Negro Universities Press, 1969.

Daly, Mary. *Gyn/Ecology: The Metaethics of Radical Feminism.* Boston: Beacon, 1978.

Davis, Angela Y. "Black Nationalism: The Sixties and the Nineties." *Black Popular Culture.* Ed. Gina Dent. Seattle: Bay Press, 1992: 317–324.

———. *Women, Race, and Class.* New York: Random House, 1981.

Davis, David Brion. *The Problem of Slavery in Western Culture.* 1966. New York: Oxford University Press, 1988.

Davis, F. James. *Who Is Black? One Nation's Definition.* University Park: Pennsylvania State University Press, 1991.

Dearborn, Mary V. "Miscegenation and the Mulatto, Inheritance and Incest: The Pocahontas Marriage, Part II." *Pocahontas's Daughters: Gender and Ethnicity in American Culture.* New York: Oxford University Press, 1986: 131–158.

DeBord, Guy. *Society of the Spectacle.* Detroit: Black and Red, 1983.

The Defiant Ones. Dir. Stanley Kramer. United Artists, 1958.

Delacampagne, Christian. *L'Invention du racism.* Paris: Fayard, 1983.

———. "Racism and the West: From Praxis to Logos." Trans. Michael Edwards. *The Anatomy of Racism.* Ed. David Theo Goldberg. Minneapolis: University of Minnesota Press, 1990: 83–88.

de Lauretis, Teresa. *Alice Doesn't: Feminism, Semiotics, Cinema.* Bloomington: Indiana University Press, 1984.

———. "The Essence of the Triangle or, Taking the Risk of Essentialism Seriously: Feminist Theory in Italy, the U.S., and Britain." *differences* 1.2 (Summer 1989): 3–37.

Dill, Bonnie Thornton. "Race, Class, and Gender: Prospects for an All-Inclusive Sisterhood." *Feminist Studies* 9.1 (Spring 1983): 131–150.

DiStefano, Christine. *Configurations of Masculinity: A Feminist Perspective on Modern Political Theory.* Ithaca, New York: Cornell University Press, 1991.

———. "Dilemmas of Difference: Feminism, Modernity, and Postmodernism." *Feminism/Postmodernism.* Ed. Linda Nicholson. New York: Routledge, 1990: 63–82.

Docherty, Thomas, ed. *Postmodernism: A Reader.* New York: Columbia University Press, 1993.

Donaldson, Laura E. *Decolonizing Feminisms: Race, Gender, and Empire-Building.* Chapel Hill: University of North Carolina Press, 1992.

Douglas, Ann. *The Feminization of American Culture.* 1977. New York: Avon, 1978.

Douglass, Frederick. "The Heroic Slave." *Violence in the Black Imagination: Essays and Documents.* Ed. Ronald T. Takaki. New York: G. P. Putnam's, 1972: 37–77.

Drake, St. Clair. *Black Folk Here and There: An Essay in History and Anthropology.* 2 volumes. Los Angeles: UCLA Center for Afro-American Studies, 1987.

Dreyfus, Hubert, and Paul Rabinow. *Michel Foucault: Beyond Structuralism and Hermeneutics.* 2nd ed. Chicago: University of Chicago Press, 1983.

DuBois, Ellen Carol. *Feminism and Suffrage: The Emergence of an Independent Women's Movement in America, 1848–1869.* Ithaca, New York: Cornell University Press, 1978.

During, Simon, ed. *The Cultural Studies Reader.* London and New York: Routledge, 1993.

Duvall, Severn. "*Uncle Tom's Cabin:* The Sinister Side of the Patriarchy." *Images of the Negro in American Literature.* Ed. Seymour L. Gross and John Edward Hardy. Chicago: University of Chicago Press, 1966: 163–180.

Dyer, Richard. "Don't Look Now—the Male Pin-Up." *Screen* 23.3–4 (Sept–Oct 1982): 61–73.

———. *Heavenly Bodies: Film Stars and Society.* New York: St. Martin's, 1986.

———. "White." *Screen* 29.4 (Autumn 1988): 44–65.

Dyson, Michael Eric. *Reflecting Black: African-American Cultural Criticism.* Minneapolis: University of Minnesota Press, 1993.

Eisenstein, Zillah R. *The Color of Gender: Reimaging Democracy.* Berkeley and Los Angeles: University of California Press, 1994.

Elam, Diane. *Romancing the Postmodern.* London and New York: Routledge, 1992.

———, and Robyn Wiegman, eds. *Feminism beside Itself.* New York: Routledge, 1995.

Ellis, John. *Visible Fictions: Cinema, Television, Video.* London and Boston: Routledge, 1982.

Ellison, Ralph. "The Birthmark." *New Masses* 36 (July 2, 1940): 16–17.

———. *Invisible Man.* New York: Random House, 1952.

Enemy Mine. Dir. Wolfgang Petersen. Twentieth Century Fox, 1985.

Fanon, Frantz. *Black Skin, White Masks.* 1952. Trans. Charles Lam Markmann. Reprint, New York: Grove Weidenfeld, 1967.

Faulkner, William. *Light in August.* 1932. Reprint, New York: Modern Library, 1968.

Fetterley, Judith. *The Resisting Reader: A Feminist Approach to American Fiction.* Bloomington: Indiana University Press, 1978.

Fiedler, Leslie. "Come Back to the Raft Ag'in, Huck Honey!" *The Collected Essays of Leslie Fiedler.* Vol 1. New York: Stein & Day, 1971: 142–151.

———. *Love and Death in the American Novel.* 1960. Reprint, New York: Stein & Day, 1966.

———. *What Was Literature? Class Culture and Mass Society.* New York: Simon & Schuster, 1982.

———, and Houston Baker Jr., eds. *English Literature: Opening Up the Canon.* Baltimore: Johns Hopkins University Press, 1981.

Fisher, Philip. *Hard Facts: Setting and Form in the American Novel.* New York: Oxford University Press, 1985.

———. "Introduction." *The New American Studies: Essays from Representations.* Berkeley: University of California Press, 1991: vii–xxii.

Flax, Jane. "The End of Innocence." *Feminists Theorize the Political.* Ed. Judith Butler and Joan W. Scott. New York: Routledge, 1992: 445–463.

Foner, Eric. *Reconstruction: America's Unfinished Revolution 1863–1877.* New York: Harper & Row, 1988.

Foner, Philip S. *American Socialism and Black Americans: From the Age of Jackson to World War II.* Westport, Connecticut: Greenwood, 1977.

Foster, Hal. "'Primitive' Scenes." *Critical Inquiry* 20.1 (Autumn 1993): 69–102.

———, ed. *Vision and Visuality.* Seattle: Bay Press, 1988.

Foucault, Michel. *The Birth of the Clinic: An Archaeology of Medical Perception.* 1963. Trans. A. M. Sheridan Smith. Reprint, New York: Pantheon, 1973.

———. *Discipline and Punish: The Birth of the Prison.* 1975. Trans. Alan Sheridan. Reprint, New York: Pantheon, 1977.

———. *The Order of Things: An Archaeology of the Human Sciences.* 1966. Reprint, New York: Vintage, 1973.

———. "What Is Enlightenment?" *The Foucault Reader.* Ed. Paul Rabinow. New York: Pantheon, 1984: 32–50.

Fowles, Diane L. *White Political Women: Paths from Privilege to Empowerment.* Knoxville: University of Tennessee Press, 1992.

Frankenberg, Ruth. *White Women, Race Matters: The Social Construction of Whiteness.* Minneapolis: University of Minnesota Press, 1993.

Franklin, Sarah, Celia Lury, and Jackie Stacey, eds. *Off-Centre: Feminism and Cultural Studies.* London: HarperCollins Academic, 1991.

Fraser, Nancy. *Unruly Practices: Power, Discourse and Gender in Contemporary Social Theory.* Minneapolis: University of Minnesota Press, 1989.

————, and Linda Nicholson. "Social Criticism without Philosophy: An Encounter between Feminism and Postmodernism." *Feminism/Postmodernism.* Ed. Nicholson. New York: Routledge, 1990: 19–38.

Fredrickson, George M. *The Black Image in the White Mind: The Debate on Afro-American Destiny 1817–1914.* 1971. Reprint, New York: Harper & Row, 1972.

————. *White Supremacy: A Comparative Study of American and South African History.* New York and Oxford: Oxford University Press, 1981.

Frye, Marilyn. "On Being White: Toward a Feminist Understanding of Race and Race Supremacy." *The Politics of Reality: Essays in Feminist Theory.* Trumansburg, New York: Crossing Press, 1983: 110–127.

Fuss, Diana. *Essentially Speaking: Feminism, Nature and Difference.* New York: Routledge, 1989.

————, ed. *Inside/Out: Lesbian Theories, Gay Theories.* New York and London: Routledge, 1991.

Gaines, Jane. "White Privilege and Looking Relations — Race and Gender in Feminist Film Theory." *Screen* 29.4 (Autumn 1988): 12–27.

Gallop, Jane. *Around 1981: Academic Feminist Literary Theory.* New York: Routledge, 1992.

Gatens, Moira. *Feminism and Philosophy: Perspectives on Difference and Equality.* Bloomington: Indiana University Press, 1991.

Gates, Henry Louis, Jr. "Literary Theory and the Black Tradition." *Figures in Black: Words, Signs and the "Racial" Self.* Oxford and New York: Oxford University Press, 1987: 3–62.

————. "The Trope of the New Negro and the Reconstruction of the Image of the Black." *Representations* 24 (Fall 1988): 129–155.

Giddings, Paula. *When and Where I Enter: The Impact of Black Women on Race and Sex in America.* New York: William Morrow, 1984.

Gilman, Sander. "Black Bodies, White Bodies: Toward an Iconography of Female Sexuality in Late Nineteenth-Century Art, Medicine, and Literature." *"Race," Writing, and Difference.* Ed. Henry Louis Gates Jr. Chicago: University of Chicago Press, 1986: 223–261.

Gilroy, Paul. *The Black Atlantic: Modernity and Double Consciousness.* Cambridge, Massachusetts: Harvard University Press, 1993.

Giroux, Henry. "Living Dangerously: Identity Politics and the New Cultural Racism:

Towards a Critical Pedagogy of Representation." *Cultural Studies* 7.1 (Jan 1993): 1–27.

———. "Post-Colonial Ruptures and Democratic Possibilities: Multiculturalism as Anti-Racist Pedagogy." *Cultural Critique* 21 (Spring 1992): 5–39.

Goldberg, David Theo. *Racist Culture: Philosophy and the Politics of Meaning.* Oxford and Cambridge, Massachusetts: Basil Blackwell, 1993.

———. "The Social Formation of Racist Discourse." *The Anatomy of Racism.* Ed. Goldberg. Minneapolis: University of Minnesota Press, 1990: 295–318.

Goldfield, Michael. "The Color of Politics in the United States: White Supremacy as the Main Explanation for the Peculiarities of American Politics from Colonial Times to the Present." *The Bounds of Race: Perspectives on Hegemony and Resistance.* Ed. Dominick LaCapra. Ithaca, New York: Cornell University Press, 1991: 104–133.

Gooding-Williams, Robert, ed. *Reading Rodney King, Reading Urban Uprising.* New York and London: Routledge, 1993.

Gossett, Thomas F. *Race: The History of an Idea in America.* 1963. Reprint, New York: Schocken, 1965.

———. *Uncle Tom's Cabin and American Culture.* Dallas, Texas: Southern Methodist University Press, 1985.

Gould, Stephen Jay. *The Mismeasure of Man.* New York: W. W. Norton, 1981.

Graham, Thomas. "Harriet Beecher Stowe and the Question of Race," *New England Quarterly* 46.4 (Dec 1973): 614–622.

Grossberg, Lawrence. "History, Politics and Postmodernism: Stuart Hall and Cultural Studies." *Journal of Communication Inquiry* 10.2 (1986): 61–77.

———, Cary Nelson, and Paula A. Treichler. "Cultural Studies: An Introduction." *Cultural Studies.* Ed. Grossberg, Nelson, and Treichler. New York: Routledge, 1992: 1–22.

Grosz, Elizabeth. "Bodies and Knowledges: Feminism and the Crisis of Reason." *Feminist Epistemologies.* Ed. Linda Alcoff and Elizabeth Potter. New York and London: Routledge, 1993: 187–215.

———. *Volatile Bodies.* Bloomington: Indiana University Press, 1994.

Guillaumin, Colette. "Race and Nature: The System of Marks." *Feminist Issues* 8.2 (Fall 1988): 25–43.

Habermas, Jurgen. "The Critique of Reason as an Unmasking of the Human Sciences: Michel Foucault." *The Philosophical Discourse of Modernity: Twelve Lectures.* 1985. Trans. Frederick G. Lawrence. Reprint, Cambridge, Massachusetts: MIT Press, 1987: 238–265.

———. "Modernity—An Incomplete Project." *The Anti-Aesthetic: Essays on Postmodern Culture.* Ed. Hal Foster. Port Townsend, Washington: Bay Press, 1983: 3–15.

———. "Some Questions Concerning the Theory of Power: Foucault Again." *The Philosophical Discourse of Modernity: Twelve Lectures.* 1985. Trans. Frederick G. Lawrence. Reprint, Cambridge, Massachusetts: MIT Press, 1987: 266–293.

———. "Taking Aim at the Heart of the Present." *Foucault: A Critical Reader.* Ed. David Couzens Hoy. Oxford and New York: Basil Blackwell, 1986: 103–108.

Hall, Jacquelyn Dowd. *Revolt against Chivalry: Jessie Daniel Ames and the Women's Campaign against Lynching.* New York: Columbia University Press, 1979.

Hall, Stuart. "Cultural Studies and Its Theoretical Legacies." *Cultural Studies.* Ed. Lawrence Grossberg, Cary Nelson, and Paula A. Treichler. New York: Routledge, 1992: 277–294.

———. "The Emergence of Cultural Studies and the Crisis of the Humanities." *October* 53 (Fall 1990): 11–90.

———. "Ethnicity: Identity and Difference." *Radical America* 23.4 (Oct–Dec 1991): 9–20.

———. "What Is This 'Black' in Black Popular Culture?" *Black Popular Culture.* Ed. Gina Dent. Seattle: Bay Press, 1992: 21–33.

Haller, John S., and Robin M. Haller. *The Physician and Sexuality in Victorian America.* Urbana: University of Illinois Press, 1974.

Haraway, Donna. "A Manifesto for Cyborgs: Science, Technology, and Socialist Feminism in the 1980s." *Feminism/Postmodernism.* Ed. Linda J. Nicholson. New York: Routledge, 1990: 190–233.

———. *Primate Visions: Gender, Race, and Nature in the World of Modern Science.* New York: Routledge, 1989.

———. "Situated Knowledges: The Science Question in Feminism and the Privilege of Partial Perspective." *Feminist Studies* 14.3 (Fall 1988): 575–599.

Harding, Sandra G. "The Instability of the Analytical Categories of Feminist Theory." *Feminist Theory in Practice and Process.* Ed. Micheline R. Malson, Jean F. O'Barr, Sarah Westphal-Wihl, and Mary Wyer. Chicago: University of Chicago Press, 1989: 15–34.

———. *The Science Question in Feminism.* Ithaca, New York: Cornell University Press, 1986.

———. "Subjectivity, Experience and Knowledge: An Epistemology from/for Rainbow Coalition Politics." *Who Can Speak? Authority and Critical Identity.* Ed. Judith Roof and Robyn Wiegman. Urbana: University of Illinois Press, forthcoming.

———, ed. *The "Racial" Economy of Science: Toward a Democratic Future.* Bloomington: Indiana University Press, 1993.

Hare, Nathan. "The Frustrated Masculinity of the Negro Male." *The Black Family: Essays and Studies.* Ed. Robert Staples. Belmont, California: Wadsworth, 1971: 131–134.

Harper, Phillip Brian. *Framing the Margins: The Social Logic of Postmodern Culture.* New York and Oxford: Oxford University Press, 1994.

Harris, Trudier. *Exorcising Blackness: Historical and Literary Lynching and Burning Rituals.* Bloomington: Indiana University Press, 1984.

———. "Native Sons and Foreign Daughters." *New Essays on Native Son.* Ed.

Keneth Kinnamon. New York and Cambridge: Cambridge University Press, 1990: 63–84.

Hartsock, Nancy. "Foucault on Power: A Theory for Women?" *Feminism/Postmodernism*. Ed. Linda J. Nicholson. New York: Routledge, 1990: 157–175.

———. "Postmodernism and Political Change: Issues for Feminist Theory." *Cultural Critique* 14 (Winter 1989–1990): 15–33.

Hawthorne, Nathaniel. "The Birthmark." 1843. *The Scarlet Letter and Other Tales of the Puritans*. Ed. Harry Levin. Reprint, Boston: Houghton Mifflin, 1961: 368–386.

Hearn, Jeff, and David Morgan, eds. *Men, Masculinities and Social Theory*. London: Unwin Hyman, 1990.

Hegel, Georg Wilhelm Friedrich. *The Philosophy of History*. New York: Dover, 1956.

Hekman, Susan J. *Gender and Knowledge: Elements of a Postmodern Feminism*. Boston: Northeastern University Press, 1990.

Helly, Dorothy O., and Susan M. Reverby, eds. *Gendered Domains: Rethinking Public and Private in Women's History*. Ithaca, New York: Cornell University Press, 1992.

Hennessy, Rosemary. *Materialist Feminism and the Politics of Discourse*. New York and London: Routledge, 1993.

———. "Subjects, Knowledges . . . And All the Rest: Speaking for What?" *Who Can Speak? Authority and Critical Identity*. Ed. Judith Roof and Robyn Wiegman. Urbana: University of Illinois Press, forthcoming.

Hersh, Blanche Glassman. *The Slavery of Sex: Feminist-Abolitionists in America*. Urbana: University of Illinois Press, 1978.

Higginbotham, Evelyn Brooks. "African-American Women's History and the Metalanguage of Race." *Signs* 17.2 (Winter 1992): 251–274.

hooks, bell. *Ain't I a Woman: Black Women and Feminism*. Boston: South End Press, 1981.

———. *Feminist Theory: From Margin to Center*. Boston: South End Press, 1984.

———. *Yearning: Race, Gender and Cultural Politics*. Boston: South End Press, 1990.

Horsman, Reginald. *Race and Manifest Destiny: The Origins of American Racial Anglo-Saxonism*. Cambridge, Massachusetts: Harvard University Press, 1981.

Howard, June. *Form and History in American Literary Naturalism*. Chapel Hill: University of North Carolina Press, 1985.

Hoy, David Couzens. "Introduction." *Foucault: A Critical Reader*. Ed. Hoy. Oxford and New York: Basil Blackwell, 1986: 1–25.

———. "Power, Repression, Progress: Foucault, Lukes, and the Frankfurt School." *Foucault: A Critical Reader*. Ed. Hoy. Oxford and New York: Basil Blackwell, 1986: 123–147.

Hull, Gloria T., Patricia Bell Scott, and Barbara Smith, eds. *All the Women Are White, All the Blacks Are Men, but Some of Us Are Brave: Black Women's Studies*. Old Westbury, New York: Feminist Press, 1982.

Hume, David. "Of National Characters." *The Philosophical Works.* 1886. Ed. Thomas Hill Green and Thomas Hodge Grose. vol. 3. Reprint, Aalen: Scientia Verlag, 1964.

In the Heat of the Night. Dir. Norman Jewison. United Artists, 1967.

Irigaray, Luce. *This Sex Which Is Not One.* 1977. Trans. Catherine Porter with Carolyn Burke. Reprint, Ithaca, New York: Cornell University Press, 1985.

James, Stanlie M., and Abena P. A. Busia, eds. *Theorizing Black Feminisms: The Visionary Pragmatism of Black Women.* London and New York: Routledge, 1993.

Jameson, Fredric. *Signatures of the Visible.* New York: Routledge, 1990.

Jardine, Alice, and Paul Smith, eds. *Men in Feminism.* New York: Methuen, 1987.

Jay, Martin. *Downcast Eyes: The Denigration of Vision in Twentieth-Century French Thought.* Berkeley: University of California Press, 1993.

——. "In the Empire of the Gaze: Foucault and the Denigration of Vision in Twentieth-Century French Thought." *Foucault: A Reader.* Ed. David Couzens Hoy. Oxford and New York: Basil Blackwell, 1986: 175–204.

——. "Scopic Regimes of Modernity." *Vision and Visuality.* Ed. Hal Foster. Seattle: Bay Press, 1988: 3–23.

Jefferson, Thomas. *Notes on the State of Virginia.* 1782. Reprint, New York: Harper and Row, 1964.

Jeffords, Susan. *The Remasculinization of America: Gender and the Vietnam War.* Bloomington: Indiana University Press, 1989.

Jones, Jacqueline. *Labor of Love, Labor of Sorrow: Black Women, Work and the Family, From Slavery to the Present.* New York: Basic Books, 1985.

Jordan, Winthrop D. *White over Black: American Attitudes toward the Negro, 1550–1812.* 1968. Reprint, New York: W. W. Norton, 1977.

Kant, Immanuel. "An Answer to the Question: 'What Is Enlightenment?'" *Kant's Political Writings.* Ed. Hans Reiss. Trans. H. B. Nisbet. Cambridge: Cambridge University Press, 1970: 54–60.

Kaplan, Caren. "Deterritorializations: The Rewriting of Home and Exile in Western Feminist Discourse." *The Nature and Context of Minority Discourse.* Ed. Abdul R. JanMohamed and David Lloyd. New York: Oxford University Press, 1990: 357–368.

Kaufman, Michael, ed. *Beyond Patriarchy: Essays by Men on Pleasure, Power, and Change.* Toronto and New York: Oxford University Press, 1987.

Kelley, Mary. *Private Woman, Public Stage: Literary Domesticity in Nineteenth-Century America.* New York: Oxford University Press, 1984.

Kerber, Linda. "Separate Spheres, Female Worlds, Woman's Place: The Rhetoric of Women's History." *Journal of American History* 75.1 (June 1988): 9–39.

Kimmel, Michael S., ed. *Changing Men: New Directions in Research on Men and Masculinity.* Newbury Park, California: Sage, 1987.

Kolodny, Annette. *The Lay of the Land: Metaphor as Experience and History in American Life and Letters.* Chapel Hill: University of North Carolina, 1975.

Ladner, Joyce. *Tomorrow's Tomorrow: The Black Woman.* Garden City, New York: Doubleday, 1971.

Larsen, Nella. *Passing.* 1929. New York: Collier, 1971.

Lawrence, D. H. *Studies in Classic American Literature.* 1923. Reprint, New York: Viking Press, 1964.

Leab, Daniel J. *From Sambo to Superspade: The Black Experience in Motion Pictures.* Boston: Houghton Mifflin, 1975.

Lemke, Sieglinde. "White on White." *Transition* 60 (1993): 145–154.

Lerner, Gerda. *The Creation of Patriarchy.* New York: Oxford University Press, 1986.

———, ed. *Black Women in White America: A Documentary History.* New York: Pantheon, 1972.

———. *The Creation of Patriarchy.* New York: Oxford University Press, 1986.

Lethal Weapon. Dir. Richard Donner. Warner Brothers, 1987.

Levin, David Michael, ed. *Modernity and the Hegemony of Vision.* Berkeley and Los Angeles: University of California Press, 1993.

Lewis, R. W. B. *The American Adam: Innocence, Tragedy, and Tradition in the Nineteenth Century.* Chicago: University of Chicago Press, 1955.

Lloyd, David. "Race under Representation." *Oxford Literary Review* 13.1–2 (1991): 62–94.

The Lords of Discipline. Dir. Franc Roddam. Paramount, 1983.

Lott, Eric. *Love and Theft: Blackface Minstrelsy and the American Working Class.* New York and Oxford: Oxford University Press, 1993.

———. "White Like Me: Racial Cross-Dressing and the Construction of American Whiteness." *Cultures of United States Imperialism.* Ed. Amy Kaplan and Donald E. Pease. Durham, North Carolina: Duke University Press, 1993: 474–495.

Love, Nancy. "Politics and Voice(s): An Empowerment/Knowledge Regime." *differences* 3.1 (Spring 1991): 85–103.

Lubiano, Wahneema. "Black Ladies, Welfare Queens, and State Minstrels: Ideological War by Narrative Means." *Race-ing Justice, En-gendering Power: Essays on Anita Hill, Clarence Thomas, and the Construction of Social Reality.* Ed. Toni Morrison. New York: Pantheon, 1992: 323–363.

———. "Shuckin Off the African-American Native Other: What's 'Postmodernism' Got to Do with It?" *Cultural Critique* 18 (Spring 1991): 149–186.

Lyotard, Jean-François. *The Postmodern Condition: A Report on Knowledge.* 1979. Trans. Geoff Bennington and Brian Massumi. Reprint, Minneapolis: University of Minnesota Press, 1984.

———. "Re-writing Modernity." *Sub-Stance 54* 16.3 (1987): 3–9.

Mann, Susan A. "Slavery, Sharecropping, and Sexual Inequality." *Black Women in America: Social Science Perspectives.* Ed. Micheline R. Malson, Elisabeth Mudimbe-Boyi, Jean F. O'Barr, and Mary Wyer. Chicago: University of Chicago Press, 1990: 133–157.

Marable, Manning. *How Capitalism Underdeveloped Black America: Problems in Race, Political Economy and Society.* Boston: South End Press, 1983.

——. *Race, Reform and Rebellion: The Second Reconstruction in Black America, 1945–1982.* Jackson: University Press of Mississippi, 1984.

Martin, Emily. "Science and Women's Bodies: Forms of Anthropological Knowledge." *Body/Politics: Women and the Discourses of Science.* Ed. Mary Jacobus, Evelyn Fox Keller, and Sally Shuttleworth. New York and London: Routledge, 1990: 69–82.

Martin, Robert K. *Hero, Captain, and Stranger: Male Friendship, Social Critique, and Literary Form in the Sea Novels of Herman Melville.* Chapel Hill: University of North Carolina Press, 1986.

McDowell, Deborah. "Transferences: Black Feminist 'Practice' in the Age of 'Theory.'" *Feminism Beside Itself.* Ed. Diane Elam and Robyn Wiegman. New York: Routledge, 1995.

McGovern, James R. *Anatomy of a Lynching: The Killing of Claude Neal.* Baton Rouge: Louisiana State University Press, 1982.

McRobbie, Angela. "Feminism, Postmodernism and the Real Me." *Theory, Culture & Society* 10.4 (Nov 1993): 127–142.

——. "New Times in Cultural Studies." *New Formations* 13 (Spring 1991): 1–17.

Mencke, John G. *Mulattoes and Race Mixture: American Attitudes and Images, 1865–1918.* Ann Arbor, Michigan: UMI Research Press, 1979.

Mercer, Kobena. "'1968': Periodizing Politics and Identity." *Cultural Studies.* Ed. Lawrence Grossberg, Cary Nelson, and Paula A. Treichler. New York: Routledge, 1992: 424–449.

——. "Skin Head Sex Thing: Racial Difference and the Homoerotic Imaginary." *How Do I Look? Queer Film and Video.* Ed. Bad Object-Choices. Seattle: Bay Press, 1991: 169–222.

——. "Welcome to the Jungle: Identity and Diversity in Postmodern Politics." *Identity: Community, Culture, Difference.* Ed. Jonathan Rutherford. London: Lawrence & Wishart, 1990: 43–71.

——, and Isaac Julien. "Introduction: De Margin and De Centre." *Screen* 29.4 (Autumn 1988): 2–10.

——, and Isaac Julien. "Race, Sexual Politics and Black Masculinity: A Dossier." *Male Order: Unwrapping Masculinity.* Ed. Rowena Chapman and Jonathan Rutherford. London: Lawrence & Wishart, 1988: 97–164.

——, and Isaac Julien. "True Confessions: A Discourse on Images of Black Male Sexuality." *Ten* 8.22 (1986): 4–8.

Minh-ha, Trinh T. *Woman, Native, Other: Writing Postcoloniality and Feminism.* Bloomington: Indiana University Press, 1989.

Mitchell, Lee Clark. "Face, Race, and Disfiguration in Stephen Crane's *The Monster. Critical Inquiry* 17.1 (Autumn 1990): 174–192.

Mohanty, Chandra Talpade. "Feminist Encounters: Locating the Politics of Experience." *Destabilizing Theory: Contemporary Feminist Debates.* Ed. Michèle Barrett and Anne Phillips. Stanford, California: Stanford University Press, 1992: 74–92.

———. "On Race and Voice: Challenges for Liberal Education in the 1990s." *Cultural Critique* 14 (Winter 1989–90): 179–208.

———, Ann Russo, and Lourdes Torres, eds. *Third World Women and the Politics of Feminism.* Bloomington: Indiana University Press, 1991.

Moraga, Cherrìe, and Gloria Anzaldúa, eds. *This Bridge Called My Back: Writings by Radical Women of Color.* Watertown, Massachusetts: Persephone, 1981.

Morrison, Toni. *The Bluest Eye.* New York: Washington Square Press, 1970.

———, ed. *Race-ing Justice, En-gendering Power: Essays on Anita Hill, Clarence Thomas, and the Construction of Social Reality.* New York: Pantheon, 1992.

Mulvey, Laura. "Visual Pleasure and Narrative Cinema." *Feminism and Film Theory.* Ed. Constance Penley. New York: Routledge, 1988: 57–68.

National Association for the Advancement of Colored People. *Thirty Years of Lynching in the United States, 1889–1918.* 1919. Reprint, New York: Negro Universities Press, 1969.

Neale, Steve. "Masculinity as Spectacle: Reflections on Men and Mainstream Cinema." *Screen* 24.6 (Nov–Dec 1983): 2–16.

Nelson, Cary. "Always Already Cultural Studies: Two Conferences and a Manifesto." *Journal of the Midwest Modern Language Association* 24.1 (Spring 1991): 24–38.

Nelson, Dana D. *The Word in Black and White: Reading "Race" in American Literature 1638–1867.* New York and Oxford: Oxford University Press, 1993.

Newfield, Christopher. "The Politics of Male Suffering: Masochism and Hegemony in the American Renaissance." *differences* 1.3 (Fall 1989): 55–87.

———. "What Was Political Correctness? Race, the Right, and Managerial Democracy in the Humanities." *Critical Inquiry* 19.2 (Winter 1993): 308–336.

Nicholson, Linda J. "Feminism and the Politics of Postmodernism." *Feminism and Postmodernism.* Ed. Jennifer Wicke and Margaret Ferguson. Durham, North Carolina and London: Duke University Press, 1994: 69–85.

Off Limits. Dir. Christopher Crowe. Twentieth Century Fox, 1988.

Ogunyemi, Chikwenye Okonjo. "Womanism: The Dynamics of the Contemporary Black Female Novel in English." *Signs* 11.1 (Autumn 1985): 63–80.

Omi, Michael, and Howard Winant. *Racial Formation in the United States: From the 1960s to the 1980s.* New York and London: Routledge, 1986.

Outlaw, Lucius. "Toward a Critical Theory of 'Race.'" *The Anatomy of Racism.* Ed. David Theo Goldberg. Minneapolis: University of Minnesota Press, 1990: 58–82.

Pateman, Carole. "Feminist Critiques of the Public/Private Dichotomy." *The Disorder of Women: Democracy, Feminism, and Political Theory.* Cambridge: Polity Press, 1989: 118–140.

Peavy, Charles D. "Myth, Magic, and Manhood in LeRoi Jones' *Madheart.*" *Imamu Amiri Baraka (LeRoi Jones): A Collection of Critical Essays.* Ed. Kimberly W. Benston. Englewood Cliffs, New Jersey: Prentice-Hall, 1978: 167–173.

Penley, Constance, ed. *Feminism and Film Theory.* New York: Routledge, 1988.

Phelan, Shane. *Identity Politics: Lesbian Feminism and the Limits of Community.* Philadelphia, Pennsylvania: Temple University Press, 1989.

Philadelphia. Dir. Jonathan Demme. Tristar Pictures, 1993.

Phillips, Anne. *Democracy and Difference.* University Park: Pennsylvania State University Press, 1993.

———. "Universal Pretensions in Political Thought." *Destabilizing Theory: Contemporary Feminist Debates.* Ed. Michèle Barrett and Anne Phillips. Stanford, California: Stanford University Press, 1992: 10–30.

Pieterse, Jan Nederveen. *White on Black: Images of Africa and Blacks in Western Popular Culture.* New Haven and London: Yale University Press, 1992.

Platoon. Dir. Oliver Stone. Orion Pictures, 1986.

Pollack, Griselda. *Vision and Difference: Femininity, Feminism and the Histories of Art.* London: Routledge, 1988.

Popkin, Richard H. "Medicine, Racism, Anti-Semitism: A Dimension of Enlightenment Culture." *The Languages of Psyche: Mind and Body in Enlightenment Thought: Clark Library Lectures, 1985–1986.* Ed. G. S. Rousseau. Berkeley: University of California Press, 1990: 405–442.

———. "The Philosophical Basis of Eighteenth-Century Racism." *Racism in the Eighteenth Century.* Ed. Harold E. Pagliaro. Cleveland and London: The Press of Case Western Reserve University, 1973: 245–262.

Poster, Mark. "Postmodernity and the Politics of Multiculturalism: The Lyotard-Habermas Debate over Social Theory." *Modern Fiction Studies* 38.3 (Autumn 1992): 567–580.

Pratt, Minnie Bruce. "Identity: Skin Blood Heart." *Yours in Struggle: Three Feminist Perspectives on Anti-Semitism and Racism.* 1984. Ed. Elly Bulkin, Pratt, and Barbara Smith. Reprint, Ithaca, New York: Firebrand, 1988: 9–63.

Probyn, Elspeth. "Technologizing the Self: A Future Anterior for Cultural Studies." *Cultural Studies.* Ed. Lawrence Grossberg, Cary Nelson, and Paula A. Treichler. New York: Routledge, 1992: 501–511.

Pryse, Marjorie, and Hortense J. Spillers, eds. *Conjuring: Black Women, Fiction, and Literary Tradition.* Bloomington: Indiana University Press, 1985.

Radhakrishnan, R. "Ethnic Identity and Post-Structuralist Differance." *The Nature and Context of Minority Discourse.* Ed. Abdul R. JanMohamed and David Lloyd. New York: Oxford University Press, 1990: 50–71.

Ramazanoglu, Caroline. "What Can You Do with a Man? Feminism and the Critical Appraisal of Masculinity." *Women's Studies International Forum* 15.3 (May–June 1992): 339–350.

Readings, Bill. *Introducing Lyotard: Art and Politics.* London and New York: Routledge, 1991.

———, and Stephen Melville, eds. *Vision and Textuality.* New York: Macmillan, 1995.

Reagon, Bernice Johnson. "Coalition Politics: Turning the Century." *Home Girls: A*

Black Feminist Anthology. Ed. Barbara Smith. New York: Kitchen Table Women of Color Press, 1983: 356–369.

Record, Wilson. "The Development of the Communist Position on the Negro Question in the United States." *Phylon* 19.3 (Fall 1958): 306–326.

Rex, John, and David Mason, eds. *Theories of Race and Ethnic Relations.* New York and Cambridge: Cambridge University Press, 1986.

Rich, Adrienne. "Disloyal to Civilization: Feminism, Racism, Gynephobia." *On Lies, Secrets, and Silence.* New York: W. W. Norton, 1979: 275–310.

Riley, Denise. *"Am I That Name?" Feminism and the Category of "Women" in History.* Minneapolis: University of Minnesota Press, 1988.

Robbins, Bruce. "Men in Feminism." *Camera Obscura* 17 (May 1988): 206–214.

Robinson, Cedric J. *Black Marxism: The Making of the Black Radical Tradition.* London: Zed Press, 1983.

Roediger, David R. *Towards the Abolition of Whiteness: Essays on Race, Politics, and Working Class History.* London and New York: Verso, 1994.

Rogin, Michael. "'The Sword Became a Flashing Vision': D. W. Griffith's *The Birth of a Nation.*" *Representations* 9 (Winter 1985): 150–195.

Romero, Lora. "Bio-Political Resistance in Domestic Ideology and *Uncle Tom's Cabin.*" *American Literary History* 1.4 (Winter 1989): 715–734.

Roof, Judith, and Robyn Wiegman, eds. *Who Can Speak? Authority and Critical Identity.* Urbana: University of Illinois Press, forthcoming.

Rorty, Richard. "Foucault and Epistemology." *Foucault: A Critical Reader.* Ed. David Couzens Hoy. Oxford and New York: Basil Blackwell, 1986: 41–49.

Ross, Andrew, ed. *Universal Abandon? The Politics of Postmodernism.* Minneapolis: University of Minnesota Press, 1988.

Rousseau, G. S. "Foucault and Enlightenment." *Enlightenment Crossings: Pre- and Post-modern Discourses, Anthropological.* Manchester and New York: Manchester University Press, 1991: 40–60.

Rutherford, Jonathan. *Men's Silences: Predicaments in Masculinity.* London and New York: Routledge, 1992.

———, ed. *Identity: Community, Culture, Difference.* London: Lawrence & Wishart, 1990.

Ryan, Mary P. "Gender and Public Access: Women's Politics in Nineteenth-Century America." *Habermas and the Public Sphere.* Ed. Craig Calhoun. Cambridge, Massachusetts: MIT Press, 1992: 259–288.

———. *Women in Public: Between Banners and Ballots, 1825–1880.* Baltimore: Johns Hopkins University Press, 1990.

Sanchez-Eppler, Karen. "Bodily Bonds: The Intersecting Rhetorics of Feminism and Abolition." *Representations* 24 (Fall 1988): 28–59.

Sawhney, Sabina. "The Joke and the Hoax: (Not) Speaking as the Other." *Who Can Speak? Authority and Critical Identity.* Ed. Judith Roof and Robyn Wiegman. Urbana: University of Illinois Press, forthcoming.

Saxon, Alexander. *The Rise and Fall of the White Republic: Class Politics and Mass Culture in Nineteenth-Century America*. London and New York: Verso, 1990.

"Scapegoating the Black Family: Black Women Speak." *Nation* 249.4 (July 24/31, 1989).

Schiebinger, Londa. *Nature's Body: Gender in the Making of Modern Science*. Boston: Beacon, 1993.

Scott, Ann Firor. *The Southern Lady: From Pedestal to Politics, 1830–1930*. Chicago: University of Chicago Press, 1970.

Sedgwick, Eve Kosofsky. *Between Men: English Literature and Male Homosocial Desire*. New York: Columbia University Press, 1985.

Sharistanian, Janet, ed. *Beyond the Public/Domestic Dichotomy: Contemporary Perspectives on Women's Public Lives*. New York: Greenwood, 1987.

Shoot to Kill. Dir. Robert Spottiswoode. Touchstone Pictures, 1988.

Singer, Linda. *Erotic Warfare: Sexual Theory and Politics in the Age of Epidemic*. New York: Routledge, 1993.

Skidmore, Thomas E. *Black into White: Race and Nationality in Brazilian Thought*. 1974. Durham, North Carolina and London: Duke University Press, 1993.

Smith, Samuel Stanhope. *An Essay on the Causes of the Variety of Complexion and Figure in the Human Species*. 1787. Ed. Winthrop D. Jordan. Reprint, Cambridge, Massachusetts: Harvard University Press, 1965.

Smith, Valerie. "Split Affinities: The Case of Interracial Rape." *Conflicts in Feminism*. Ed. Marianne Hirsch and Evelyn Fox Keller. New York and London: Routledge, 1990: 271–287.

Snead, James. "Racist Traces in Postmodernist Theory and Literature." *Critical Quarterly* 33.1 (Spring 1991): 31–39.

Spelman, Elizabeth V. *Inessential Woman: Problems of Exclusion in Feminist Thought*. Boston: Beacon, 1988.

Spillers, Hortense J. "Mama's Baby, Papa's Maybe: An American Grammar Book." *diacritics* 17.2 (Summer 1987): 65–81.

Spivak, Gayatri Chakravorty. "Can the Subaltern Speak?" *Marxism and the Interpretation of Culture*. Ed. Cary Nelson and Lawrence Grossberg. Urbana and Chicago: University of Illinois Press, 1988: 271–313.

———. "In a Word: Interview." *differences* 1.2 (Summer 1989): 124–156.

———, and Sneja Gunew. "Questions of Multiculturalism." *The Cultural Studies Reader*. Ed. Simon During. London and New York: Routledge, 1993: 193–202.

Stam, Robert, and Louise Spence. "Colonialism, Racism and Representation." *Screen* 24.2 (Mar–Apr 1983): 2–20.

Stanton, William. *The Leopard's Spots: Scientific Attitudes toward Race in America 1815–59*. Chicago: University of Chicago Press, 1960.

Staples, Robert. "The Myth of Black Matriarchy." *The Black Family: Essays and Studies*. Ed. Staples. Belmont, California: Wadsworth, 1971: 149–159.

Stepan, Nancy. *The Idea of Race in Science: Great Britain 1800–1960*. Hamden, Connecticut: Archon, 1982.

————. "Race and Gender: The Role of Analogy in Science." *The Anatomy of Racism.* Ed. David Theo Goldberg. Minneapolis: University of Minnesota Press, 1990: 38–57.

————, and Sander Gilman. "Appropriating the Idioms of Science: The Rejection of Scientific Racism." *The Bounds of Race: Perspectives on Hegemony and Resistance.* Ed. Dominick LaCapra. Ithaca, New York: Cornell University Press, 1991: 72–103.

Stocking, George W., Jr. *Race, Culture, and Evolution: Essays in the History of Anthropology.* New York: Free Press, 1968.

Stowe, Harriet Beecher. *Uncle Tom's Cabin.* 1851-52. Reprint, New York: Bantam, 1981.

Streets of Gold. Dir. Joe Roth. United Artists, 1986.

Suleiman, Susan Rubin, ed. *The Female Body in Western Culture.* Cambridge, Massachusetts: Harvard University Press, 1986.

Taylor, Charles. "Foucault on Freedom and Truth." *Foucault: A Critical Reader.* Ed. David Couzens Hoy. Oxford and New York: Basil Blackwell, 1986: 69–102.

Tillman, Ben. "The Black Peril." 1907. *Justice Denied: The Black Man in White America.* Ed. William Chace and Peter Collier. Reprint, New York: Harcourt, Brace 1970: 180–185.

Tompkins, Jane. *Sensational Designs: The Cultural Work of American Fiction, 1790–1860.* New York: Oxford University Press, 1985.

Turner, Graeme. *British Cultural Studies: An Introduction.* Boston: Unwin Hyman, 1990.

Twain, Mark. *The Adventures of Huckleberry Finn.* 1885. Reprint, New York: New American Library, 1959.

Van Deburg, William L. *Slavery and Race in American Popular Culture.* Madison: University of Wisconsin Press, 1984.

Vogt, Carl. *Lectures on Man, His Place in Creation, and in the History of the Earth.* London: Longman, Green, and Roberts, 1864.

Walker, Alice. *In Search of Our Mothers' Gardens: Womanist Prose.* San Diego and New York: Harcourt Brace Jovanovich, 1983.

Wall, Cheryl, ed. *Changing Our Own Words: Essays on Criticism, Theory, and Writing by Black Women.* New Brunswick, New Jersey: Rutgers University Press, 1989.

Wallace, Michele. *Black Macho and the Myth of the Superwoman.* 1979. Reprint, London and New York: Verso, 1990.

————. *Invisibility Blues: From Pop to Theory.* London and New York: Verso, 1990.

————. "Modernism, Postmodernism and the Problem of the Visual in Afro-American Culture." *Out There: Marginalization and Contemporary Cultures.* Ed. Russell Ferguson, Martha Gever, Trinh T. Minh-ha, and Cornel West. Cambridge, Massachusetts: New Museum of Contemporary Art and MIT Press, 1990: 39–50.

Walzer, Michael. "The Politics of Michel Foucault." *Foucault: A Critical Reader.* Ed. David Couzens Hoy. Oxford and New York: Basil Blackwell, 1986: 51–68.

Warner, Michael. "The Mass Public and the Mass Subject." *Habermas and the Public Sphere.* Ed. Craig Calhoun. Cambridge, Massachusetts: MIT Press, 1992: 377–401.

Weed, Elizabeth, ed. "Introduction: Terms of Reference." *Coming to Terms: Feminism, Theory, Politics.* New York: Routledge, 1989: ix–xxxi.

Wells-Barnett, Ida B. *On Lynchings: Southern Horrors; A Red Record; Mob Rule in New Orleans.* 1892, 1895, 1900. Reprint, New York: Arno Press, 1969.

Welter, Barbara. "The Cult of True Womanhood, 1820–1860." *Dimity Convictions: The American Woman in the Nineteenth Century.* Athens: Ohio University Press, 1976: 21–41.

West, Cornel. "Marxist Theory and the Specificity of Afro-American Oppression." *Marxism and the Interpretation of Culture.* Ed. Cary Nelson and Lawrence Grossberg. Urbana and Chicago: University of Illinois Press, 1988: 17–33.

———. "The New Cultural Politics of Difference." *Out There: Marginalization and Contemporary Cultures.* Ed. Russell Ferguson, Martha Gever, Trinh T. Minh-ha, and Cornel West. New York and Cambridge, Massachusetts: New Museum of Contemporary Art and MIT Press, 1990: 19–36.

Wheeler, John. *Touched with Fire: The Future of the Vietnam Generation.* New York: Avon, 1984.

White, Deborah Gray. *Ar'n't I a Woman: Female Slaves in the Plantation South.* New York: Norton, 1985.

White Nights. Dir. Taylor Hackford. Columbia Pictures, 1985.

Wicke, Jennifer, and Margaret Ferguson, eds. *Feminism and Postmodernism.* Durham, North Carolina and London: Duke University Press, 1994.

Wiegman, Robyn. "Feminism and Its Mal(e)Contents." *Masculinities* 2.1 (Spring 1994): 1–7.

———. "Feminism, the *Boyz,* and Other Matters Regarding the Male." *Screening the Male: Exploring Masculinities in Hollywood Cinema.* Ed. Steven Cohan and Ina Rae Hark. New York and London: Routledge, 1993: 173–193.

———. "Melville's Geography of Gender." *American Literary History* 1.4 (Fall 1989): 735–753.

———. "Toward a Political Economy of Race and Gender." *Bucknell Review* Special Issue: "Turning the Century: Feminist Theory in the 1990s." Ed. Glynis Carr. Lewisburg, Pennsylvania: Bucknell University Press, 1992: 47–67.

Williams, Linda. *Hard Core: Power, Pleasure, and the "Frenzy of the Visible."* Berkeley: University of California Press, 1989.

Williams, Patricia J. *The Alchemy of Race and Rights.* Cambridge, Massachusetts, and London: Harvard University Press, 1991.

Williams, Raymond. "The Future of Cultural Studies." *The Politics of Modernism: Against the New Conformists.* Ed. Tony Pinkney. London and New York: Verso, 1989: 151–162.

Williams, Sherley Anne. "Some Implications of Womanist Theory." *Reading Black,*

Reading Feminist: A Critical Anthology. Ed. Henry Louis Gates Jr. New York: Meridian, 1990: 68–75.

Williamson, Joel. *The Crucible of Race: Black-White Relations in the American South since Emancipation.* New York: Oxford University Press, 1984.

Wilson, William Julius. *The Declining Significance of Race: Blacks and Changing American Institutions.* 2nd ed. Chicago: University of Chicago Press, 1980.

Wokler, Robert. "From *l'homme physique* to *l'homme moral* and Back: Towards a History of Enlightenment Anthropology." *History of the Human Sciences* 6.1 (Feb 1993): 121–138.

Wollstonecraft, Mary. *A Vindication of the Rights of Woman.* 1792. Reprint, London: Penguin Books, 1992.

Woodward, C. Vann. *The Strange Career of Jim Crow.* 3rd ed. New York: Oxford University Press, 1974.

Wright, Richard. "How 'Bigger' Was Born." *Native Son.* New York: Harper & Row, 1966: vii–xxxiv.

———. *Native Son.* 1940. Reprint, New York: Harper & Row, 1966.

Yarborough, Richard. "Strategies of Black Characterization in *Uncle Tom's Cabin* and the Early Afro-American Novel." *New Essays on Uncle Tom's Cabin.* Ed. Eric Sundquist. New York and Cambridge: Cambridge University Press, 1986: 45–84.

Yellin, Jean Fagan. "Doing It Herself: *Uncle Tom's Cabin* and Woman's Role in the Slavery Crisis." *New Essays on Uncle Tom's Cabin.* Ed. Eric Sundquist. New York and Cambridge: Cambridge University Press, 1986: 85–105.

———. *The Intricate Knot: Black Figures in American Literature, 1776–1863.* New York: New York University Press, 1972.

Yingling, Thomas E. "How the Eye Is Caste — Robert Mapplethorpe and the Limits of Controversy." *Discourse* 12.2 (Spring–Summer 1990): 3–28.

Young, Robert. *White Mythologies: Writing History and the West.* London and New York: Routledge, 1990.

Young-Bruehl, Elisabeth. "Discriminations." *Transition* 60 (1993): 53–69.

Index

About the Author. Robyn Wiegman is Associate Professor
of Women's Studies, English, and Comparative Literature
and Director of Women's Studies at the University of
California, Irvine.

Library of Congress Cataloging-in-Publication Data
Wiegman, Robyn.
American anatomies : theorizing race and gender.
p.   cm. — (New Americanists)
Includes bibliographical references and index.
ISBN 0-8223-1576-9. — ISBN 0-8223-1591-2 (pbk.)
1. United States — Race relations.   2. Sex role — United States.
3. Afro-American women.   I. Title.   II. Series
E185.615.W48 1995
305.8′00973 — dc20   94-36882 CIP